Who Would
You Be Without
Your Story?

Who Would You Be Without Your Story?

Dialogues with

BYRON KATIE

Edited by Carol Williams

HAY HOUSE, INC.
Carlsbad, California • New York City
London • Sydney • Johannesburg
Vancouver • Hong Kong • New Delhi

Published and distributed in the United States by: Hay House, Inc.: www.hayhouse.
com • *Published and distributed in Australia by:* Hay House Australia Pty. Ltd.: www.
hayhouse.com.au • *Published and distributed in the United Kingdom by:* Hay House
UK, Ltd.: www.hayhouse.co.uk • *Published and distributed in the Republic of South
Africa by:* Hay House SA (Pty), Ltd.: www.hayhouse.co.za • *Distributed in Canada by:*
Raincoast: www.raincoast.com • *Published in India by:* Hay House Publishers India:
www.hayhouse.co.in

Editorial supervision: Jill Kramer • *Design:* Tricia Breidenthal

Special thanks to Elizabeth Lavine for transcribing these dialogues.

Library of Congress Cataloging-in-Publication Data

Katie, Byron.
  Who would you be without your story? : dialogues with Byron Katie / edited by Carol
Williams. -- 1st ed.
      p. cm.
  ISBN 978-1-4019-2179-8 (tradepaper : alk. paper) 1. Self-actualization (Psychology) 2.
Self-evaluation. I. Williams, Carol. II. Title.
  BF637.S4K338 2008
  158--dc22
                                   2008016186

ISBN: 978-1-4019-2179-8

14 13 12 11   8 7 6 5
1st edition, October 2008
5th edition, September 2011

Printed in the United States of America

CONTENTS

Foreword by Carol Williams vii

DIALOGUES:

1. Joe Is Irresponsible. 1

2. Sleep Disorder 19

3. My Mother Wouldn't Approve 39

4. I Can't Stand It That George Fell in Love with Linda. 47

5. The Rent Increase 81

6. Welcome to Al-Anon! 91

7. Frank Bosses Me Around 117

8. My Mother Manipulates Me 123

9. Cancer Ruined My Life 153

10. My Sister the Prostitute 185

11. My Mother Made Me a Victim 211

12. My Husband Shouldn't Have Left Me. 227

13. I'm Not Enough—and Some People Are Better Than Others. . .251

14. My Father Abused Me 267

15. Scared and Angry at God. 299

Afterword by Carol Williams. 309
Appendix 311
Index of Topics. 315
About the Author 317

FOREWORD

by Carol Williams

Over the past twenty years, Byron Katie has become known around the world as one of the clearest and most inspiring teachers of our time. She teaches a way to happiness, and those who meet her respond instantly to the delight she takes in whoever and whatever is in front of her. Yet, as she is quick to explain, her own teacher was suffering.

Amid the circumstances of what should have been a satisfying life in a California desert town—successful business career, healthy children, beauty—Byron Kathleen Reid (everyone calls her Katie) was overcome by a depression that lasted more than ten years. She kept to her bed in deepening rage and despair. Eventually she committed herself to a shelter for women with eating disorders—the only place that would take her health insurance. One day she woke up in her attic room to find that all her suffering was gone, replaced by a joy that was unlike anything she had ever known:

> I discovered that when I believed my thoughts, I suffered, but that when I didn't believe them, I didn't suffer, and that this is true for every human being. Freedom is as simple as that. I found that suffering is optional. I found a joy within me that has never disappeared, not for a single moment. That joy is in everyone, always.

The difference between her experience and other experiences of spiritual opening is that in the moment of waking up, she discovered a method of sustaining that extraordinary lightness. The four questions and turnaround that she later called The Work were already present in that first moment.

Katie knew that the joyous clarity she was experiencing is available to everyone. And, in her down-to-earth American way, she began to share her method of self-inquiry with the many people who were immediately drawn to her. Katie's primary realization was that every painful feeling—anger, loneliness, fear—is the result of believing a thought that isn't true. To notice what that thought is and then to examine it with the questions that Katie discovered has an unimaginable power—unimaginable until you do it for yourself.

To do The Work, alone or with others, you begin by finding the particular thoughts that are causing you stress. Perhaps one thought is: *My husband doesn't love me.* You write the thoughts down on what is called a Worksheet (see the Appendix of this book for more information), then examine the thought using these four questions:

- *Is it true?*
- *Can you absolutely know that it's true?*
- *How do you react when you believe that thought?*
- *Who would you be without the thought?*

After this, you turn the thought around to its several opposites—for example, *My husband does love me, I don't love my husband,* and *I don't love myself*—and you find three genuine examples of how each turnaround is as true as or truer than the original thought.

The conversations in this book show the kinds of things that happen when people who are suffering answer these questions, slowly and accurately. They are edited dialogues between Katie and fifteen participants at various public workshops and Schools for The Work that took place around the United States and in Europe. Some of the participants had painful illnesses; others were lovelorn or in messy divorces; some were simply irritated with a co-worker or worried about a rent increase. What they all had in common was a willingness to question, with Katie's help, the painful thoughts that they came to see were the true cause of their suffering.

The dialogues aren't organized by their ostensible topics—family, illness, and so on—because the real subject here is the process of The Work and the various paths it can take. Some of the participants were new to The Work, while others had been practicing it for some time but had hit particular walls. In every case, we see how Katie's acute mind and fierce kindness helped each person dismantle for themselves what was felt to be unshakeable reality.

Although these dialogues make fascinating reading—some are both hilarious and deeply moving at once—they are intended primarily as teaching tools. Each took place in front of an audience. Katie never lost her connection with that audience, repeatedly reminding each person in the room to follow the dialogues inwardly and to ask themselves the questions the participant must ask.

This is the way this book should be read to be most useful. The dialogues between Katie and these volunteers is an external enactment of precisely the kind of dialogue each reader can have with his or her own thoughts. The result, even in the seemingly direst situation, can be an unimagined freedom and joy.

Two Things to Know Before You Begin Reading

Each participant in the dialogue has been given a copy of Katie's Worksheet to fill out before the workshop begins. (There is also a copy of it in the Appendix at the back of this book; you are encouraged to look at it and use it yourself.) The Worksheet—which asks questions such as "Who angers, frustrates, disappoints, or confuses you, and why? What is it about them that you don't like?"—helps identify and pin down the thoughts that are the causes of suffering. Usually the conversation begins with the participant reading from the Worksheet, and they return to it again throughout the conversation. In this book, each time a participant reads from the Worksheet, their words appear in italics. This is to make the process clear.

Some readers might be puzzled when Katie addresses the workshop participants as "Sweetheart" or "Honey." This doesn't mean that she knows them or that she is being insincere. For Katie, the one she is with is always the dearest person in the world, and

I hope some of the intensity of her attention comes through in these transcriptions.

1. JOE IS IRRESPONSIBLE

If there's someone who makes your blood boil, thank him. He's showing you what you need to know to become a kinder person. He's doing the best he can, and so are you.

Brian: [in the audience, reading from his Worksheet] *I am angry at Joe because he's inconsiderate, arrogant, a jackass, money hungry, unethical, uncaring, irresponsible, slimy—and he doesn't care about the staff or the client.* [The audience laughs.]

Katie: Basically, that's about it.

Brian: I ran out of space.

Katie: Thank you. That is the mind. So what do we do with a mind like this? The mind has a process—I've noticed it has a job; it's a seeker. We believe the thought "He is selfish." And then the mind immediately begins to give us all the stories that prove it, and all the pictures that prove it. It's not enough that he was selfish then—the mind has to prove it, prove it, prove it.

So what happens is that the mind is attacking that person. Usually we're married to them when we have these thoughts! So the mind absolutely annihilates that person. It does its job. And it swerves around and attacks you for attacking him. And it exhausts itself. And throughout that, the addictions have kicked in—you light the cigarette, you go to the refrigerator after you've just eaten

1

a full meal, you turn on the television. It's a blur to you—you don't really care.

What do we do with a mind like this? We can't stop the thoughts. We outwait them. We rationalize them. We medicate them down. We meditate them down. I have come to see that this mind is seeking a place to rest. It's seeking peace. In that scenario I just showed you—where it's attacking him and attacking you— there's no peace in it. And yet that is how the mind works. And that's how we have been dealing with these thoughts, since we first believed thoughts.

Notice the thought "He's so selfish!" and feel what the body does, the stories and the pictures that come along with that thought. Feel what that does to your arms and your shoulders, to your body, to your system: how the heart races. And how you set the glass down on the cabinet a little too hard—just in case he doesn't notice that you're angry.

But I noticed one day that those stressful thoughts that I was believing weren't necessarily true. I discovered that it's the truth that sets us free. And so I began to deal with my thoughts as though they were my children. I used to sit with that wild-child mind as though it were the beloved.

It's just like when you're talking to your children or someone you love, and you're thinking these wonderful thoughts about them, and you're not trying to force yourself, because it's genuine. "Isn't he wonderful, isn't she talented, isn't she kind?"—those thoughts. Feel what your body does when you're thinking *those* thoughts genuinely. And look at the difference between the two states, depending on what you're believing.

So I've come to see that if I question my stressful thoughts, the mind can rest. And so that's what we're going to play with this evening. So, sweetheart, do you want to come up here? Do you want to step into my parlor, and we'll do The Work on Joe?

[Brian joins Katie on stage.]

Okay, sweetheart, read it again.

Brian: *I am angry at Joe because he's inconsiderate, arrogant, a jack-ass, money hungry, unethical, uncaring, irresponsible, slimy—and he doesn't care about the staff or the clients.*

Katie: Absolutely. So now let's look at these. I heard you say "irresponsible." That one just kind of came out at me. That's really frustrating.

Brian: It's *really* frustrating.

Katie: Yes. So "He's irresponsible"—is that true? [To the audience] Find someone in your life who's irresponsible. It could be someone you knew a long time ago, who drove you nuts with that quality, or it could be someone you're living with. So, "He's irresponsible"—is that true?

Brian: In my world, yes.

Katie: Well, that's the only world you ever have to deal with.

Brian: Yes. Sad but true.

Katie: Yes. So "He's irresponsible"—how do you react when you believe that thought?

Brian: I get . . . I feel tension, and the blood-boil kind of feeling of percolating anger.

Katie: Yes.

Brian: The injustice, or that kind of indignant—

Katie: Absolutely. So where does your mind travel when you believe the thought "He's irresponsible"? What pictures do you see, what concepts do you experience?

Brian: Well, it's totally negative and dark. And it's not a happy spot. It's uncomfortable.

Katie: And who would you be without that thought—"He's irresponsible"?

Brian: I'd be the same person.

Katie: So describe it. Close your eyes. Now get a picture of him being irresponsible. Can you see it?

Brian: Oh, yeah. [The audience laughs.]

Katie: Okay. Now see the same picture.

Brian: Okay.

Katie: And just watch him. Look at his eyes, look at his face, and drop your story. Watch him. What do you see?

Brian: He's doing the best he can.

Katie: Wow!

Brian: He's trying.

Katie: Yes, honey. So "He's irresponsible"—turn it around. The turnaround is where you find the opposite of what you believe and really experience it. So "He's irresponsible"—turn it around.

Brian: He's doing the best he can. He's—

Katie: He's responsible. He's as responsible as he can be.

Brian: With what tools he has, and . . .

Katie: That's very good to know. Because if you can see this in him, you can see it when you're with the rest of us. And also something dear happens, something very powerful, out of that: You come to see that *you're* as responsible as *you* can be, and that you always have been.

Brian: And just saying it, I felt softer, like a relaxing almost, physically.

Katie: You got a glimpse of what's really going on. Because the mind tells you, "He's doing it on purpose, he's doing it just to make me angry." The mind is like that. It becomes a personal thing.

But thoughts aren't personal. I noticed that one morning. My self-esteem was so low I used to sleep on the floor, and I thought that's what I deserved—I didn't think I deserved to sleep in a bed, because I was so full of self-hatred. And one morning I woke up and was lying on the floor, and just for no reason, I noticed that I was being breathed. And really, *it* was being breathed. It wasn't even me; the body wasn't even mine. I got a glimpse of . . . nothing personal. And then I noticed that I was being thought.

I invite you to experience this for yourself. When you're asleep at night, when you're not dreaming, where is the world? It doesn't begin until the I begins. "I." "I am." "I'm late for work." "I need to go to the bathroom." "I, I, I, I, I, me, me, me." And then it starts to really think you're a this. Or a that. An "I."

So we begin to question our thoughts, and we find something new happening. We come to see that thoughts aren't personal. And when we see that, miracles take place. It's unconditional love.

The next time you see this man and he's being irresponsible—to everyone else—you may wonder why *you* aren't seeing it that way. You're seeing someone just doing the best he can. It's a radical shift—this glimpsing into oneself.

Brian: It would have to be, because if you feel this way every day, it's not even conscious, really, after a point. He could be a saint, and I would still . . .

Katie: . . . miss it. That's right, honey. He could be a saint, and you attach your story to him, and your story is who he is. The truth is that no two people have ever met. You are who I believe you to be. I believe the thoughts about you, so that's who you are. Okay, sweetheart, we're fighting perceptions actually.

So "He is irresponsible"—turn it around.

Brian: He's doing the best he can, and his belief is that he cares or he wouldn't be doing what he is doing.

Katie: Okay, but let's keep the words as close as possible to your original statement. "He is irresponsible" turned around is "He is responsible."

Brian: He is responsible.

Katie: Okay, so that can be just a concept. It may not be genuine for you. The mind's not satisfied unless it sees that the turnaround is genuine. So give me three examples of where this man *is* responsible. Three genuine examples, and make them as specific as you can. When we do this, we begin to think in another polarity, in a polarity that's much kinder than the one we've been living in.

[To the audience] I invite all of you to do this when you're at home.

[To Brian] So, give me three examples of where he is responsible.

Brian: He shows up every day he's supposed to show up.

Katie: That's amazing.

Brian: Yes. [The audience laughs.] He works hard, and a lot of times he's working overtime and past his shift, technically—you know, extra hours.

Katie: My goodness!

Brian: And there are actually instances when he's caring and responsible. I've seen it.

Katie: Okay, so for me, my mind would need more than "There are actually instances when he's caring and responsible." That's vague. I need specifics. So I suggest that you really look for specific examples. The mind is finding a new way to live. It's finding a way to live in what's real.

Brian: So, he would go to classes to keep up with continuing education to bring to the table. Is that specific enough?

Katie: Yes, honey, yes. Now, when you go back to work, you may want to share this with him. "Joe, I find that you're responsible." [The audience laughs.]

1. Joe Is Irresponsible

Brian: *You* have to come with me.

Katie: Okay, honey. I want to meet this man. He sounds like a very caring, hardworking man, who, as you say, is as responsible as he can be, and even goes over the line in trying to be. So at work you may want to let him know: "I have been thinking about you. And I appreciate the classes you take, and how you show up every day you're supposed to, and . . ." And you give him your list.

Brian: Without the first part, though. [The audience laughs.] I actually have a sponsor who's having me do work like that.

Katie: Excellent. And eventually you can also tell him your answers to that third question, "How do you react when you believe that thought?" It shows you amazing things about what you can talk to these people about. How do you treat him when you believe the thought "He's uncaring and irresponsible"?

Brian: It's probably not very kind.

Katie: I would drop the "probably," and get real.

Brian: Okay. Yes, I'm sure I have put him off . . .

Katie: Specifically, what have you done to put him off?

Brian: I've avoided his eye contact. I've rolled my eyes. I've probably—not "probably". . .

Katie: Very good!

Brian: . . . shared my feeling with other people . . . like gossip.

Katie: Basically, you've gossiped about him.

Brian: Yes.

Katie: Okay. So you may want to take care of that, too.

Brian: I feel like a scumbag now.

Katie: Sweetheart, you haven't had a choice. That's the point of this. When you believe the thought "He is uncaring and irresponsible," you don't have a choice. You *have* to live out of that belief.

Brian: I see.

Katie: You feel bad? But it's pure innocence. If I believe it, I have to live out of it. I can try and try and try, I can use positive affirmations, but *under* these affirmations, what I really believe is what drives me to act. And it rules me. And I pretend, and I hate myself. Feel it. It's violence. Feel what it's like to believe the thought "He's irresponsible and unkind." I'm not saying that he's not. We could also do this list in areas where he *is* irresponsible. But that's playing with a full deck. It's called reality. And when the mind balances, it's clear. He's responsible here; he's not responsible there.

And he appears to be unkind here, but I can't know his mind. Maybe he sees it as helpful. So the mind begins to clear, as we begin to give the truth a chance, your truth. Now, "He's unkind and irresponsible"—feel what that feels like inside, and look at the thoughts.

Brian: Icky.

Katie: And they're violent.

Brian: And dark.

Katie: Yes. We want war to end in the world, but basically we think that war works in our lives. Feel that—that violence inside us, and we think somehow it's making us more responsible; that kind of self-talk, as if we're above him. And look how we treat him.

Okay, sweetheart, can you find another turnaround? "He is irresponsible"—can you find another opposite?

Brian: He's caring.

Katie: "He is irresponsible." "I am . . ."

1. Joe Is Irresponsible

Brian: I am irresponsible.

Katie: Yes.

Brian: I get it.

Katie: Good, good. If I see someone as irresponsible, in that moment I am irresponsible. If I see someone as uncaring, in that moment I am uncaring. Look at the thoughts that you're thinking in the moment you see someone as uncaring. Who is being uncaring? And you know why I care about loving someone? It hurts until I do.

I am someone who knows the difference between what hurts and what doesn't. I discovered what masochism really is, and that discovery left me as someone who loves you. I walk into a space like this, with hundreds of people, and I know that everyone here loves me. I just don't expect them to realize it yet. [The audience laughs.] But if you hate me, you hate you. If you love me, you love you. And every time you question what you believe, you become a kinder human being.

Brian: It's freeing.

Katie: It's so freeing. That is what's meant by freedom. Free the mind, and the body follows.

Okay, sweetheart, so where are *you* irresponsible at work? Where are you irresponsible with him? And where are you unkind to him, and where are you unkind to yourself? This Work is meditation. Get real with it, and you come out radically changed.

So, sweetheart, let's hear your list again, the one that you read. [Brian shakes his head.] Ah, you got it. You got it that fast.

Brian: I don't even want to look at it.

Katie: Yes, well, it was okay for *him*. But not really. In fact, let's go tell our friends about him. You know who our friends are? People who agree with us. Those are our friends. You say, "He's irresponsible and unkind." They say, "Oh, I know it, I know it. Isn't that awful? You must be so frustrated." And if anyone argues with that, you have to convince them that he's irresponsible.

Brian: Through stories.

Katie: Yes, even if you have to exaggerate them. Because these are your friends—they have to agree. And people who don't agree become our enemies, and then we find another group that will agree with us about him, whoever it is.

And we do it in our family. We side against each other. We do it in our workplace, and we do it in our communities. There are "those people"—and then there's us. And we all agree.

But a so-called enemy will point out what I want to know, because he's awake to me. And what would happen if I listened? He could be right, after all. So when the mind is open to questioning, oh my goodness! There ceases to be an enemy in the world. You can't find one.

Someone says, "Katie, you're irresponsible!" I'm supposed to say, "What do you mean, I'm irresponsible?! How dare you say that to me! I'm *totally* responsible!" War, right? But if I were as open as you are now and someone walked up to me and said, "Katie, you are irresponsible," I would say, "Okay, let me take that in. You could be right." And we could sit down and talk about it. And they could enlighten me to me, and I could learn. The mind loves to learn. But when it's in that negative polarity, it's so limited. We're only learning the stress that's been taught from the beginning.

Brian: Well, it's so easy to fall back on your old stuff.

Katie: Unless you've done what you're doing here today. Okay, so read that sentence again.

Brian: *I am angry at Joe because he's inconsiderate, arrogant—*

Katie: So let's turn the whole thing around. "I'm angry at myself . . ."

Brian: I'm angry at myself because I'm inconsiderate.

Katie: Yes, and then I would sit down and really look at that statement. Where am I inconsiderate? Again, this Work is meditation.

10

1. Joe Is Irresponsible

Where am I inconsiderate, especially toward Joe? Where have I been inconsiderate? And the next word?

Brian: Arrogant.

Katie: Where have I been arrogant? As soon as we sit in these judgments and we can see where they are true about ourselves, our whole life changes. And that's the power of truth.

Okay, sweetheart, let's look at the second statement: "I want . . ."

Brian: *I want Joe to acknowledge his problems, be honest about his motives, and learn to have true compassion.*

Katie: "He doesn't have true compassion"—is that true?

Brian: No.

Katie: Nice to know. How do you react when you believe the thought "He doesn't have true compassion"?

Brian: It's that icky feeling of indignant anger, justifying—

Katie: And who would you be without this thought, without this lie?

Brian: A better person.

Katie: I can say "lie" because I hear from you that it's not true. Look at the lies we believe because the mind will give us all the proof. And until we question it, it's just a lost child; and we come out as angry, frustrated, confused. I've come to see that confusion is the only suffering on this planet. So, sweetheart, turn it around.

Brian: I want myself to acknowledge *my* problems, be honest about *my* motives. Right.

Katie: Let's look at the next statement.

Brian: *Joe should follow his own program, think about others' welfare, be honest. I would offer the advice of following his own twelve-step program and listening to other people.*

Katie: Okay, turn it around. We all move at our own speed.

Brian: I should follow *my* own program.

Katie: Yes.

Brian: Ouch. I should think about others' welfare, which, if you look at . . . How ironic that I wrote that! Oh my God! *I* should be honest.

Katie: Yes. Especially about him.

Brian: . . . and take my own advice.

Katie: Yes, honey, yes. All that wisdom we put out to other people is for *us* to hear. Have you noticed how they're not listening? [The audience laughs.] If it's such great wisdom, let *me* live it.

Brian: Yes. And I feel icky about the next statement. *I need Joe . . . for me to be happy . . . I need Joe to quit.*

Katie: Yes.

Brian: I'm laughing because I'm really ashamed of that statement.

Katie: Well, what if you don't have time for shame? It's innocent. You believed your thoughts.

Brian: Well, I believed he was my problem.

Katie: Yes. You're not guilty; you're simply believing what you think. But guilt and shame are all we've had available to us as human beings, because we haven't known how to question the mind. In my experience, guilt and shame are outmoded. They're ancient ways of dealing with reality, and they don't work.

12

1. Joe Is Irresponsible

Brian: They don't serve me.

Katie: They don't serve you or him or us, because you continue to teach that there's something terrible in the world. And here is this person just doing the best he can, as you've come to see.

So we're asleep. We're simply believing what we think. *No* one is guilty. I work in San Quentin—I work in a lot of prisons. And the inmates robbed and murdered because they believed what they thought—that's why they're in there.

Why are *you* where you are? You believe what you think. If your life isn't going the way you want it to go, it's because you believe what you think. You believe your stressful thoughts. When you question them, it leaves you in a space where you're free to act. You're free to be a kind, loving, mature human being.

Brian: Can I ask a question?

Katie: Of course.

Brian: Why is it that my mind can readily accept a negative thought before it will start to believe a positive thing?

Katie: It's the way we have been taught the world is, and so we just automatically believe it. It's like—what is your name?

Brian: Brian.

Katie: Is that true? Do you believe everything you think? Your mother said, "You're Brian," and you believed it?

Brian: Yeah.

Katie: So *that's* how.

Brian: Okay.

Katie: Yes. You really think you are a you! You may not be. And your identity is being radically shifted right now. You were the man who saw him as unkind, and now you're the man who

13

doesn't believe that anymore. And he hasn't changed at all. It's you who have changed. You've changed your identification, and that makes you a kinder human being.

Brian: That's true.

Katie: So who changes the world? You do.

Brian: I do.

Katie: If I live in an ugly world, I need to work with the mind that sees it that way. Because if I start working with the ugly world, I get it all squared away over here, and then there's a whole ugly mess over there. My goodness! There are just not enough hours in the day! [The audience laughs].

You take care of the war in this area, and it breaks out over there. What's a human being to do? We've done the best that we can, and there's shame and guilt . . . it's hard. And out of that comes frustration and self-hatred, and we strike out. And we do things that we don't like ourselves for. "Why did I do that? I promised myself I would never do it again!"

Well, you *have* to do it because you believe what you think. But when you work with the mind, the world changes. That's how it is. Mind is the projector, and the world is the projected. Work with mind and the world follows. It's so simple.

We've been trying to change the world. And we've missed this.

So, sweetheart, read that statement again.

Brian: *I need Joe to quit.*

Katie: Turn it around.

Brian: I need to quit.

Katie: Yes. Not quit your job . . . What is it you need to quit?

Brian: My thought pattern.

Katie: Yes. Every time you see someone as less than you, question it, turn it around, and give yourself some peace. And give yourself a life. It's your birthright—to be an unlimited, free, loving, caring human being.

Do you know how I know that our nature is good? Every thought that would oppose that or attack it feels like stress. I use the term *God*—and for me, reality is God, because it rules—but I sometimes say, "God is everything, God is good." People who truly live that don't need The Work. It's over, because out of that comes peace.

Brian: Yes, I can tell the difference in the kinds of thoughts pretty easily.

Katie: So put the stressful thoughts on paper and question them. The reason I invite you to put them on paper is that they can't move away. You can't say, "I didn't really mean that," because there it is in black and white.

Brian: "I didn't really say that."

Katie: Right! So, "I need to quit"—give me three examples of how that is as true as or truer than your original statement, "I need Joe to quit."

Brian: I need to quit my thought pattern.

Katie: Yes, that's one.

Brian: I need to quit judging people.

Katie: Yes, sweetheart, and that's impossible. Judging is what the mind does, I discovered. But what you can begin to do is write your judgments down and question them. That will give you a sane, happy life.

And a third example?

Brian: I need to quit gossiping.

Katie: Good. Let's look at the next statement.

Brian: I wasn't sure about this one. "What do you think of them? Make a list." This wasn't the good stuff, right?

Katie: Right. You followed the directions perfectly.

Brian: Okay. *He's selfish, self-seeking, self-centered.*

Katie: Turn it around.

Brian: I am selfish, self-seeking, self-centered.

Katie: Yes. You are so selfish in your unquestioned mind that you wouldn't see . . .

Brian: The good parts of him.

Katie: Yes. Okay, honey, the next statement?

Brian: "What is it that you don't want to experience with that person again?" I thought this one was powerful—I couldn't even finish writing it.

Katie: Yes.

Brian: I wrote, *I don't ever want to feel like a nobody.*

Katie: Yes.

Brian: And what I would have written if I could have was: "I don't ever want to feel unacknowledged and unimportant."

Katie: Good. "I don't ever want to feel unacknowledged and unimportant." So now, "I'm willing to . . ."

Brian: I'm willing to . . .

Katie: ". . . feel . . ."

1. Joe Is Irresponsible

Brian: . . . feel . . .

Katie: ". . . unacknowledged . . ."

Brian: . . . unacknowledged and unimportant.

Katie: "I look forward to . . ."

Brian: Whoa! I look forward to feeling unacknowledged and unimportant.

Katie: Yes. Because when you think that and feel that—and feelings will let you know what you're thinking—then you can . . .

Brian: I can change it.

Katie: You can put your thoughts on paper and begin again. You do this until, when someone says, "You're not good enough; we don't want to acknowledge you," you can say, "Well, I used to believe that about me, too." So it levels the field.

Okay, so what was the statement you actually wrote?

Brian: *I don't ever want to feel like a nobody.*

Katie: Okay, "I'm willing . . ."

Brian: I'm willing to feel like a nobody.

Katie: "I look forward to . . ."

Brian: I look forward to feeling like a nobody.

Katie: Yes, and if you feel that, then it's time to do The Work again. It's time to question your stressful thoughts. And for me, when I used to think, "I'm a nobody," it was like a knife in my heart. Today I think, "I'm a nobody," and I'm just elated! I can *be* that. In fact, I *am* that. Thank you, sweetheart. Nice Work.

Brian: Thank you, Katie.

2. Sleep Disorder

"I have a disease"—is that true? You can either scare yourself or you can question your mind.

Valerie: *I don't ever want to experience a sleep disorder again without the help of medication.* I've been doing The Work a lot over the past few months, on people, because I wasn't ready to do it on this. And I'm ready to do it on this today.

Katie: Yes, I see. I'd love it if you'd take a good look—really go inside.

So those of you in the audience: Find a disease, whatever you have. It could even be the flu, if you don't have a disease like cancer or MS or AIDS. And as I ask Valerie the questions, go inside yourselves and find your own answers, because to wait for her answers is of zero value. We've all heard other people's answers all our lives. But to go inside and to know for yourself, that's what's truly valuable. So as I ask her the questions, go *inside*—that is self-inquiry. You're the one you've been waiting for. Ask for yourself, answer for yourself—or not.

So, sweetheart, let's look at your first statement.

Valerie: *I don't like chronic fatigue syndrome because it makes me unable to work.*

Katie: Okay, "You have chronic fatigue syndrome"—can you absolutely know that that's true? I'm not trying to change your mind about your disease. The doctor says you have it, yes?

Valerie: Yes.

Katie: This is not about changing anyone's mind; this is inquiry. "You have chronic fatigue syndrome"—can you absolutely know that that's true?

Valerie: It's a concept. I can only know my experience. I don't always feel fatigued. But I sometimes do. The sleep disorder is the most scary.

Katie: "You have a sleep disorder"—can you absolutely know that that's true? And again, I am not trying to change your mind.

Valerie: I understand.

Katie: "You have a sleep disorder"—can you absolutely know that that's true?

Valerie: It *feels* like I can know that it's true.

Katie: Yes. Because you're supposed to sleep eight hours every night—everyone knows that. It's in every book.

Valerie: Because I'm on medications to sleep, and when I don't take them—before I went on them—I was very dedicated to not going on anything. And I was in disastrous physical condition and going downhill every day, but that was eight years ago. And when I've tried to go off the medications . . .

Katie: Sweetheart, you're really going into a story here.

Valerie: Oh, I am?

Katie: Which is okay, it's just not inquiry.

2. SLEEP DISORDER

Valerie: I have a big story about this problem.

Katie: Well, the story keeps you from inquiry. To inquire honestly, with intention, is to wait for an answer within you to meet the question. Your wisdom is always there to speak, and it will give you the answer to the question. But the I-know mind, rather than wait for the answer, will give itself its own story back again.

Valerie: Okay.

Katie: So to ask with intention. "You have a sleep disorder"—can you absolutely know that that's true?

Valerie: It *feels* true.

Katie: Yes. If I answered that question for myself, if I were to not-sleep to the death, this would be normal for me. Normal is what is going on now. And for those of you new to The Work, "normal" doesn't mean that I'm not going to go to a doctor. It doesn't mean that I'm not going to take medication. It doesn't mean anything—this is about inquiry. But if I'm on a planet with no medication and no doctors, no sleep would be normal for me, to the death. What is is.

Valerie: That's what it feels like—dying. That is it.

Katie: I am very comfortable not-sleeping to the death, until I have the expectation that I should be doing something else—like sleep. This is confusion, and confusion is the only suffering.

I'm one of two things: I'm a lover of what is, or I'm godless. Which is okay, too—except that there's a separation there and a loneliness and a pain and a suffering that we've been experiencing throughout all the ages. When I argue with what is, it hurts. It hurts more than sleep deprivation. And that still doesn't mean that I'm not going to a doctor. So to argue with what is, that's the emotional pain, the confusion. And to be a lover of what is is the end of suffering, because there's no decision to be made there.

So if I don't sleep, I love that! That's what is. And in the peace of that, I know where to go, what to do. It's not even me doing it.

It's a knowing. It's what is, moving itself as itself—God. So it's no longer confused.

How do you live your life when you believe the thought that you have chronic fatigue syndrome? How do you treat yourself when you believe the thought that you're supposed to sleep at night?

Valerie: This is so hard; I need you to repeat the question.

Katie: That's okay, sweetheart, I'll stay with you as long as you would like that. How do you live, how do you treat yourself, when you believe the thought that you need more sleep and you're not getting it?

Valerie: I feel like I'm protecting myself all the time. I'm afraid all the time.

Katie: Yes . . . afraid all the time. I'm not asking you to drop the thought. What I'm asking you is: Can you see a *reason* to drop the thought "I need more sleep"?

Valerie: Yes. I don't want to keep living like this.

Katie: Would you rather be crawling to the bathroom because you're so tired, or living in fear? Which is more painful?

Valerie: The memory of before I went on the medication, of how I lived then . . . this feels less painful than that. But I'm not sure that that's true.

Katie: So you live in fear when you believe the thought that you need more sleep and you're not getting it. Can you see a stress-free reason to keep the story that you need more sleep?

[To the audience] She attaches to it and to fear. I ask, "Can you see a reason to drop it?" "Yes," she says.

[To Valerie] Can you see a reason to keep the story "I need more sleep" that is *not* stressful?

2. Sleep Disorder

Valerie: This is where I get confused. If I keep the story, then I have a solution—a so-called solution, which isn't a solution I like. I have all this stuff around it. It protects me from dying.

Katie: Sweetheart, "You would die if you dropped the thought"— can you absolutely know that that's true? You're going to die anyway. No one makes it.

Valerie: Right. It's not the being dead that I care about. It's the process of . . . the suffering.

Katie: So this is your story: "If I dropped the story, I would suffer and have no control over my sleep."

Valerie: That's it.

Katie: Can you absolutely know that that's true? [Pause] "Without the story, I would have no protection"—can you absolutely know that that's true?

Valerie: I just have the memory, from when it was true before— before I was on medication—and I felt like I would go out of my mind.

Katie: I *love* how you don't answer the question!

Valerie: I didn't? Say it again, please.

Katie: To live in the past is how we miss being here, which is the only reality.

Valerie: This is my hardest story.

Katie: Yes. Can you really know that if you dropped the story "I need more sleep" you would be worse off?

Valerie: I'm sorry, I'm really having a hard time! I am!

Katie: Oh, honey, you just take your time. I'll repeat it as many times as you'd like to hear it.

Valerie: I'm hearing the words, but it's just not going in!

Katie: This messes with your sacred story, and that's what you worship. Without this? God. But this attachment to a thought—that's a false god. And to even have it questioned, the mind just tweaks all over the place. That's the power of investigation. So, "Without the story that I need more sleep, I would be worse off"—can you absolutely know that that's true?

Valerie: I can't know that it's true. It's fear in my mind—terror.

Katie: Yes, I hear you. Who would you be without the story "I need more sleep"? Who would you be if you'd never heard that story, if it had never been implanted, if you could never think it again?

Valerie: I wouldn't be worried; I'd be happy. I'd just be alive. I'd be going about my business.

Katie: So, "I need more sleep"—turn it around. "I don't . . ."

Valerie: I *don't* need more sleep?

Katie: How does that feel?

Valerie: [laughing] Like a sacrilege.

Katie: Well, it is. You're betraying the illusion. It's a betrayal of your god—of what you worship. Does it feel a little more flexible?

Valerie: I haven't entertained this! [Laughing] What am I supposed to be doing with this now?

Katie: Just laugh.

Valerie: I don't need more sleep—that's a good one!

Katie: No one ever has. No one needs more sleep than they get. That's the good news. It has never happened. It won't ever happen.

Valerie: So that means that if I'm considering what isn't enough sleep, that's what's happening?

Katie: Well, that's the way it's always been. Except for your story, that's the way it's always been, the way it's supposed to be.

Valerie: Then if it doesn't mean to go to a doctor, and it doesn't mean to take medication, how does that all fit in here?

Katie: You're going to take the trip. You're going to go to the doctor one way or the other—but *how* are you going to take the trip? You can go there in peace, or you can go there full of stress and fear. *You* don't take you there in the first place.

Valerie: Okay.

Katie: What is is. I love that you don't sleep—you can do The Work instead. There's nothing else to do.

Valerie: I could take a lot of Worksheets home with me.

Katie: Yes. How do I know I'm supposed to do self-inquiry? I'm awake. Let's see . . . what am I supposed to do now? Hmm. I can start to scare myself, or I can question my mind.

So let's make this even more real for you. Give me three genuine examples of how the turnaround "I don't need more sleep" is true in your life.

Valerie: Hmm . . . well, I guess I'm carrying on okay with the sleep I'm getting.

Katie: I would drop the "I guess."

Valerie: Okay. And second, I don't need more sleep because I don't know how much sleep my body really needs. Maybe it's less than what other people need. I just don't know.

Katie: That's huge, sweetheart! And a third reason?

Valerie: [long pause] I just can't think of a third one right now.

Katie: That's okay. The Work is meditation. This can be part of your homework. You have all the time in the world to find another example. Let's look at the next statement.

Valerie: *I want the chronic fatigue syndrome to disappear.*

Katie: What for?

Valerie: So I could have peace.

Katie: How does it feel to believe the story that you want it to go away, and you're wide awake at two o'clock in the morning, and exhausted?

Valerie: The thing is, I never am, because I'm on medication.

Katie: Okay, so—

Valerie: See, I'm not in the experience of it, but I'm always living in fear of it.

Katie: Okay, so, "You have chronic sleep disorder"—can you really know that that's true? [Pause] You see, you don't. You're sleeping at night. That's the reality of it.

Valerie: Yes, because I'm on drugs.

Katie: What's not okay about taking drugs, to sleep?

Valerie: I have a big judgment over it.

Katie: I noticed.

Valerie: *Huge* judgment.

Katie: Well, then you're the one to ask—you're the expert. What's wrong with taking drugs to sleep at night? And I'm not advocating using drugs to sleep.

Valerie: I don't want to take drugs to sleep—and I do it. So the question was?

Katie: What is not okay about using drugs to sleep at night? Do you want to sleep or not? Do you see how you are wanting two things at once? You want to sleep; you don't want to take drugs. Welcome to hell.

How do I know that you want to take drugs? You're taking them—that's it. Own it.

Valerie: Right.

Katie: "I don't want to take drugs"—turn it around. "I do . . ."

Valerie: I do want to take drugs.

Katie: Yes. Welcome to some integrity.

Valerie: Okay.

Katie: "I want to take drugs, because I want to sleep." Someone asks, "Do you take drugs?" And you can say, "Yes. I want to sleep."

Valerie: Then I hate myself for it.

Katie: Well, it's because you haven't been honest about it. People say, "I hate to take drugs, I don't want to take drugs." But that's a lie. The reason I know you want to take drugs is that you do. You *want* to take drugs so that you can sleep.

Valerie: Right.

Katie: So now you get to sleep, and you're doing what you approve of to do it. But it's a lie to say, "I don't want to take drugs," if that's how you sleep. So read that one again.

Valerie: *I want the sleep disorder to disappear.*

Katie: So "You have a sleep disorder"—is that true?

Valerie: It feels like it's true.

Katie: It would *have* to feel like it's true, because you're attached to the thought that you have it. You're feeling the thought.

Valerie: And experiencing it in my body is a thought?

Katie: It would have to be. You don't have those feelings at night when you're asleep and your mind is quiet. You open your eyes, you have the thought, and you feel it.

Valerie: Right.

Katie: The thought is the cause, and the feeling is the effect.

Valerie: Right. So is it true that I have a sleep disorder?

Katie: Can you absolutely know that that's true?

Valerie: My experience now, as I'm dropping into this, is that I've told myself so many times that I have it—a million times or more. I have to dive under all these times. It's like a million voices around me.

Katie: Yes, what fun just to dive into yourself and wait. You see, I absolutely know that I don't have a sleep disorder, that there's nothing the matter. But the thinking disorder! If I *think* that something's the matter . . .

Valerie: That's true. This is still really hard for me to get to, the experience that it's true that I don't have a sleep disorder.

Katie: Well, don't bother. Don't even expect the experience of it. Just go in, find the answer and—

Valerie: How is that different from the experience?

Katie: The expectation prejudges what the answer's going to be.

2. Sleep Disorder

Valerie: Okay. [Pause]

Katie: "You have a sleep disorder"—can you absolutely know that that's true?

[To the audience] Are you putting your AIDS on it? Are you putting your cancer on it? Are you applying your colds or flus or broken bones?

Valerie: [after a pause] How do I go in and get this, with the million concepts and the million voices? It's like a broken record. There are a million voices.

Katie: Ask each voice, "Sweetheart, is it true? Can I absolutely know that it's true?" And let's don't look at the future. Just right here in this chair: "You have a sleep disorder"—can you really know that that's true? Not tonight, not later—just right now.

Valerie: I'm getting what a large volume this story really is. It's like a thousand pages, maybe two thousand. And I keep doing it to myself.

Katie: As it should be. I just love that you're noticing. Let's look at the next statement.

Valerie: It's all about the same stuff.

Katie: It always is.

Valerie: *I want the sleep disorder to leave my body, I want the sleep disorder to leave so I can go off the medication.* So what else is new?

Katie: Let's turn it around, and where you have the phrase "sleep disorder," where you have the word "sleep," put the word "thinking." Read it just that way again and switch the words.

Valerie: I want the thinking disorder to leave my mind—instead of "my body"?

Katie: Yes. Everything is mind. So read the whole thing that way.

Valerie: I want the thinking disorder to disappear. I want the thinking disorder to leave my mind, I want the thinking disorder to leave so I can go off the medication.

Katie: Does that sound as true or truer?

Valerie: I see at this point, after all this time that the story has been going on, that I don't really know what's true under the medications. All I know is that my thinking has me in fear, and it's a whole ritual around this.

Katie: So it's a thinking disorder!

Valerie: Yes, it's fear. It creates fear, and it amplifies itself as it goes around.

Katie: What happens to you when you believe the thought that you need to sleep?

Valerie: I go into a fear—I would say, almost a panic—imagining the not-sleeping, remembering the wretchedness of it.

Katie: Can you see a reason to drop the story?

Valerie: The story scares me so much.

Katie: Can you see a reason to drop the story, if it brings you so much fear?

Valerie: Yes.

Katie: Can you see a reason to keep the story that is not stressful?

Valerie: No! It would probably help me heal, if I dropped the story.

Katie: Okay. And I would say that's none of our business. We're investigating the mind; we're healing the mind, not the body. Heal the mind, and the body will follow. It doesn't have a choice.

Valerie: If I dropped the story, I'd have less stress.

Katie: I'm not asking you to drop the story. I love the story—what else is there? We're just meeting it with a little understanding here. No one has ever dropped a story. It just appears. We didn't create it. We're not doing it. It's a happening, like air.

Valerie: We're not doing it?

Katie: Are *you* thinking you? Do you wake up in the morning and say, "I think I'll think this morning." Doesn't it just happen? It's what is. There are no friendly or unfriendly stories. There are just stories that are misunderstood—all of them. There are some stories that are very frightening, so we're just meeting them with some understanding.

Valerie: Right.

Katie: Do *you* think you? Do you think on purpose?

Valerie: No, I do meditation to try *not* to think, and that doesn't work. [The audience laughs.] Sometimes I'm lucky enough to watch it, and I'm not all in it, and I think, "Oh, I'm doing it right!" Most of the time I'm not doing it how I would consider right.

Katie: So who would you be without this story, "I need to sleep." And I'm not asking you to drop it.

Valerie: Who would I be without it? I don't know. I don't know.

Katie: You could be someone who doesn't sleep, someone who takes medication happily.

Valerie: Say that again?

Katie: You could be just living your life happily, the way that it is, without any confusion, without wanting two contradictory things at the same time. You've been living this way for eight years—in hell—so you may as well live this way without the hell.

Valerie: So what you're saying is that I should change my thoughts about it, that I should accept it?

Katie: No. You can't change your thoughts. No one can. That's not possible. I *am* suggesting that you just investigate your thoughts and meet them with some understanding. Sleep deprivation is not hurting you. It's your *thinking* that is so painful.

Let's look at the next statement.

Valerie: Again: *The chronic fatigue syndrome, the sleep disorder, shouldn't be in my body.*

Katie: Is that true? *Is* it in your body?

Valerie: Is it true that it shouldn't be in my body?

Katie: You say it's there.

Valerie: It is. It's there.

Katie: Okay, so how do you live when you believe the thought that it shouldn't be in your body, and it is, according to you?

Valerie: I fight it.

Katie: And how does that feel, to be at war?

Valerie: It makes me feel defeated.

Katie: And how does that feel? Depressing, dead, frightening, lonely—what?

Valerie: Kind of like deflated.

Katie: How does that make you feel, to be deflated?

Valerie: Depressing.

Katie: Okay, can you see a reason to drop the story?

Valerie: Yes.

Katie: Can you see a reason to keep the story that isn't depressing?

Valerie: No.

Katie: Who would you be without the story?

Valerie: I'd be more at peace.

Katie: Okay. Now let's turn it around.

Valerie: *I need chronic fatigue syndrome to leave my body.* How do I turn this around? I need my thinking to leave my body. Maybe I need my thinking to leave my mind.

Katie: On the turnarounds, you just find it. You find what you find. So, sweetheart, my mind stopped—it stopped! I met my concepts, *the* concepts that everyone has, with understanding. So it's a wash. They're there; they're of no meaning. Ultimately, words have no meaning when you investigate them. So that's all that happened. Thoughts are like the rain or the wind; they're just not personal. And if you're not under stress, it's simple how to live. You're just lived. It amazes me how people think we have some control here. It's very painful to think that.
  Can you find another turnaround?

Valerie: I need chronic fatigue syndrome—

Katie: I *don't* need . . .

Valerie: I don't need chronic fatigue syndrome to leave my body. But I do! [The audience laughs.]

Katie: Sweetheart, see if you can just experience this turnaround right now. This is a chance for you to really sink into the opposite of what you so firmly believe, your sacred religion, your "I need chronic fatigue syndrome to leave" religion. So give me three genuine examples of how the turnaround could be true in your life.

Valerie: This is really hard, Katie.

Katie: I know. So just start with one example.

Valerie: [pause] Well, I would still have a life if it didn't leave. I would still be me. So I guess ultimately, I don't absolutely *need* it to leave.

Katie: Wow!

Valerie: And if it didn't leave and I was awake at night a lot, I could write a lot of Worksheets.

Katie: Yes, you could. And a third reason?

Valerie: Maybe it's here to teach me something, and I've been spending so much time fighting it that I haven't been able to listen.

Katie: Wonderful, sweetheart. You're really going in for your own answers.
   Let's look at the next statement.

Valerie: *Chronic fatigue syndrome is cruel. Chronic fatigue syndrome is painful, frightening, and ego smashing.*

Katie: Okay. "My thinking . . ."

Valerie: My thinking is cruel. My thinking is uncaring. My thinking is painful. My thinking is frightening. My thinking is ego smashing.

Katie: Yes, it tells you there is something to be frightened of when you don't sleep, and there's something to be frightened of if you take drugs to sleep. There's always something to be frightened of. That's what this thinking is about—to keep you totally body-identified. "I, I." So this Work is just about a noticing. I: survival, I: comfort, I: pleasure. Pleasure, pain—all pleasure is pain.

2. Sleep Disorder

Valerie: All pleasure is pain?

Katie: In my experience. Every thought is about body, the body's survival, its comfort, its pleasure, and all pleasure is pain. It's hopeless. No wonder you're so frightened. So, at home, investigate. I love that you are used to meditation. You can ask one of these questions, like "'I need more sleep'—is it true?" And you can go in and have a wonderful time. It's very exciting!
  Let's look at the last one.

Valerie: The thing that I don't ever want to experience? *I don't ever want to experience sleep disorder again without the help of medication.*

Katie: "I'm willing . . ."

Valerie: I'm willing to experience the sleep disorder without the medication.

Katie: Yes, because that can put you back in The Work. Do it *with* your medication or *without* your medication. "I look forward to . . ."

Valerie: I look forward to experiencing the sleep disorder without the medication. I really do look forward to it.

Katie: Yes, it can put you back into The Work. That's what everything is for—self-realization. You've been drug-realized, sleep-realized, doctor-realized. Now be self-realized. You're good at this. There's no right or wrong here in my experience. Just work on the mind and the rest will follow. And the worst that can happen already is happening. You have nothing to lose with inquiry, and what you have to gain is freedom, so investigate this story. It's good that you don't sleep. You know what to do now. Why do you want to sleep anyway?

Valerie: To be able to function.

Katie: Why?

Valerie: So that I can take care of myself.

Katie: Why?

Valerie: Because I don't want other people to have to take care of me.

Katie: Why?

Valerie: That's a good one to investigate. I've never gone there. That's a really scary place to go!

Katie: You would deprive us of that privilege?

Valerie: *I'm* supposed to be the caretaker.

Katie: Oh, really?

Valerie: Yes.

Katie: Is that true?

Valerie: No, no.

Katie: Can you receive? You know how to give. Step into receiving. Step into the good part—it's equal. Complete it. So you don't want us to take care of you—why?

Valerie: Because it's embarrassing.

Katie: Why?

Valerie: I don't know.

Katie: So you don't want to be embarrassed—why?

Valerie: I should never have to be taken care of. Listen to this: I should always be the one who is taking care of others. I should never, ever be taken care of—ever. It's like it's a mortal sin or something. The Catholic Church, you know?

Katie: So that's frightening. That would be a frightening place. I've come to see that I've never taken care of myself—not ever. It's just a story that I attached to when it appeared.

Where are your hands now? [Valerie looks surprised. Her right hand is on her cheek; her left hand is in her lap.] Did you put them there? Did you plan that? Did you plan to put your hands where they are now?

Valerie: What? Now? Not consciously. No.

Katie: Interesting. Maybe you don't do it. Maybe you're being done. Do *you* breathe you?

Valerie: I was actually asking that question, in meditating earlier today. Who's breathing? I wasn't sure.

Katie: Well, just answer the question: Who's breathing?

Valerie: [after a pause] I don't know!

Katie: I would go with that one. Thank you, angel. It's a very sweet position. "I don't know." Good.

Valerie: Thank you.

Katie: There's a lot of freedom in "I don't know." It's being a child. This is very sweet. There's nothing *to* know. It's level ground.

3. MY MOTHER WOULDN'T APPROVE

Are you trying to spare someone's feelings by denying yourself?
Free yourself from that prison. How can you know that they'll
disapprove? And if they do, whose business is that?

Rebecca: I'm very new at this; a friend just invited me to come to
your event today, and voilà! Here I am. My question refers to the
parent-child relationship. Actually, it sort of stems from a problem
that I have with my mother. And I lied when I filled in the Worksheet. The problem was not with [choking back tears] relationships that I have now. It's . . . probably something that I didn't
work out with her . . . probably am unable to.

Katie: So what is it with your mother that you haven't worked out
yet?

Rebecca: Well, I come from a conservative Jamaican family, and
I've been living in America now for twelve years, so I don't have my
family with me. And I have to depend on myself, to pat myself on
the back and say, "You're doing okay!" I find myself, though . . .

Katie: Sweetheart, what's the problem with your mother?

Rebecca: I'm not certain I can get her approval to do what I really,
really want to do.

Katie: And what is that?

Rebecca: Well, it's music . . . yes. They've told me in the past that I shouldn't. In a conservative family, you do something practical.

Katie: So if your life became all about music as an occupation . . .

Rebecca: Well, I can't even imagine that. I think of it all the time, and it's . . . [She chokes back tears.]

Katie: . . . and it's overflowing.

Rebecca: I teach business English, and my business is going very well, and this is something my mother approves of, especially when I'm so far away.

Katie: So what is it she would not approve of?

Rebecca: Doing something impractical, something that's so risky.

Katie: Like what?

Rebecca: Singing . . . yes.

Katie: Singing where, how? As an occupation?

Rebecca: Possibly, yes.

Katie: So "if you dropped your profession . . .

Rebecca: I dare not.

Katie: . . . and you became a singer, your mother wouldn't approve"—is that true?

Rebecca: She would kill herself with worry.

Katie: That was a very quick answer. Sweetheart, this is inquiry. This is where you look for answers that are not on the surface. This is where you open your mind and heart to what you don't already know. "If you dropped your occupation and became a singer, your mother wouldn't approve"—can you absolutely know that that's true?

Rebecca: Absolutely? I can't absolutely know, but I know her well enough to know. . . . It's not . . . not 100 percent certain, but . . .

Katie: Drop your philosophy. Drop your qualifications, and just give me a straight yes or no. This is meditation. "If you become a singer, your mother would not approve"—can you absolutely know that that's true?

Close your eyes and really look for your answer. It's okay to say *yes* or no. Get a picture of your mother. Can you absolutely know she wouldn't approve?

Rebecca: [crying] I know the reality that she lives. It's not a yes or no answer, but I know her reality.

Katie: I understand. You think for her. She thinks for you, and you think for her. [Rebecca laughs.] Have you ever said things and not really meant it? "She wouldn't approve of you"—can you absolutely know that that's true?

Rebecca: Can we redefine that word *approve?*

Katie: No. Can you absolutely know that it's true she would not approve if you became a singer?

Rebecca: [after a long pause] No.

Katie: Feel that. Now, how do you react when you believe the thought "My mother would not approve"?

Rebecca: Katie, she's a worrier; she's a professional worrier.

Katie: Notice that you didn't follow the simple direction. You get to be right, and you don't answer the question.

Rebecca: Can you repeat the question?

Katie: How do you react when you believe the thought "My mother would not approve"? How do you live your life when you believe that thought?

Rebecca: Strained, disappointed, unfulfilled.

Katie: So you're living out everything you don't want *her* to experience!

Rebecca: That's true.

Katie: Close your eyes, and look at her look at you—singing. Now drop your story, just for a moment, and look at her face. Who would you be without that thought?

Rebecca: Freer! Not so cramped, not so unhappy. Not so uncertain, not so hopeless and helpless.

Katie: "My mother would be disappointed"—turn it around.

Rebecca: My mother would not be disappointed.

Katie: Could that be as true?

Rebecca: It could be. She might even be excited!

Katie: Who knows?

Rebecca: But it has its flip side. She's got enough worries, and I don't want to be the problem.

Katie: Now we're out of inquiry.

Rebecca: Oh.

Katie: Can you see how you moved out of answering the questions and into another story?

Rebecca: Yes, I see that.

Katie: So you turned around the statement "My mother would be disappointed" to "My mother would be excited." Now give me three reasons why she would be excited if you were singing and loved it.

Rebecca: Because I would be doing what I want. Because I would be doing something she possibly never had the courage to do. And because I'd be happy.

Katie: So she might be excited because you're doing something you love, because you're happy, and because it's possibly something that she wanted to do herself and didn't. "My mother would be disappointed"—can you find another turnaround?

Rebecca: Because it's another thing to worry about.

Katie: That's a reason, not a turnaround. "My mother would be disappointed"—can you find another turnaround?

Rebecca: I'm not sure I understand how to turn it around.

Katie: "My mother would be disappointed." Turn it around to yourself. "I would be . . ."

Rebecca: *I* would be disappointed—if I didn't do it.

Katie: Is your mother disappointed a lot?

Rebecca: Yes.

Katie: So if you sang, would she be any less disappointed? She's already disappointed!

Rebecca: But she's not disappointed in *me*.

Katie: What's the worst that could happen if your mother was absolutely blown away disappointed—in you? You drop your occupation, you're out there singing, and she is *very* disappointed in you. This is your nightmare. What's the worst that could happen if she was disappointed in you? [Pause]

So you take on the role of your mother, disappointed. Even exaggerate it. And I'm going to be her daughter, the one who loves her very much, the one who is singing her heart out, and loving it. I'll be you. This is your chance to experience what you think your mother would say.

Katie: [as Rebecca] "Hello, mom. Guess what? I quit my job. I'm singing now."

Rebecca: [as her mother] "Rebecca? Have you totally lost it? Have you lost your mind?"

Katie: "Oh, mom, I've lost my job, my occupation, everything. I *have* lost it."

Rebecca: "What happened to you?"

Katie: "I decided to be a singer. That's what I want to do. I love it."

Rebecca: "Rebecca, how are you going to make a living?"

Katie: "I don't know."

Rebecca: "Lord help us!" [The audience laughs.]

Katie: "That's what I'm counting on." [The audience laughs and applauds.] "So, are you disappointed, Mom?"

Rebecca: "You know we don't have a lot; I can't send you any money. I've got your father here to worry about; I've got your brothers; I've got your sister; I've got your nephew."

Katie: "Mom, I don't know how you do it. Would you like to hear me sing?"

3. My Mother Wouldn't Approve

Rebecca: "That's not funny."

Katie: "I was serious. It brings me so much joy, I thought maybe you'd want to hear what I was doing."

Rebecca: "Rebecca, this is probably not the time and place for that."

Katie: "You have a major burden on your hands, Mom. What I can tell you is, I'm going to help you in any way that I can. And I just don't know how you do it. You're an amazing woman."
[As herself] Is that all she would say, honey?

Rebecca: No, she'd say [resuming the dialogue as her mother], "Rebecca, we all worry about you, I worry about you . . . you're so far away! Who's going to feed you?"

Katie: "If I get hungry, I promise I'll call."

Rebecca: "Rebecca, we love you. I love you. And it's important—it's important for me that you're happy."

Katie: "Mom, you are so amazing. . . . Do you realize that not one time have you said that you were disappointed in me? I asked you the question and it was as though you didn't even hear me. You're incredible. You've been that way all my life. You've only wanted my happiness."

Rebecca: "Yes."

Katie: [as herself] So, "Your mother would be disappointed"—can you absolutely know that that's true?

Rebecca: [pause] No, I really can't. That's just incredible. I feel so much lighter. Thank you.

Katie: You're welcome. Sweetheart, when you believe what you think, it's as though you're living in a horrible prison. And when you question what you believe, you set yourself free. The mind becomes so open that it sees ways that you can have it all—your job, a singing career, you can have it all. But one thing you can know: When you go to work, it's because you choose it. It could be that you'll never say, "I didn't live out my passion because of my mother. I couldn't sing because I didn't want to disappoint her." It just doesn't sound reasonable.

Rebecca: It makes me sound unreasonable, yes.

Katie: Thank you. So, sweetheart, would you like to sing right now? [The audience whistles and applauds.]

Rebecca: Sure! Now this is not exactly a song my mother would approve of.

Katie: And can you absolutely know that that's true?
    [Rebecca laughs, then belts out a torrid love song. The audience applauds wildly.]

4. I Can't Stand It That George Fell in Love with Linda

You think, "I can't stand it!" Take a trip through your feelings, and find out what you really can't stand.

Katie: Welcome. Thank you for raising your hand.

Sandra: So shall I just read, or shall I tell a little bit about what's happening?

Katie: Well . . . read it.

Sandra: [choking back tears] *I can't stand it that George fell in love with Linda and has sex with her almost every day.*

Katie: Is George your husband, sweetheart?

Sandra: Yes.

Katie: "You can't stand it"—is that true?

Sandra: Yes, it's true—I can't stand it. Well, I can barely stand it. [Pause] But I *have* stood it, actually.

Katie: It was a nice trip. [The audience laughs.] The truth is that sometimes you just kind of take a trip. So your first answer was yes, but when you actually considered it for a moment, you saw that your statement was absolutely not true. *Can* you stand it?

Sandra: I can stand it—yes. I *have* been standing it.

Katie: How do you react when you believe that thought—"I can't stand it that he has sex with Linda almost every day"?

Sandra: It makes me feel like—the picture is that I'm just throwing myself backward and falling on the ground. So I guess it makes me feel . . . it's hard for me to find that right now.

Katie: Well, I get it . . . from that last graphic. How do you treat George and Linda when you believe the thought "I can't stand it"—and they walk into the room, either of them, or both?

Sandra: I want them not to exist. I want them to go away. I want them to disappear.

Katie: And what do you do just to let them know this?

Sandra: Well, either I fake how I feel about them, or—

Katie: How do you treat them specifically?

Sandra: Hmm . . .

Katie: See how hard it is to go there? We can talk about our feelings, but what do you do with your face? What do you do with your voice? How do you treat them when you believe this thought?

Sandra: Well, I don't talk to them as much. I'm not going to say that I should treat them more kindly than I do . . .

Katie: Well, I hope not, because you don't.

Sandra: I don't.

Katie: So how does that look? What do you do with your face?

Sandra: My face is more passive. I don't smile, I don't . . . I'm not happy. I don't *really* care what they're feeling.

4. I Can't Stand It . . .

Katie: So can you see a reason to drop the story "I can't stand it"?

Sandra: Yes.

Katie: Give me a peaceful reason to keep this story.

Sandra: No, there isn't one.

Katie: How do you react when you believe the thought "I can't stand it"? Feel it. Maybe your shoulders slump, your head goes down, or there's a feeling of tiredness. Now you have to live that, even at the grocery store, to prove to people that you're a person who can't stand it. This is your identity. "I can't stand it. I'm a person who can't stand it."
So who would you be without this lie, "I can't stand it"?

Sandra: Well, I would feel a lot better about myself, because actually, I *have* stood it.

Katie: Exactly so.

Sandra: And when I *see* that I've stood it, I feel very good about myself.

Katie: And when you believe you can't stand it, you have to live out that belief.

Sandra: That's right.

Katie: You *believe* you can't stand it because you haven't inquired. You haven't enlightened yourself about how the mind works. So you have to live out "I can't stand it." And when your partner comes into the room and asks, "How are you?" you say [in a depressed tone], "Oh, honey, I'm okay."
"Are you sure?"
Well, how do you live your identity? He has to believe you can't stand it because you believe it. Or you're pretending to believe it. You're pretending to believe that you believe it—because when we inquire, I hear that the truth is that you *can* stand it.

So he asks, "Are you sure?"

And you say, "Yes, honey, I'm fine."

And then you say that he's cold, because he's supposed to be psychic and realize that you're not fine. Can't he *see* that you can't stand it?

This is your identity, and you're blind to it. You think, "What's the matter with me?" Well, what's the matter is that you haven't asked. The easiest way to say it is that you're not enlightened to the thought you're attached to in the moment.

"I can't stand it"—turn it around.

Sandra: I *can* stand it.

Katie: And you do. Here's what's difficult to stand: the attachment to a lie. Not George, not Linda, not their sex—but this lie. In fact, they may be having sex at this very moment, and you're not affected.

Sandra: Right.

Katie: So if someone *tells* me they're having sex, what's the difference? I was fine before; I'm fine now. But if I attach to the thought "I can't stand it," then I have to live that out. "Oh, no! Oh my God, they're having sex!" Rather than: "Wow! I thought I couldn't stand it, and I *am* standing it!"

Sandra: I've noticed, through these months that I've been dealing with this, that there's this sort of emotional acting out. If I can just be in the place of the truth—as you're bringing it out—then I have nothing to fight with. So I'm fighting with these playing-outs, and they don't do any good. I've learned that.

Katie: Yes, that's enlightenment. I'm enlightened to the truth that I thought it was them, and it wasn't. It was my mind confused about itself.

So now we're using mind to enlighten mind, because there isn't anything else. But what we're taking here are just baby steps—and at the same time, they're huge. When we realize that it's our own mind that is causing our suffering, then The Work begins, then the fun begins. It's living in a whole other polarity, a whole other realm. And what I love about it is we no longer believe that the world is causing our suffering, that it *can* cause our suffering. It can't, not ever—no chance of it.

So, now give me three genuine examples of how the turn-around is as true as or truer than your original statement.

Sandra: I can stand it. That's so much truer. I have stood it all this time. "I can't stand it" is an out-and-out lie.

Katie: That's one.

Sandra: I've stayed with him. I haven't left—not yet, anyway. So I can stand it.

Katie: That's two.

Sandra: And even though I hate what he's doing, I still love him. If I really couldn't stand it, I would have done something else. Or I'd be in the loony bin.

Katie: Thank you for telling yourself the simple truth. Let's look at the next statement.

Sandra: *It hurts me when George tells me that he is happier now than he has ever been in his life.*

Katie: So, sweetheart, turn it around.

Sandra: It hurts me when I tell myself that *I* . . . [She breaks into laughter.]

Katie: Did you go there?

Sandra: That's actually true. [The audience laughs.]

Katie: Yes, we *hate* to lose. We lose the identity of the one who can't stand it. And we see that in reality we're the one who has always been happy. That's what it leaves.

Say it the way you turned it around.

Sandra: It hurts me when I tell myself that I am happier now than I have ever been in my life.

Katie: So tell me about that.

Sandra: I'm going to say it again: It hurts me when I tell myself that I am happier now than I have ever been in my life. I'm a little confused.

Katie: What did you understand the first time?

Sandra: Well, I *am* happier than I have ever been. It's *not* that it hurts me.

Katie: There you have it. That's it!

Sandra: I *am* happier.

Katie: Well, it hurts when we lose. When you find out the truth, that you're happier than you've ever been, there's goes the identity of "I can't stand this!" There goes your suffering. It hurts you to admit that you're happier than you've ever been.

Sandra: In comparison to who I thought I was, and what I thought I needed . . . to lose that . . . and at the same time I'm standing in a feeling of fullness of myself more than I have been. It's true: It's both things. It's both things.

Katie: I hear that. Yes, you *would* be happier than you've ever been in your life—until you attach to a story that isn't true for you.

Sandra: So . . . why would I want to attach to that story so strongly?

Katie: Because you don't know you're attached to it! You haven't asked *you*. Your mother said, "It's a tree." You said, "Okay." She said, "It's a sky." You said, "Sky . . . I'll go with that." She told you your name, and you said, "Okay." And you never asked you.

Sandra: So in your experience, is it the attaching—the strong attaching—that's the pain?

Katie: The ignorance—I call it ignorance. If my mother tells me it's a tree, and I don't ask me, then I teach the world my own ignorance. "It's a tree." I didn't ask me. If I asked me, maybe I would be awake to it—to whatever it is for me. So ignorance is the only suffering. I call it confusion.

And The Work is education, because these are questions that take you *in* to your truth, not ours. You are your own wisdom. I love this Work because it has everyone's own fingerprint on it. So, sweetheart, do you want him to be happy?

Sandra: Well . . . yes . . . well . . . [The audience laughs.] I'm struggling with this one because there's a part of me . . . I almost wrote it down . . . that wants George to be free.

Katie: So let's hear it the way you just read it.

Sandra: Okay. *It hurts me when George tells me that he is happier now than he has ever been in his life.*

Katie: Do you want him to be happy?

Sandra: I feel he's being happy . . .

Katie: Here's a good one: Close your eyes. Now, picture him; get a picture of his face while he's having sex with Linda.

Sandra: Oh . . . okay.

Katie: Just picture his face.

Sandra: Yes . . .

Katie: Okay, now look at him for just a moment without your story. What do you see?

Sandra: I see that he's happy.

Katie: Is that what you want?

Sandra: Yes. I'm happy for him.

Katie: There you have it. You know, it's just like the part where I want you to be happy—but only if I'm the one who can give you that.

Sandra: That's right.

Katie: The question is, do you want him to be happy or not? That's love. And until you find it, there's no happiness for you. Because you're denying the truth. And the truth is that you don't care *who* makes him happy, as long as he's happy.

There's nothing we can do about that except attach to thoughts that would tell us otherwise. And we call this "proof." But when we put those on paper, they fall apart.

Do you really care if it's you or her who gives him this happiness?

Sandra: Well, I do. I *do* care, and that's my problem. A part of me can see it not that way, and a part of me is still in the other way.

Katie: Okay, so you know that you're placing a condition on his happiness. "I want him to be happy, but I need to be the one."

Sandra: Yes.

Katie: So the truth is, "I *don't* want him to be happy. If I'm not the one, then I want him to be miserable." So you *don't* want his happiness.

Sandra: That would be more truthful.

Katie: And that's not love. So it's really nice that he's with *her,* since you don't love him anyway. [The audience laughs.] He knows it. Now you know it.

Just be with it a moment. Do you want him to live with someone he's not happy with?

Sandra: Well, I have to admit that a part of me does!

4. I Can't Stand It . . .

Katie: So it's wonderful to tell him all these things. Maybe *that* will attract him. [The audience laughs again.]

Sandra: To tell him . . .

Katie: "I don't love you, and I don't care about your happiness, and I want you to live with me whether you like it or not."

Sandra: That's what I feel *he's* been telling *me.* So I guess, yes . . .

Katie: And you're the last to know. Read the statement again.

Sandra: *It hurts me when George tells me that he is happier now than he has ever been in his life.* So I'm still feeling that I'm the one who wants to make him happy, and he can't be happy if it's not me. That's the truth.

Katie: So there it is . . . you're enlightened to it. And when he asks, "Do you love me?" you can say, "No, I notice I don't care a lot about you . . . and I still want to live with you. And I don't care if you're happy about it or not—that's where I am." It's called an honest, straight-up partner. And in that truth, you understand why he sleeps with her—or not. This is why people fight.

Sandra: I'm not sure about the sleeping-with-her part. But I am sure about where the truth is for me, right now, that is true, what I said.

Katie: Good, honey, good Work. Let's look at the next statement.

Sandra: *I don't like George telling me that I need this experience, and that it is for my spiritual growth.*

Katie: Turn it around: "I don't like me telling him . . ."

Sandra: I don't like me telling him that I need this experience . . . yes. And that it is for my spiritual growth. That's right. I don't like feeling the humiliation of that, in front of him. That's true.

Katie: Okay, read it like that again.

Sandra: I don't like me telling him that . . .

Katie: ". . . that living with me . . ."

Sandra: I don't like me telling him that living with me . . .

Katie: ". . . is best for his . . ."

Sandra: . . . is best for his experience. I'm getting confused.

Katie: ". . . is best for his spiritual growth."

Sandra: Is best for his spiritual growth. But I *do* like telling him that it is. [The audience laughs.]

Katie: Well, he does, too! [The audience laughs even more.]

Sandra: Or I could say I *like* telling George that living with me is best for his spiritual growth.

Katie: And he likes telling you what's best for your spiritual growth, just as you like telling him what's best for his spiritual growth.

Sandra: Oh, that's true.

Katie: You both really like that.

Sandra: [laughing] Yes! Yes . . . okay.

Katie: Let's look at the next statement.

Sandra: *I don't like George finding deeper sexual fulfillment with Linda than he did with me.*

Katie: Is that true?

Sandra: It might take me a little while to find this.

Katie: That's okay, sweetheart, very few humans have gone that deep . . . to the truth that waits for us, whether we meet it or not.

Sandra: [after a very long pause] I'm just screaming and screaming inside: "You can't, you can't, you can't!"

Katie: And does he?

Sandra: I think he does.

Katie: Can that screaming change reality?

Sandra: No, no. But in the absence of the screaming, I'm faced with such terrible feelings. I have to have *him* be different . . . I have to have *life* be different so that I don't feel those ways that I don't know how to not feel. Once those feelings start, it's like a deep black hole. So I can feel them, and I've been with them as much as I can, and still I'm really afraid of dying in that place and never coming out.

Katie: So, "If you went into that place, you would never come out"—can you absolutely know that that's true? Be slow with that one.
   [After a long pause] Can you absolutely know that you would never come out if you went into that place?

Sandra: No.

Katie: And how do you react when you believe that?

Sandra: Terrible fear . . . and all the compulsion toward him, and all the futile living to keep from dying in that place and never coming out.

Katie: Yes. Can you see a reason to drop the story "If I went into that place I would never come out"?

Sandra: Well, I can see a reason. But I have to say that I can't say that I truly know that I wouldn't.

Katie: That's okay.

Sandra: Because the only way that I know to come out of *that* place is by being in what I would call false places. And I don't want to go there, so I don't know how.

Katie: Yes.

Sandra: I don't know how to come out of that place. That is really what the truth is.

Katie: What about inquiry? [Pause] I simply asked, can you see a *reason* to drop the story "I would never come out of that place if I went there."

Sandra: Well, yes, I can see a reason, because that's really making it difficult.

Katie: So now, give me a reason to believe that thought that doesn't cause fear or stress. Give me something legitimate, something that's useful about it.

Sandra: Something useful—

Katie: That's not stressful. There must be a reason for that thought other than masochism.

Sandra: [after a long pause] I don't know. It seems, now, like an unnecessary thought.

Katie: Unless you're looking for fear on purpose, misery on purpose.

Sandra: I would need to really look into that.

Katie: That's wonderful. I respect that you will do that. Who would you be if you didn't have the ability to believe that thought?

Sandra: That I would never come out?

Katie: Yes. Who would you be without that, going in—if you didn't have the ability to believe that thought? Who would you be, going into that place?

Sandra: Well, I think I would probably feel the blackness. I wouldn't be crushing myself down psychologically. I think I would be just noticing what that place was.

Katie: Maybe even enjoying it—maybe you'd be finding things in there that you could never have imagined, that are beautiful rather than the opposite. That's the power of love, the power of peace. Fear is blind. So, "If I went into that place, I would never come out"—turn it around.

Sandra: If I went into that place, I *would* come out.

Katie: Could be just as true.

Sandra: It could be just as true. It's an area of life that is very unfamiliar to me.

Katie: It's very unfamiliar to most people, because they haven't had inquiry. I've been to that place, and inquiry was alive because I stayed in it. You go into that dark place, and when you think, "I can't come out," the mate to that thought—"Is it true?" or "Who would I be without that story?"—meets any thought that would lead you to believe that there's a dark place at all. And in that, there's a balance, and you come back to what I call the last judgment—woman sitting in chair with friend. It could even be as simple as seeing his smile and recognizing it as something you *are* familiar with.

Sandra: Thank you very much for that.

Katie: You're welcome. Thank you for *your* part. I ask the questions; you answer. That gives us a friendship, an equal friendship. A balance that's intimate.

Sandra: Yes.

Katie: And I love that you don't need me for it. Let's look at the next statement.

Sandra: *I want George to stop getting stoned as a way of life and believing that he is wiser as a result.*

Katie: "He believes he's wiser"—can you really know that that's true?

Sandra: Yes.

Katie: He says so . . .

Sandra: He says so.

Katie: He swears to it.

Sandra: Yes.

Katie: So, "He believes he's wiser"—can you absolutely know that that's true, that he believes that?

Sandra: Well, I guess I could say he's telling me, but I don't know if it's completely true *inside* him.

Katie: Yes. So if I tell you that I'm wiser than you are, I'm going to have to get pretty fierce with it because I'm never going to believe it. So this is where war breaks out. And if you don't see me as wiser, then we part ways.
   One day I noticed that I *don't* believe that, and it's not a humble thing, it's simply that I *can't* know. So I dropped the contest. How do you react when you believe that he believes he's wiser?

Sandra: I think he's a fool.

Katie: And how do you treat him when you believe this thought and you think he's a fool?

Sandra: I treat him with contempt. That's really true.

Katie: And how does that look, graphically?

Sandra: Well, I don't know how that looks to him, but for me, there's a hardening in my heart, hardening in my jaw, just hardening.

Katie: And what does it look like on your face, when you look at him?

Sandra: I'll look at you like that?

Katie: Yes. [Sandra gives Katie "the look"—full of projected judgment.] Yes, feel it, feel it. Good. How does it feel to treat someone you love this way? To hold him in contempt? How does it feel *inside* you?

Sandra: Well, to be completely honest, there's a belief somewhere that if I do that, I'll get what I want.

Katie: And has it worked so far?

Sandra: No.

Katie: Does it work in the long run, even?

Sandra: No, no, it hasn't worked.

Katie: So can you see a reason to drop the story?

Sandra: Again, it's the mixed feeling of having to lose something that I've been trying to get. Maybe you could speak about that a little bit? I'm willing to maintain these hurtful behaviors—hurtful to me, hurtful to him—because I can't stand the consequences of not holding on.

Katie: Is that true?

Sandra: Oh! Okay, wait a second . . . I don't know. . . . The consequences aren't the way I think they should be. I want something else. So to say I can't stand it is compounding that problem. I see that . . . and then the chagrin, utter chagrin of not getting him the way I want him, I can't let go of that. Okay, so that's a belief—"I can't let go of that."

Katie: You've got it, very good.

Sandra: So by saying I can't let go of that—I'm telling myself I can't let go of that, so I'm imprisoning myself, enslaving myself to this—

Katie: Lie.

Sandra: . . . pattern . . .

Katie: To this lie.

Sandra: . . . to this lie. The first lie is that I can't let go of it. But there's also the lie that he should be different.

Katie: And the way you treat him has changed. "He's different"— is it true? No.

Sandra: No.

Katie: So can you see a reason to drop the story that he thinks he's wiser than you are?

Sandra: Well, maybe I *could* stand it, if I dropped it. I mean, I've been believing that I *can't* stand it. So, yes.

Katie: Feel your face now.

Sandra: [laughing] A lot better!

Katie: There's nothing more fun than going inward rather than outward to them. Outward to them—we treat them with contempt and anger and coldness, and then wonder why they're happier with someone else. After all, don't we give them our whole life? What a life! Who would you be without this identity: "I am the woman who . . ."

Sandra: Who would I be if—

Katie: Read it again, the way you wrote it.

Sandra: Okay. *I want George to stop getting stoned as a way of life and believing that he is wiser as a result.* So who would I be if I didn't think that way, right?

Katie: Yes. Let's turn it around. I think it will show us.

Sandra: Okay. I want *me* to stop getting stoned as a way of life . . .

Katie: On George.

Sandra: I want me to stop getting stoned on George . . .

Katie: As a way of life.

Sandra: As a way of life. [She bursts into laughter.]

Katie: He does marijuana; you do George . . .

Sandra: As a way of life—right.

Katie: Look what marijuana does to his mind, in your opinion. And look what the thoughts of George do to your mind. Who's more stoned?

Sandra: I actually can't say who's more stoned.

Katie: Okay, honey. Let's look at the next statement.

Sandra: *I want George to want me more than he wants Linda.*

Katie: Is that true?

Sandra: It's only half true.

Katie: And how do you react when you believe it?

Sandra: I'm infuriated.

Katie: So can you see a reason to drop the story? And I'm not asking you to drop it.

Sandra: I'd like to go to this place again. If I drop that story, then I'm left in a place that is unfamiliar to me, where I don't have that thing out there that I've always had.

Katie: And what does that leave?

Sandra: Well, it leaves me, but I feel alone.

Katie: It leaves you in the unknown.

Sandra: Yes, it leaves me alone in the unknown.

Katie: Okay, is that true? "It leaves you alone in an unfamiliar place"—is that true? Have you ever sat in a chair before?

Sandra: Yes.

Katie: Been with the trees? Inside a home? That's where you're going to be.

Sandra: Okay, but psychologically I'm not there.

Katie: Without a story, it leaves you where you are. And it's a very beautiful place: woman standing, sitting, or lying horizontal somewhere. That's it. Rather than out of herself in the world of George.

"I would be on unfamiliar ground and alone"—is that true? There's a planet of humans here; you can't be alone. And if you're out in the desert, you can't be alone. There are lizards and cactuses even in the most desolate place. I've been there. It's alive; it's not dead! You can't be alone, and you can't be in an unfamiliar place. Only a story would lead you to believe that there is such a place!

Sandra: Right.

Katie: And it is so frightening that eventually it brings you back to "woman sitting in chair"—feel the chair hold you. It's there for you to notice. And the ground—we have gravity here; this is amazing! It will hold you. And your mind will do this, and air will support you. It's not unfamiliar ground, and you're not alone. Nothing you can do about that either.

Sandra: So the inquiry would help me rediscover that or experience that.

Katie: Read it again.

Sandra: *I want George to want me more than he wants Linda.*

Katie: And who would you be without that story?

Sandra: Okay . . . it's like I lose my boundaries.

Katie: I don't see that you need boundaries. You're doing fine without them. I don't see anyone attacking *you*. I hear that you attack George occasionally.

Sandra: I do.

Katie: No wonder you project that you need boundaries. Look how you attack *him*. I discovered one day that for me, boundaries are an act of selfishness. And I'm not saying drop your boundaries. Play with them.

Sandra: Okay.

Katie: Okay, angel, let's look at the next statement.

Sandra: *George shouldn't think that he has really found his happiness by being in love with and being passionate with Linda.*

Katie: Is that true? "He shouldn't think that"—is that true?

Sandra: I don't *want* him to think it. That's what's true.

Katie: Is that true?

Sandra: That I don't want him to think it? Yes, I don't. I don't.

Katie: Can anyone change *your* thinking?

Sandra: I can't change it, but I don't want it.

Katie: How does it feel when you believe that thought?

Sandra: That I don't want it? In your words, I'm at war.

Katie: Then that's what you get. Now—do you want that? Is that what you want?

Sandra: No. I don't want that.

Katie: Ah! That's interesting Work. That's why I'm a lover of what is. I want what *is* because I noticed what you just noticed.

Sandra: Because you don't want to feel that way.

Katie: Exactly. I call it self-love. Read it again.

Sandra: *George shouldn't think that he has really found his happiness by being in love with, and being passionate with, Linda.*

Katie: "He shouldn't think that"—is that true? Can you absolutely know that that's true? That's like saying the tree shouldn't be out there in the yard.

Sandra: Right. That's right.

Katie: How do you react when you believe this thought, that he shouldn't think that?

4. I Can't Stand It . . .

Sandra: I'm in a constant state of contraction and beating. That's how I'm living.

Katie: Can you see a reason to drop the thought?

Sandra: Yes. [Laughing] Yes, I can see it. And I can't see any reason to keep it that wouldn't feel bad.

Katie: Yes. And who would you be without the story that people shouldn't think their thoughts?

Sandra: Let's say *this* thought, if you don't mind.

Katie: I don't at all.

Sandra: Okay.

Katie: This thought, that thought . . .

Sandra: Well . . . again, I'm faced with a dilemma of seeing the relief and still desperately grasping onto something that I think I need out there. If I allow that thought to exist, then I see myself in a way that I don't like. If I allow the thinking to exist—that he's found his happiness—then I feel all those thoughts about myself. Then I guess I could ask, "Are those true?"

Katie: You could. Because those are your proof. Without them, your whole case falls apart.

Sandra: That's my case.

Katie: And as you write your case down and put it up against inquiry, it leaves you with no proof. But it's something you have to do, to realize it. You can't just say, "Oh, I realize it." It's not enough.

Sandra: The Work, as I usually try to do it, is to focus outward. I don't take that menu of myself, that horrible menu that is the reason I can't move into peace because I'm going to lose the hope that I could possibly be proven to be okay, acceptable, or loved. So—while I'm sitting here—can I do one with you, like "I am not good enough"?

Katie: [to the audience] Is she going for it, or what?
Yes, you're doing our Work for us. I love your gentle tenacity.

Sandra: Okay, so the thought, among many thoughts, "I'm not good enough," is the thing I'm trying to keep from being proven by George's thinking that he's happier with her than with me. Because if he is, then . . .

Katie: Yes. Your story is "He's with her, and happier with her, because I'm not good enough."

Sandra: Right.

Katie: Can you know that that's true? Can you absolutely know that that's true, that that's why he's with her?

Sandra: So, okay, just a minute . . . I believe it, and the worst thing is that it's almost like I *want* to believe it. I *want* to believe that thought, and I don't know why.

Katie: It gives you an identity of the woman who hurts.

Sandra: Yes, it gives me an identity. One thing that I really love about The Work—as opposed to so many of these other things—is that you don't just stick something else in there. You don't just stick "I'm okay" in there.

Katie: I love when you stick something else there. We just look at that, too.

Sandra: Okay.

Katie: Can you absolutely know that he's happier with her because you aren't good enough?

4. I Can't Stand It . . .

[To the men in the audience] Men, do you go shopping for women? Do you never look at another woman until you think, "The one I'm with is not good enough; now I'll go shopping"? Is that how it works?

Men in audience: [in unison] No!

Katie: No. [Sandra bursts into laughter.] Just checking it out, just taking a poll here—a little census reading. So how do you react when you believe this thought?

Sandra: Oh, it's terrible. It's terrible! I feel so low, so bad.

Katie: Not good enough?

Sandra: Yes.

Katie: Not like *you?*

Sandra: Not like me . . . yes, I guess that's true.

Katie: And then we say, "He's doing it." But it's a lie. It's attachment to an uninvestigated story: "I'm not good enough." Who would you be without this mantra: "I'm not good enough. He's with her because I'm not good enough"?

Sandra: [pause] No thought. No thought.

Katie: "I'm not good enough"—turn it around.

Sandra: I *am* good enough.

Katie: That could be just as true.

Sandra: Yes. It could be just as true.

Katie: Which one feels truer?

Sandra: "I am good enough" feels truer.

Katie: Don't you hate it? [Laughter.] We know, we know. We use our story of another to delude ourselves. I heard a woman say, in one of the sessions yesterday, "I just realized that my father did what he did not because of me, but because of his story!" Did you hear that?

Sandra: Yes, I did.

Katie: So it could be as simple as that. You do what you do because of your story. Because of your story, you attack him in a manner that doesn't feel like you. And because of his story—who knows? It's not your business. Just watch your own story. And if it doesn't feel right, then put that concept up against inquiry.

Sandra: Right. I hear you.

Katie: There's only mind meeting mind. What a chase! And once it's over, the mind that says "I'm not good enough" and the mind that through the questions knows it *is* good enough come together. Mind is infinite. I *am* that infinite mind; I am everything, everything, and there's no confusion in it. It's clear; it's the mind meeting itself. Question, answer—they never travel separately again. And it eventually knows that it's nothing and wants to see itself, so its reflection looks like something, but it understands— it's nothing. It looks like *that*.

So, can you find three genuine examples of how the turn-around is true in your life? "I am good enough."

Sandra: Well, there are times when I do feel attractive—sexy, even.

Katie: Good. And a second example?

Sandra: I'm bright. I'm really good at what I do professionally. I like that about myself.

Katie: And can you find a third example?

Sandra: Well, I'm a good daughter. I'm a good friend . . . except when I want to kill George. [The audience laughs.]

4. I Can't Stand It . . .

Katie: Okay, sweetheart, let's look at the next statement.

Sandra: Thank you.

Katie: You're welcome, angel. It's a privilege to sit with you. It's all so simple, isn't it?

Sandra: Yes, it is. *George should feel bad for what he's doing.*

Katie: Is that true?

Sandra: I don't like how I feel when I think that way, so . . .

Katie: Let's go back to the other one, just before this one, and turn it around.

Sandra: I shouldn't think that I have really found *my* happiness by being in love with and being passionate about George. . . . Yes.

Katie: You're doing with him what you don't want *him* to do!

Sandra: That's true!

Katie: Yes. Good. I like the part where "It's okay for me, but not you, honey. It's working for me, but you give it up." Now read the next statement.

Sandra: Okay. *I need George to meet me with a clear consciousness at all times.*

Katie: Is that true? Is that what you need?

Sandra: No. I can see that by demanding that, I'm moving away from that place that we're talking about.

Katie: Who would you be without this story?

Sandra: Just fine.

Katie: I see that statement as meaning: "If he stopped smoking marijuana, he would prefer you to her." Can you really know that that's true? [Sandra laughs.] I like these little back doors that we've got going.

Sandra: Right, because if he stopped smoking marijuana, he would come to his senses. [The audience laughs.]

Katie: Right.

Sandra: Well, let's see. Well, I guess that's that same chase again.

Katie: So how do you react when you believe that? How do you treat him when you believe that if he gave up smoking, he would choose you?

Sandra: Well, self-righteous, punishing, like a know-it-all. . . . Ah, I'm not an attractive woman in that state, either to him *or* to me.

Katie: Yes. And to you is where you feel it. And when he looks at you, he reflects back to you what you feel about yourself. Even if he smiled, you would perceive what you feel inside as being what that smile is about.

Sandra: Yes.

Katie: Can you see a reason to drop this story?

Sandra: Yes.

Katie: Give me a reason to keep it that is not stressful. Give me a reason to keep it as a tool in your life.

Sandra: That's a good word.

Katie: "If he didn't smoke". . . Well, haven't we been using these as tools, to protect our boundaries?

Sandra: Yes. Okay . . . so now I give you a peaceful reason to keep this tool?

Katie: Yes. "He would prefer me to her if he stopped smoking."

Sandra: There isn't one.

Katie: Who would you be without this story in the presence of George?

Sandra: I feel very light.

Katie: And respecting his choices—stoned or not.

Sandra: Actually, it's much less interesting to me. This space is much more interesting to me.

Katie: Oh my! You do inquiry for a while and no human can compete with what you've got going *inside* you. They're just a bonus, because they bring you back again. There's no separation; it's all *inside* you, awake.

Sandra: Awake.

Katie: That's my experience. What you speak of—that's it. He can't compete with that.

Sandra: Right. And I'm just toppling that over, time after time after time after time.

Katie: Isn't that it?

Sandra: Yes.

Katie: We've been looking for love in all the wrong places, but only *all* the wrong places. [The audience laughs.] Okay, sweetie, let's turn that one around.

Sandra: I want me to meet me with a clear consciousness at all times. That's true, right.

Katie: There's another one.

Sandra: I want me to meet George—that's beautiful—with a clear consciousness at all times.

Katie: Yes! The man smokes—see it clearly. He prefers her—see it clearly. And you prefer meeting yourself with a clear consciousness.

Sandra: Yes.

Katie: You have your lover; he has his. . . . For some of us, falling in love with ourselves is the ultimate. There can be no other lover.

Sandra: Uh-huh.

Katie: Even though it may appear we have one. There's no competition.

Sandra: I hear that.

Katie: Even our own body can't compete with this thing you call consciousness. Let's look at the next.

Sandra: *George is deluded, self-indulgent, looking outside for happiness, rationalizing, not really in touch, excited, happy, and satisfied.*

Katie: "George is deluded"—can you absolutely know that that's true?

Sandra: I can see the poison in myself by thinking that.

Katie: Yes. "George is deluded"—can you absolutely know that that's true? He sounds very clear to me. He wants to smoke, he wants her . . .

Sandra: I don't know if he's deluded or not!

Katie: Isn't that fine?

Sandra: I mean, I don't even want to speculate on it. Because if I speculate on it, I don't like how I feel! So why should I?

Katie: Yes, it's a waste of time, being out of yourself. It's all happening from here, anyway! You may as well just save yourself the trip.

Sandra: So you're saying that inquiry will bring you back to this place, right?

Katie: Well, I don't bother saying it. I notice that that's how it is for you. So *you* can ask you.

Sandra: Well, certainly it is. Certainly it has.

Katie: So there you have it. That's my experience, also.

Sandra: I would say that the experience I've had of this when I'm by myself is more fleeting. And now that we're really focused, I can see it more as unchanging.

Katie: I like that we sit together like this. Because I don't move, you get a taste of what you are inside that doesn't move. And when you sit with inquiry, you know the power of it. You know your possibility of just sitting with "Is it true?"—of just sitting with the questions and going in and not moving as the questioner, like this one.

Sandra: Right.

Katie: People say, "I've done The Work, and it doesn't work!" Well, of course it doesn't. It doesn't work unless you really answer the questions. The questions are nothing; it's your *answers* that count!

It's really sweet watching how you do that, and don't settle for less. You are our possibility. Let's look at the next statement.

Sandra: *George is self-indulgent.*

Katie: No, let's go back and turn that last one around.

Sandra: I am deluded, when I see him as deluded.

Katie: In that moment.

Sandra: Yes. The same craziness that I think he is, I actually feel in my own mind when I look at it that way.

Katie: "He's crazy"—is it true? Can you really know that it's true? Smoking marijuana would be crazy for you; we can't know what it is for him. How do you treat him when you believe "He's crazy"?

Sandra: I don't want to touch him or look at him.

Katie: Who would you be without the story that he or anyone on this planet is crazy?

Sandra: Hmm . . . I don't know. I need to spend time with that.

Katie: Isn't that delicious?

Sandra: Yes.

Katie: Finally, a game we can understand, because this world is not possible to understand when we see it as a physical world. But as we start working with mind, it all begins to make sense. So we work with our thoughts about the world, and we include the world when we do it. I love it; it's a balance. That way we don't *leave* it; we respect it.
So "He's crazy"—turn it around.

Sandra: I am crazy when I see him as crazy.

Katie: Yes, the man is on his path. It requires marijuana. That's his job—he's doing it. Your job is *not* to smoke marijuana—you're doing it.

Sandra: Right.

Katie: We all have our job. Until it changes, we're doing it.

4. I Can't Stand It . . .

Sandra: I would just say, by sitting here, the choice is to tangle myself up or be at ease. And I would rather be at ease. And I've been tangling myself up, moment after moment after moment.

Katie: Yes. And the next statement?

Sandra: *George is self-indulgent.* I don't know. I mean, that's my basis, looking at him and making myself feel shitty thinking like that.

Katie: And self-indulgent.

Sandra: And self-indulgent.

Katie: George-indulgent.

Sandra: George-indulgent. Yes! That's true. That's really true.
George is looking outside for happiness. Well, obviously . . . [The audience laughs.]
George is rationalizing, and I actually can't say that I really know that that's true, although a half hour ago I would have said I *did* know that that's true. And I can see that *I* certainly am—with all these rationalizations about him.
George is not really in touch. Again, that's connected to what I want. I don't know if he's really not in touch.

Katie: Sounds like he's perfectly in touch. He wants to smoke; he wants to have sex with Linda. He sounds like he's in touch. No matter what you say or do, the man doesn't move.

Sandra: That's right.

Katie: He's very in touch. So turn it around.

Sandra: I am not really in touch.

Katie: Especially about George.

Sandra: Especially about George—that is the truth. That's what I'm avoiding feeling. That's exactly what I'm avoiding feeling. So you're sitting here and you look like you're okay, you know, that these things have fallen away, and you're still here.

Katie: Well, whether they fall away or not, I'm still here. There are two ways to be here: One feels right, and the other feels the way we've looked at.

Sandra: Yes.

Katie: So there are two ways to be with George—or anyone. Okay, honey.

Sandra: *George is excited*—I'm excited. I'm actually . . . that's true.
    George is happy—I'm happy . . . that's true.
    George is satisfied—I'm satisfied, that's true. That's true; that's true. Just let the truth be known.

Katie: I love how you meet it. It really is the end of war. Let's look at the next statement.

Sandra: This is number six. *I don't ever want to experience George preferring Linda again.*

Katie: "I'm willing . . ."

Sandra: I'm willing to experience George preferring Linda again.

Katie: "I look forward to . . ."

Sandra: I look forward to George preferring Linda again?

Katie: Yes, because that will show you what's left of your delusional thinking. And it takes you into what you love: you—and your freedom. That's the *only* reason he would be with Linda. That's how it is.

Sandra: Wow!

Katie: He has to do that until you get it. And then when that's okay with you, then it's done. So good, look forward to it. Sweet Work.

Sandra: Thank you.

Katie: It's lovely to be in the position where you know how to reach that place inside you that rings true.

Sandra: Thank you, Katie.

5. The Rent Increase

In the following dialogue, which took place in Germany, we learn that a rent increase is a gift and the law is a guru. The way to accomplish change is to know that your enemy is your friend. That's obvious when you inquire into it.

Ernst: *I'm angry at my landlord—the federal government—because they're trying to raise my rent above the legal level.*

Katie: "People shouldn't break the law"—is it true?

Ernst: Yes.

Katie: So you're paying them to break the law.

Ernst: I don't want to pay!

Katie: And *are* you paying them?

Ernst: I may not. I'm trying to fight it in court.

Katie: That sounds very honest to me.

Ernst: But it's causing me bad feelings. It's not just a thought. I feel personally hurt by this.

Katie: So, "People shouldn't break the law"—is it true? *Do* they break it?

Ernst: Yes.

Katie: And, "People shouldn't raise the rent"—is it true?

Ernst: It is true, but they do it.

Katie: For me, what's true is whatever is really happening. Whether you like it or not, they're raising the rent. In reality, there is no such thing as a *should* or a *shouldn't*. These are only thoughts that we superimpose onto reality. Without the *shoulds* and *shouldn'ts,* we can see reality as it is; and this leaves us free to act efficiently, clearly, and sanely. *Are* they raising your rent?

Ernst: Yes.

Katie: So people *should* raise the rent. Why? Because they do. That's what's true. That's what we do. We break the law. We raise the rent, until we don't. And do you want to keep your money?

Ernst: Yes.

Katie: And *they* want to keep *their* money. So you have everything in common. What happens inside you when you attach to this lie: "People shouldn't raise the rent"? The reason I call it a lie is that when you look at the reality of it, you can see that you've been arguing with what is.

Ernst: I can feel that in me.

Katie: You're attached to that lie. You really believe that people shouldn't raise the rent, even though the reality of it is that they *do* raise the rent. You're reading what's right in front of you. The notice is right here—your rent has been raised. If we stop and inquire, we get to see that we really are lovers of what is. Who would you be without your story that people shouldn't raise the rent?

5. The Rent Increase

Ernst: I'd have more time for other things. I'd feel freer.

Katie: That sounds good to me. Can you turn the statement around?

Ernst: *I* shouldn't raise the rent?

Katie: You're raising your *internal* rent and costing yourself a lot of time and energy. Now, can you give me three examples of how this turnaround is as true as or truer than your original statement?

Ernst: I shouldn't raise my internal rent. Yes, I can see that.

Katie: And two more examples?

Ernst: I shouldn't raise the rent if I am ever a landlord. Hmm. I might have a problem with that. [The audience laughs.]

Katie: Oh, well! You might find that it's not so easy for you to do what you want them to do, especially if your expenses start going up. But this is *your* philosophy. So practice it. And a third example?

Ernst: I shouldn't raise the rent on my girlfriend. When I'm upset with her, I shouldn't start charging her more in my mind, demanding more of her, or taking things out on her.

Katie: Good, sweetheart. Let's look at the next statement.

Ernst: *I want them to obey the law.*

Katie: Hopeless. That's the judge's business, the business of the courts. Turn it around.

Ernst: I want me to obey the law. But I *don't* necessarily want to obey the law. [The audience laughs.]

Katie: [to the audience] Is this you? [The audience laughs again.] [To Ernst] So what laws don't you want to obey?

Ernst: Parking regulations.

Katie: Is that true? Do you want to get a ticket? Or do you want to obey the law?

Ernst: I want to get away with it.

Katie: [laughing] This is *our* voice! Tell me, sweetheart, what's easier: to take this wonderful illegal parking spot and risk getting a ticket or to keep looking for a legal parking spot?

Ernst: The easiest would be to just be like you. Somebody to tell you: "Do this or that," and you do it. Very easy.

Katie: Well, the law makes it very easy. It tells us what to do like a great guru. It's absolutely clear. Park here, you get a ticket. Park there, you don't. Simple. There's no confusion in it.

When you jump out of a plane and you pull the parachute cord and it doesn't open, you feel fear because you have the next cord to pull. So you pull that one and it doesn't open—and that's the last cord. Now there's no decision to make. When there's no decision, there's no fear, so you just enjoy the trip!

Obeying the law is peace. Arguing with the law, trying to get away with something, creates a lot of stress in your life. I love the laws of the land. They make my life very simple. And when you're free inside, there is no government that can take that freedom from you. So, read the next statement you wrote.

Ernst: *They shouldn't try to find weird ways to get my money.*

Katie: Turn it around.

Ernst: I shouldn't try to find weird ways to lose my money.

Katie: "I shouldn't try to find weird ways to *keep* my money."

Ernst: Yes. And my turnaround is also true, because if I go to court, it might turn out to be more expensive than paying the higher rent.

5. The Rent Increase

Katie: That's a good one. With some of these statements, you may find six turnarounds, each one truer than what you wrote. "They shouldn't try to get your money"—is that true?

Ernst: No.

Katie: And how do you react when you believe the thought that they're trying to get your money?

Ernst: Every month when I send them the money, I get really angry—and whenever I think about it.

Katie: Yes, and then how do you live?

Ernst: Stressed. Unhappy.

Katie: So, it's becoming obvious that attaching to an untrue story causes a lot of stress. And stress is a gift. It lets us know that our thinking is out of balance in the moment. Every uncomfortable feeling is a gift. We've been trying for centuries to change the feeling by changing the world, and that just doesn't work. But when we investigate the thought that causes the stress, the feeling changes by itself. It has to. We change the projector—mind— and the world it projects has to change. We can't feel stress unless we're believing a story that isn't true for us.

Let's look at your next statement.

Ernst: *I need them—the government—to respect my rights as a citizen.*

Katie: And can you know that they don't?

Ernst: No, not really.

Katie: How do you react when you believe the thought that they don't respect your rights as a citizen?

Ernst: I feel homeless.

Katie: Yes, this third question can take you inside for hours. You become a homeless victim at the mercy of the world, something outside it. That's terrifying, and the concept will spill over to everything and everyone else. Do you have children? Put the word *children* on it and read it again.

Ernst: I need my daughter to respect my rights as a father.

Katie: Hopeless! And it's not love. Does that statement feel loving?

Ernst: No.

Katie: How do you treat your daughter when you believe the thought that she should respect you at all, and she does something that you interpret as not respecting your rights as a father?

Ernst: Like a thing, not like a human being.

Katie: How does that feel?

Ernst: It doesn't feel good.

Katie: Who would you be without the story that we should respect you at all, ever?

Ernst: Very free.

Katie: Let's turn the statement around.

Ernst: I need to respect my rights as a citizen.

Katie: And I see you're doing that when you go to court. You leave it in their hands; it's their business. My business is to report my thinking, and then it's done. From then on, it's no longer my business. It's the court's business to decide what they think is fair.
There's another turnaround, and I love when this happens.

Ernst: I need to respect the rights of the federal government.

Katie: Yes, especially in your mind. I love this turnaround. I find great humor in it. It shows me how to live freely. When I don't respect the federal government, it's stressful. And when I find out that respecting it is the path to happiness, I feel great joy. I walk down the street in appreciation, seeing how they maintain it with my parking money. Everything I touch in my house or apartment, I know that it's provided by the government and me. It's a total merging and partnership without separation. It's heaven. It's truly heaven.

Ernst: That's the strangest way to heaven I ever heard of.

Katie: It's called the direct route. I can kiss the pavement. Without separation, I can see that I'm even that. It's nothing more than a kiss on my own body.
    Let's look at the next statement.

Ernst: *I think they are greedy, they cheat, and they look for loopholes to deceive others.*

Katie: Whose business is that?

Ernst: Their business.

Katie: And how do you feel when you mentally go into the government's business? Like a hopeless victim?
    Can you see one stress-free reason to mentally go there?

Ernst: No, I can't.

Katie: Who would you be without your story?

Ernst: I would dance; I'd be full of joy. I'd be a clown, a dancing dervish, instead of a policeman.

Katie: Yes, angel. So turn it around.

Ernst: I'm greedy, I cheat, and I look for loopholes to deceive others. It's true.

Katie: Especially the federal government.

[To the audience] Isn't this you? This is living in mental hell. If you want the government to change, turn it around and run for public office. Or simply present your case with all the information you can gather and send it to the courts. And mentally stay in your own business. If you live this way, we will follow you. You're the living example. We teach what we live, not what we talk. But until you live it, all you teach us is to be hopeless victims of the dishonest government that you project.

I love to invite people to do three things every day that are kind, good, and helpful, and that no one knows about, and if anyone finds out to start all over again. This is a way to learn freedom, a way to begin living your nature. With you, I would invite you to do three things a day to help the federal government, for your own sake.

People who do this Work begin to pay back what they owe. This is dangerous. If you file for bankruptcy, the federal government says you owe nothing. What do *you* say? If you can pay one dollar per month, do it—for your sake. It has nothing to do with the federal government. This is *your* freedom we're dealing with.

So, sweetheart, let's look at the next statement.

Ernst: *I don't want to be cheated again by people or institutions.*

Katie: I'm willing . . .

Ernst: I'm willing to be cheated again by people or institutions.

Katie: Yes, because it could only be your own mind cheating you of your freedom in the moment. And that's only a lack of understanding. "I look forward to . . ."

Ernst: I look forward to being cheated by people or institutions. Why not?

Katie: Yes, why not? Because if it hurts, it's your thinking that's hurting you. Nothing else is possible. In my experience, there's no exception to this. I am responsible for my own freedom, totally.

And when someone sympathizes with your anger or sadness, they're just supporting your insanity: "Yes, you're right, the federal government is cheating you. The world is unfair." And we call that a friend. A friend is just someone who agrees with you.

Ernst: All friends do that.

Katie: So bring me an enemy. Enemies are very clear about what I haven't discovered yet. The enemy turns out to be the friend. Where do you go, whom do you go to, to get your concepts justified? And how long does it work before they disagree with you one way or the other? You are your own freedom.

6. WELCOME TO AL-ANON!

What is sobriety? If you want someone to get sober, try getting sober about the stressful thoughts that rule your life.

Margaret: [reading from her Worksheet] *I am fearful and sad about my son Paul because he is trying to recover from using drugs and doesn't really know how to be in the world, and is really having a hard time learning how to live.*

Katie: Yes, so, "He doesn't know how to be in the world"—is that true?

Margaret: He's having to relearn everything, because he's just been using drugs, so living life is new to him, and he's really struggling.

Katie: Yes, I hear that. And "He doesn't know how to live in the world"—is that true? Does he know how to eat?

Margaret: He knows how to eat.

Katie: Does he know how to dress himself?

Margaret: Yes. Okay, he knows how to be in the world. Okay, okay.

Katie: We all know everything we need to know.

Margaret: Ahh! But you know . . . he's learning how to go grocery shopping, I mean these basic things. He's an adult, and he's learning all this stuff.

Katie: That's beautiful! He knows how to be in the world! You grow, and you learn—that's how to be in the world. If people stop growing and learning, the world gets really scary. "He's learning how to be in the world" means that he knows how to be in the world—it's growing and learning and being willing. Sounds like he's doing it.

Margaret: Okay. Thank you.

Katie: How do you react when you believe the thought "He doesn't know how to be in the world"? Where does your mind travel when you believe that thought?

Margaret: A lot of fear. A lot of pain.

Katie: So close your eyes. What pictures do you see of him when you believe the thought "He doesn't know how to be in the world"?

Margaret: Just really sad and scared and miserable—confused.

Katie: So who would you be without the thought "He doesn't know how to live in the world"—as you watch him eat breakfast, put on his shoes, go grocery shopping?

Margaret: I would be free. Yes, I'd be a free person.

Katie: Yes. You'd be free to notice that he's doing fine in the world.

Margaret: I'd be free to notice that he does know how to eat, he does know how to dress. And I'd be more focused on—

Katie: And he knows how to learn. That's amazing! Not every son goes to the grocery store.

Margaret: [laughing] Okay.

Katie: So, "He doesn't know how to live in the world"—turn it around.

Margaret: I don't know how to live in the world.

Katie: You don't know how to live in the world with your son sober.

Margaret: This is true—I don't.

Katie: So do you know how to eat?

Margaret: Yes.

Katie: Do you know how to put on your shoes?

Margaret: Yes.

Katie: Okay, that's how you live in the world with your son.

Margaret: Oh, God . . .

Katie: You just eat; you put on your shoes. When he walks in, you say, "Hello," or you don't. When he asks, "How are you?" you answer the question. When he says, "I had a miserable night, Mom," you say, "Well, can I help you?"

And when he says "No," believe him. If he says "Yes," listen. That's how to live in the world with a newborn son. How old is he?

Margaret: He's thirty-four; he's an adult.

Katie: He's like a newborn baby.

Margaret: Yes, he is really.

Katie: Yes. And he's born again, and he's learning to crawl. So how were you with him when he was little and crawling?

Margaret: I was there to help him.

Katie: And when he fell down?

Margaret: I picked him up.

Katie: And did you laugh?

Margaret: Yes.

Katie: And play?

Margaret: Yes, we played and we laughed.

Katie: So you *do* know how to be in the world with your newborn son.

Margaret: Part of the struggle, though, is for me to stay out of it and allow him to, you know, work his AA program, work with his sponsor, work with people in the program, and all of that. And for me really to stay out of it.

Katie: That sounds like a relief.

Margaret: That's the hard part. That's the part of where I don't know how to be.

Katie: "That's the hard part"—turn it around.

Margaret: Okay. That's the easy part.

Katie: Yes. He's out of your hands.

Margaret: Ah!

Katie: It's what he wants!

Margaret: [laughing] So when he's talking about a problem, it's my job—from what I'm taught in Al-Anon—to not solve his problems, but allow him to solve his own problems.

Katie: That sounds wonderful. It's not your problem.

Margaret: Right.

Katie: He doesn't think it's your problem. Al-Anon doesn't think it's your problem. You're the only one who thinks it's your problem.

Margaret: Oh God! You make it sound really easy!

Katie: Well, not living someone else's life *is* really easy. Living your own is enough.

Margaret: Yes, yes, absolutely. Should I read this next part?

Katie: Let's dialogue, okay?

Margaret: Okay.

Katie: He's got a big problem, and he's talking to me, and I am you. Think of something he would say that really would suck you in—you take on that role.

Margaret: Okay. [as her son] "Well, I'm avoiding my sponsor because I owe him homework, and I don't want to see my sponsor."

Katie: [as Margaret] "Yes, I hear that you don't want to see your sponsor, honey. I love that you shared that with me."

Margaret: "And I'm still not really feeling like a part of things with AA—I'm just out there. I'm really . . . my mind's really foggy."

Katie: "Yes, well, that's understandable, honey. Is there anything I can do to help?"

Margaret: "No, I don't think so."

Katie: "Okay. I love you."

Margaret: "Okay."

Katie: "It must be tough to be foggy and not feel a part of it."

Margaret: [as herself] And then what if he said, "Yes"? Okay, so now I'm going to be him.
   "Yes, there *is* something you can do to help."

Katie: "Good. What would that be?"

Margaret: "I don't know."

Katie: "Well, when you know, just ask."

Margaret: "Okay."

Katie: "And if it feels right to me, I'm just going to do it."

Margaret: [as herself] The big part for me as a parent is keeping my mouth shut when I see that he may be doing something that isn't supportive of his well-being.

Katie: Well, he didn't even want to see his sponsor! I just *heard* him. Why is that hard on you? He's the one it's hard on. What I did was that I just repeated it to him. My job as a mother is to listen. The solutions to his life are within him. So you find them within you, and then you understand that.

Margaret: Okay, it's not about giving advice.

Katie: Only if you take it yourself.

Margaret: Oh God!

Katie: So that keeps me very still at home. [The audience laughs.]

6. Welcome to Al-Anon!

Margaret: Okay, thank you. Yes, it all sounds so much different, reading this now. *He is exhibiting behaviors that may lead to drug use again.*

Katie: Turn it around.

Margaret: I am exhibiting behaviors that may lead to drug use again. What does that mean?

Katie: I don't know. You tell me. Give me one genuine example.

Margaret: Well, I'm exhibiting behaviors that lead to my own drug use, which is obsessiveness.

Katie: Obsessing over him.

Margaret: Yes, obsessing over him and his life, yes.

Katie: Yes, alcohol and drugs are what he obsesses over. And he is what you obsess over. So he's your drug of choice.

Margaret: Yes. Okay, okay.

Katie: So say it again, just like that. I . . .

Margaret: I am exhibiting behaviors that may lead to drug use again.

Katie: . . . to *son* use again.

Margaret: To what?

Katie: . . . to son abuse again.

Margaret: Oh! I am exhibiting behaviors that may lead to son abuse again?

Katie: Yes. Can you find examples?

Margaret: I try to give him advice when I'm in a state where *I* could use some good advice.

Katie: Good.

Margaret: And also I feel that if I keep up this being in fear and being obsessed, it'll cause him to go use, you know?

Katie: Well, he'll reflect back your own lack of sobriety, yes.

Margaret: So I *could* cause him to go use.

Katie: Well, my experience is that people mirror back my life.

Margaret: Wow! Okay.

Katie: I mean, if you're worried all the time, sobriety does not look that great.

Margaret: Yes. But then there's the part, though, where I need to know that I'm not responsible for whether he uses or not. I mean, there's this whole piece about nobody can make anybody do anything, so I'm confused.

Katie: Well, I agree with that.

Margaret: However . . .

Katie: Get sober, that's all I'm saying. If you want him to get sober, *you* get sober first.
Read your next statement.

Margaret: Okay. That's what I'm here for. Okay! *I am fearful that he could die or become homeless again.*

Katie: So, what's not okay about him being homeless?

Margaret: It's terrifying for me, not knowing where he is, or if he's dead or alive or drunk.

Katie: So, your story is: "You need to know where he is." Let's say he's drunk, he's using, he's on the streets, he's homeless. "You need to know where he is"—is that true? You're at home, and you're comfortable; he's out there. "You need to know where he is"—is that true?

Margaret: No. I don't *need*—

Katie: Where did the *no* come from?

Margaret: The *no* came from a place where there was a period of time where I didn't know where he was, and I knew he was in danger, but there was nothing I could do. I couldn't change his drug use. And the thing was, when he wasn't around me, I was able to really work on my life, because his drug use wasn't in my face. So I was able to get some semblance of joy in *my* life, even though I didn't know where he was.

Katie: Wonderful.

Margaret: That's the truth.

Katie: Yes. I don't know if you can hear this, but if I needed that and my son really loved me, that's what he would give me.

Margaret: Say that again?

Katie: If I were just a total mess and needed help, if my son *really* loved me and that's the only way I could find help, he would just live like your son. Interesting, huh? There's no mistake in the universe. Everything is for you. You've heard the expression "I'd die for you"? Well, that's the people in our lives, and it's ourselves. What does it take for you to get sober?

Margaret: Well, that's the whole thing.

Katie: One way I say it is: If your son's path were your only way to God, would you take it?

Margaret: If my son's path were my only way to God, would I take it?

Katie: If that were your only way to God, would you take it? Would you choose that son, and that pain?

Margaret: I've got my path that has plenty of pain with regards to that. And through it I *am* finding God, more God. So this is my part in it.

Katie: Yes, so thank God. Thank your son. It's what everything is about. That's how it is. No mistake.

Margaret: Okay. There's no mistake that he was out on the streets?

Katie: It's all for you.

Margaret: Just like it is for each one of us. It's all for us.

Katie: It's all for you. Each one of us? That's all for you, too. You just shifted back into your son's business. You were caretaking again.

Margaret: So is that another way of saying we always get what we need, then?

Katie: Yes. It's an example of that.

Margaret: I *did* need that—not to be in his presence while he was using.

Katie: So, "You need to know where he is"—he's out there drinking, using, he's homeless. "You need to know where he is"—how do you react when you believe that thought and you don't know where he is?

Margaret: In utter panic: "Is he dead? Is he alive? Is he in pain?"

6. Welcome to Al-Anon!

Katie: Look at all the pictures that go with that—as you're at home, thinking the thought: "I need to know where he is. He's dead; he needs me"—all the pictures.

Margaret: Or, "I should be doing something." There's always this thing going on in my mind: "Oh, my God, I'm his mother; I should be doing something, and I should be helping . . ."

Katie: That's a good one. There's another one: "If something happens to him, it's my fault. I'm his mother." That one is very powerful.

Margaret: That's a big one for me. Absolutely. It's my fault, so I have to fix it.

Katie: Yes. So again, it just leaves no regard for them. Really, it becomes about us. It's all about us. If something happens to him—what are they going to say about me, as a mother?

Margaret: Yes.

Katie: We don't grieve long.

Margaret: Wow! Or it's: "What am *I* going to say about me?" That's the thing that drives me crazy.

Katie: Okay, so, "I need to know where he is"—give me a peaceful reason to believe that.

Margaret: So that I know he's safe . . . and alive.

Katie: That's not very peaceful when you don't know where he is, when he's drinking and using. There's nothing peaceful about it. Give me a peaceful reason to believe "I need to know where he is"—when you don't know where he is.

Margaret: [after a pause] There isn't one. There isn't a peaceful reason.

Katie: Who would you be without this thought that's useful only for suffering? "I need to know where he is"—who would you be if you didn't believe that?

Margaret: I would be free and joyous and living my life.

Katie: "I need to know where he is"—turn it around.

Margaret: I don't need to know where he is.

Katie: Yes, and that would match reality. When you don't know where he is, you don't need to know where he is. It doesn't mean you're not going to make phone calls and check around. And ultimately when you don't know where he is, you don't know where he is. And panic doesn't make for a clear mind.

Margaret: No.

Katie: Not a lot of options there. Now give me three examples of how this turnaround is true in your life.

Margaret: Well, I don't need to know where he is because I can't do anything about his using even when I do know where he is. And second, I'm sometimes happy when I don't know where he is. . . .

Katie: That's two, sweetheart. Can you find a third example?

Margaret: I don't need to know where he is because he has gotten along without me in the past.

Katie: That's major! Can you find another turnaround to "I need to know where he is"?

Margaret: I need to know where *I* am?

Katie: Yes. Get sober. And just notice where *you* are and what's supporting you, the ground that's supporting you, or the chair that's supporting you, or the air that's supporting you—all the beauty of the moment. And as you notice what's supporting you, you know that the ground is supporting him, too; you know that the air is supporting him; you know that everything he needs is there.

Are *you* awake to it? He doesn't have to be. What you know is that everything that's supporting you is supporting him. To awaken to it is a wonderful thing. Because you know what's supporting him, you know where he is: He's supported. Dead or alive—he's supported.

Margaret: Ahh! Okay, got it.

Katie: Continue to read.

Margaret: I want to say this. Since he's been sober, I've noticed when I'm in his presence, when he's with me, it's just so upsetting to me to still be in that fear. I want to be in that place of absolutely just loving him to pieces.

Katie: Well, that's ahead of your time.

Margaret: Okay.

Katie: So let's continue. Read the next statement.

Margaret: *I want him not to have the disease of chemical dependency.*

Katie: Turn it around. "I want me . . ."

Margaret: I want *me* not to have the disease of chemical dependency. Meaning my obsession over his.

Katie: Well, you also want you not to have the disease of chemical dependency. That's your path. It's not his now, but that's your path.

Margaret: Yes.

Katie: So, try: "I want me not to have the disease of *son* dependency." When he's not well, you're not well.

Margaret: Wow!

Katie: But why does he have to be well for you to be well? Why don't you just skip the middleman and be well?

Margaret: Yes, yes, yes. I like that.

Katie: Take the quick route because it's happiness that you want. When you're happy, it's so much easier to serve the people you love.

Margaret: Man!

Katie: I once hung out with someone who looked like a very old man. He had a beard, and he smelled, and it was about two in the morning, and I was in an interesting neighborhood in one of these high-rise parking things. And it was dark, and I was going to my car, and I saw him.

And I thought—I don't know, what was it? It looked like a good place to sit. So I sat down beside him and reached under his tarp thing for his hand, and sat there, and put it in my lap, and just sat in the parking lot. And I see why people sit in parking lots. [Margaret laughs.]

You know, it was very pleasant. And as it turned out, he was a *young* man. He was in his early twenties or his teens. And he just looked so old—so old and so beautiful.

And we talked; we just talked. And it wasn't as terrible for him as you would imagine. This is what I heard from him. And he was miles away from home, *states* away from home. He came from New York or someplace. But he wasn't having a terrible life—that's what he said. It was his life. What do I know?

What I know is that I listened to his reality. He *loved* sharing his life with me. But his mother—if she has a mind like yours—can't share that with him. He'd say, "I spent the night in a parking lot, no food, cold, alone." And the mother might panic, because she's not listening. She thinks that being alone is terrible, maybe. She thinks that a parking lot is a terrible place to sleep, maybe.

Margaret: And that's not how he was meaning it?

Katie: Not at all! This is not uncommon. It's called listening. What is hell for you may not be hell for someone else.

Margaret: However, it was hell for my son. I mean, he's told me it was hell for him.

Katie: If you sat and really talked with him, you might be able to find that he could tell you other things. And I hear that for him it was hell. But you listening—that's wonderful.

All I can report is what people tell me. I sit in countries where children are very hungry, and they have great big smiles on their faces. They're playing; they're wonderful. How are you to know?

In other words, take care of your own reality. For all you know, your pain was greater than your son's pain, as miserable as he was. Pain is pain. That's what I know.

Margaret: Yes. Well, he was busy using, so he wasn't feeling the pain that I was feeling.

Katie: Who knows? So take care of your own sobriety. That's what you're doing here, honey. This is about getting sober: dropping your addiction to needing your son, your dependence on your son for your own happiness. It would be okay if it were kind. It's just not kind—not to you, not to him.

Margaret: Yes, I agree.

Katie: Because if he slips up, he has to worry about you. That's off. You've taught him that you're dependent on his life being a certain way. That's not sobriety.

I had a cousin who called me very late at night. The phone rang, I woke up, picked up the phone, and he said, "I have a loaded gun in my mouth, and the hammer is cocked." He was very drunk. And he said, "If you can't give me one reason why I shouldn't kill myself, I'm going to pull the trigger."

And I waited and I waited and I waited. And I just kept waiting for one good reason. And I couldn't find one. And finally I said, "You know, sweetheart, I can't find one reason why you shouldn't do it." And he burst into tears. He said that was the most honest thing he'd ever heard. Later he found AA, and he died sober.

I was just being honest. I couldn't find a reason. But what happened was that because I'm not dependent on other people, they don't have to live for me. I'm free.

Margaret: Well, it was huge when you said, "He's not here to live or die to make you happy." That really struck home. If he's going to die, it's his right to die! I don't want it, but I just realize now how disrespectful it is for me—

Katie: To use him for your happiness.

Margaret: To use him for my happiness in any way.

Katie: That's what users do, and users teach their children to use.

Margaret: Oh good God!

Katie: Yes, God is good.

Margaret: My son is using drugs, and I'm using him. So we're both users. Very clear.

Katie: Very good. Welcome to Al-Anon. Now read the next statement.

Margaret: *I want him to have an easy life.*

Katie: No, no, no, no, no. Turn it around. You don't care about his life. Turn it around. "I want *me* . . ."

Margaret: I want me to have an easy life.

Katie: Yes, and you think he has to live for you to have that. You require him to live and be sober for you to have it.

Margaret: Yes. I see that.

Katie: So that gives him a hard life.

Margaret: Ooooh! Let me write that down.

Katie: "Here are your requirements so that I can have an easy life."

Margaret: Oh God!

Katie: Yes.

Margaret: Oh man! [The audience laughs.] Okay.

Katie: [laughing with the audience] I think she's getting sober. What do you think?

He gets to live an easy life through your example. That's how our children learn, through example. They don't do what we say. We get angry and say, "Do this!" And what they're learning is "If I get angry enough, I get people to do things." Because we're always teaching—not by what we say, but by what we do.

Margaret: And yet I don't want to do it for that purpose, live that easy life. You know? Because then it's manipulation: I'm still focused over there, on him.

Katie: There's another turnaround. "I *don't* want him to . . ."

Margaret: I don't want him to have an easy life?

Katie: Well, obviously: Look at all the requirements you put on him.

Margaret: Oh man! Poor kid! [Margaret laughs with the audience.] Oh! So will these realizations help to change my behavior?

Katie: Let me know. Because stressful feelings will let you know if your behavior doesn't change. Your stressful feelings will let you know when your mind is out of order. When your mind is out of order, it's time to do The Work.

Margaret: Okay.

Katie: So "I don't want him . . ." and continue.

Margaret: I don't want him to have an easy life.

Katie: Now give me three genuine examples of how that turn-around is true for you.

Margaret: Well, like you just said, look at all the requirements I put on him.

Katie: Yes. And a second?

Margaret: [pause] Well, if I really think about it, it's arrogant of me to want an easy life for him. How would I know what's in his best interest? Maybe his life should be difficult. Maybe that's what will help him the most.

Katie: Yes. As I often say, who needs God when we have your opinion? And a third example?

Margaret: Let's see. I don't want him to have an easy life, because when I want that and his life isn't easy, I get so bent out of shape. It makes *my* life so difficult.

Katie: Good, sweetheart. Keep reading.

Margaret: *I want him to live and stay alive.*

Katie: And turn that around.

Margaret: I don't want him to live and stay alive and be in joy?

Katie: Not *his* way of life and *his* way of joy. You want him to live *your* life. That's what you've been requiring.

Margaret: Oh.

Katie: Keep reading.

6. Welcome to Al-Anon!

Margaret: *He shouldn't have the disease of chemical dependency.*

Katie: Is that true?

Margaret: No. I don't *want* him to have it.

Katie: Can you absolutely know that it's true that he shouldn't have that?

Margaret: No, I can't know that.

Katie: Who needs God when we have your opinion?
[As Margaret]: "You shouldn't be chemically dependent—I *know* this."

Margaret: Wow!

Katie: The I-know mind is very painful. It tries to run things like a dictator, and life goes on without it. And all sadness is a tantrum. It's the war with God, the war with reality—*all* sadness. And you lose.
So turn it around.

Margaret: He *should* have the disease of chemical dependency.

Katie: Yes, welcome to reality. You're catching up with him. You're out of denial. He *should* have it, because he does.

Margaret: Okay. And then I wrote, *He shouldn't have it so hard.*

Katie: Turn it around.

Margaret: He *should* have it so hard.

Katie: Yes! There's no mistake in the universe. There's another turnaround.

Margaret: *I* shouldn't have it so hard?

Katie: Yes. You're not the one living our there on the streets with a chemical dependency. But you're living as painfully as if you were. And you throw yourself out into the streets. When he's standing there with you clean and sober, in your mind you throw him out there into the streets, as though it were happening, and it's not.

Margaret: I hate that.

Katie: Well, just notice. And be kind and say to yourself, "Oh, sweetheart, you're throwing your son into the streets again." And just come back, be present. And see the real son, the one in front of you, not the one in your imagination. And put your arms around him, and just thank him for standing there with you.

That's what I loved about my daughter coming in. She was sixteen and, by her own admission, an alcoholic, and she'd come through the door and she would look at me like "Blauugh!" Just look at me as if she couldn't bear having me as her mother. And I knew why. I had done my Work. She was looking at who I used to be, worried and fearful. She had every right to look at me like that.

But she didn't see who was really sitting there. It was a different mother. I had realized who the woman was that she thought she saw. So the reality that I was present with was this: She was home; she was with me; she was alive. "Oh my God, another moment with this beautiful being."

In my imagination, before I had a clue, I had killed her a thousand times, but there she was. So that's where I learned that reality is always kinder than my story. That was just a first taste.

Margaret: That's the thing that I hate the worst—that he's here, and I don't know how long he's going to be here. We don't know how long anybody is going to be here, but—

Katie: "That's the thing I hate the worst"—turn it around.

Margaret: That's the thing I love the most.

Katie: Yes. That he's here.

Margaret: He's here. But—

Katie: And here is the only place he's ever going to be.

Margaret: Well, I want to be here, too.

Katie: You're on the right track, honey. And keep reading.

Margaret: *He should be honest and really dive into recovery and work with his sponsor.*

Katie: No, no, no, no, no. Turn that around.

Margaret: *I* should be honest, and really dive into *my* Work . . . and work with *my* sponsor.

Katie: Yes. Are you working with your sponsor?

Margaret: Yes.

Katie: Closely?

Margaret: Every day.

Katie: Very good. So you're following your—

Margaret: I'm following my advice.

Katie: Very good. That keeps you mentally out of your son's business and in your own. You live a happy life, and that sets the example. Sobriety is very attractive.

Margaret: And I haven't been sober.

Katie: No, you haven't.

Margaret: So, it's all coming clear. *I need him to not have this disease. . . .* See, I'll never be happy with what I wrote here, because it won't work. *I need him to not have the disease and to be in full sobriety* *and working his program. To be in my life sober and to live and have joy.* Jeez. It's just impossible; this is impossible.

Katie: Very good. You've been requiring . . . well, you see it.

Margaret: It's awful.

Katie: Well, you said it—it's not possible, up to now.

Margaret: No, he's got the disease. There's no denying it. I can't change that; nobody can change that, and even in full sobriety—he's sober, he's doing the best he can. And it's so clear that *he* can't make me happy—no matter what he does, ever.

You know, if I continue to worry about whether he lives or dies, or whether he's sober or not, or whether he goes back to the streets, I can't be happy—no matter what. So it's *got* to be about me. It's *got* to be about my own sobriety, which means . . . working on my life and not using the drug of being obsessed by him.

Katie: Using him as your drug. Okay, so turn it around.

Margaret: I need him to . . .

Katie: "I need me . . ."

Margaret: Oh. I need *me* to not have this disease and to be in full sobriety and working my program. To be in my life sober. Yes. Wow! That's a big deal.

Katie: Now there's another turnaround. "I *don't* need him to . . ."

Margaret: Ohhh. Yes, that's a good one. I don't need him to not have this disease or be in full sobriety and working his program. I don't need him to be in my life sober. . . . That last one is easy for me to say, but in reality if he went out and used again, it could be tough for me.

Katie: Oh, there's a plan. "I think I'll plan that." [Margaret laughs.] If you want to know your plan, look at your mind. It will show you. "That will be tough." There's a plan.

6. Welcome to Al-Anon!

Margaret: Okay.

Katie: Okay, and the next statement?

Margaret: *He is loving, passionate, sad, doesn't know how to live everyday life, confused, afraid, kind, wise, intelligent, hilariously funny.*

Katie: Yes. No wonder you love him so much.

If I had the thought "I don't know what I would do without my daughter"—it would be a lie. Sooner or later, I'd have to go to the bathroom. Then I'd eat. "I don't know what I'd do without her"? Of course I do! It's a lie. It's our thoughts that drive us crazy, not death, not the loss of a child, not life at all. Our thoughts about life—that is a lack of sobriety, that is *the* lack of sobriety. Our stressful thoughts—until we question them, we're drunk.

Okay, let's look at the next statement.

Margaret: *I never want to have him living on the streets again and to wonder if he is alive or hurting and not know where he is.*

Katie: "I'm willing . . ."

Margaret: I'm willing to have . . . aargh! Okay, I can say, "I'm willing." I'm willing to have him live on the streets again—

Katie: How many times today did you have a picture of him living on the streets?

Margaret: A few.

Katie: And he's sober! So, that's what this number six is about. "I'm willing to have him out on the streets"—well, you just were! Any time you picture him on the streets, you put your son on the streets, and you feel that. And you become worried, and sad, and stressed. So just notice that he's not putting himself on the streets; *you're* putting him on the streets. So just notice and smile and come back to reality.

Margaret: Yes.

Katie: Okay. "I'm willing . . ."

Margaret: I'm willing to have him live on the streets again and to wonder if he is alive or hurting and not know where he is.

Katie: Yes. So either in your mind or in his life, it doesn't matter—it's just as painful, because he's sober, and you're still in pain. So whether it's in reality or in your imagination, you'll feel it. And when you feel those feelings, it's time to do The Work again. Question it; turn it around.

So, "I look forward to . . ."

Margaret: I look forward to having him live on the streets. . . . Okay.

Katie: It could happen again in your mind. And it could happen again in reality. It's just that there are two ways for it to happen: One way is you sane, and the other way is you crazy. Either way, life happens. And mind happens.

It's like we're superstitious cavemen. We really believe that if we say, "I'm willing; I look forward to him being on the streets again," it will happen. That way of thinking is ancient. But that's not how it works. It's what supports denial. "Oh, I won't dare think that, or it'll really happen!"

Well, I say: Put integrity above superstition. And just face it head on. "I'm willing to, I look forward to . . ." It could happen. It's called life. And if it doesn't happen in life, it happens in my mind. Either way, it hurts. So what kind of intelligence would just wait for it to happen and suffer to the end of our days?

So do it now—be ahead of life, and then you're prepared. Your arms are open to it.

The thing that runs in me is: I love God. And for me, reality is God. I love God.

Margaret: No matter what's going on around you?

Katie: I love God. And God is what is. I weep at my devotion. Because the good in it is so clear to me. Nothing happens that is not for the good. And if I can't see that, I'm insane, and I suffer.

It's because I am seeing through a distorted mind and the gift of life is lost to me.

People say, "Open to the beauty." Well, everyone would if they could, and that's what this Work is about. The answers inside you are just waiting for the questions to be asked. And as you ask these four questions, the answers can live and enlighten you to what you already know. And there is no way I can lose a son or a daughter until it's time.

Margaret: Period.

Katie: Period.

Margaret: No matter what.

Katie: No matter what. When we stop using our children, we come to see who they really are. And then we know true love. And dependency is not love. Thank you, sweetheart.

Margaret: Yes. Thank you so much, Katie.

7. Frank Bosses Me Around

Another person is never your boss. That leaves only you to be your boss, a boss you'll always want to say yes to.

Katie: What did you write?

Gene: [reading from the Worksheet] *I am frustrated by my co-worker Frank because he takes the role of a boss and tries to give me rules. At the same time, he knocks off and doesn't assume responsibility.*

Katie: Keep reading.

Gene: *I want Frank to treat me in a respectful way.*

Katie: And continue.

Gene: *I want Frank to let go of acting like he's boss and not try to give me rules.* When we have a job to do, he plays the boss and says, "You will do this and this and this." It's not so much the job that bothers me, but rather the way he says it. And I say, "Yes, I agree," and afterward I'm mad at myself that I said yes, because basically I wanted to say no.

Katie: Ah, so you lied when you said yes.

Gene: Yes.

Katie: I didn't like me when I did that either. And then I blamed other people. But it was really me I wasn't being honest with. So rather than blame them, I just look to myself and notice and begin again.

My name is "Yes." I love living that way. I say yes to everything. For example, if you ask me to do something for you and I want to, I say yes. If you ask me to do something and I don't want to, I say no—and that no is a yes *to me*. I live as an internal yes, because I am honoring something *inside* me that has nothing to do with you.

It's so exciting to see what the answer is to that question he's asking! I don't think, "Will it hurt his feelings? What will he give me? Will he think I'm nice? Will he be disappointed?" Instead I think, "What is *my* answer to that question?"

It's very exciting. You never know what answer's going to be there! So you just walk through life waiting for people to ask for anything, so that you can hear the language of your own heart, your own intelligence.

Okay, sweetheart, begin reading again.

Gene: *I am frustrated by my co-worker Frank because he takes the role of a boss and tries to give me rules.*

Katie: So "He plays the boss"—is that true?

Gene: Yes.

Katie: Give me an example of that.

Gene: He says, "Do this and this and this."

Katie: So. Say that to me.

Gene: [as Frank] "Give me that glass over there."

Katie: [as Gene] [silence]

Gene: "You heard what I said—give me the glass!"

7. Frank Bosses Me Around

Katie: "I did hear you."

Gene: "I'm the one in charge, and you have to do what I tell you."

Katie: [silence]

Gene: "We've got a job to do, and it has to get finished."

Katie: [silence]

Gene: "You have some nerve! If we don't get finished, it will be your fault."

Katie: "I can see that. It just didn't feel right handing you the glass when it was so near to you. Is there anything else that you want? Any other ideas?"

Gene: "First, the lawn has to be mowed. And once you've done that, you could trim the front."

Katie: "Great! I'll trim after you mow."

Gene: "No, you do both. That's your job."

Katie: "I'll trim after you mow."

Gene: "I've got another job to do."

Katie: "I hear that. When do you think you'll be through mowing? I'd like to know, because I want to do my job as quickly as possible."

Gene: "You didn't understand me! I've got my job, and you've got these two jobs. And when you're done with these two, I've got a third one for you."

Katie: "I hear that, and I'll trim after you mow."

Gene: [after a pause] "I have to rethink it."

Katie: "Good! Let me know, because I want to trim as quickly as possible. And then I could be open to that other job you were talking about. I really like working with you. You're a little slow, but . . ."

Gene: [after a long pause] "All right, maybe we should work together."

Katie: "I love that. That's working together, in a really balanced way. Now if you'll give me the other job while you mow, I'll be ready to trim, and we'll just finish this in no time. I like working with you."

[As herself] You understand what happened? I didn't believe I had to do what he said. And I hear that he has really good ideas about what needs to be accomplished, so I can use that. But how it's accomplished—I have a choice in that. And being a fair person, I want to do my part.

But if I say yes to him and it's not true for me, I'm the one who throws things off balance, not him. Also, if I say yes when I mean no, I train him to order me around. Why wouldn't he order me around, when I keep saying yes? Understand?

Gene: Yes.

Katie: Thank you. So the next statement, number two?

Gene: *I want Frank to treat me in a respectful way.*

Katie: Is that true?

Gene: No. I need *me* to treat me in a respectful way—by saying no when I mean no.

Katie: And to be open! *No* is the kindest word when it's honest. It doesn't have to be bossy and hard—just honest.

Gene: There's a fantasy that we will start arguing when I say no.

7. Frank Bosses Me Around

Katie: Well, that could happen. So I didn't say no. I just told you what I would or would not do. And when you told me what to do, I just waited. You ordered me to give you the glass. And I just listened to your need. But I didn't really believe it. Because if you needed it, you would just reach out and get it.

Gene: That's true.

Katie: You're very fast, a very honest man. It's a privilege to sit with you. How do you react when you believe the thought "I need him to respect me"?

Gene: And he doesn't do it?

Katie: Yes, he's ordering you around.

Gene: I get angry—frustrated! And on the inside, I'm at war with him.

Katie: Who would you be without the thought "I need him to respect me," when he's ordering you around?

Gene: At peace. Listening to him. And I'd be open for both answers.

Katie: Oh, yes. "I need him to respect me"—turn it around.

Gene: I need me to respect me.

Katie: Yes, and when you give a dishonest yes, you lose respect for yourself. The next time that happens, you'll feel the lack of respect. And in that moment, you can change your mind if you want. You're free.

Now give me three genuine examples of how the turnaround is as true as or truer than your original statement.

Gene: Oh. Well, my respect is the most important. If I don't respect myself, how can I feel good about myself?

Katie: Yes, sweetheart. That's so true. And a second example?

Gene: If I don't respect myself, I won't believe other people when they say they respect me, so there won't be any respect at all.

Katie: Can you find a third?

Gene: I need to respect myself if I'm going to do a good job at work and in my family.

Katie: Good. Now can you find another turnaround for "I need him to respect me"?

Gene: I need me to respect him.

Katie: Yes. He was simply a man who wanted the glass. He was simply a man who wanted to get the job done—without doing it! Everyone has a right to want that. It just doesn't always work that way.

Gene: When I took on his role, I noticed that there was a good intention behind that.

Katie: You are fine. You are a giant. I think you know that. I love watching you own that. I love that you let you out of your cage. Thank you, sweetheart.

8. My Mother Manipulates Me

She's mentally and physically ill. She accuses her son of child abuse. She inflicts her suffering on those around her, and they feel responsible for making her happy. Well, we all have the perfect mother.

Doug: *I am angry at my mom because she uses her mental illness to manipulate me and my family. I can't stand the way when I confront her about any issue, she throws her many illnesses in my face—and she has every illness known to man—saying I don't understand.*

Katie: Sweetheart, why don't you step into my parlor? We'll do a little surgery here. What a mom! We all have the perfect mother. Let's see if that's true.

Doug: Okay. [Walks up onto the stage and sits opposite Katie.]

Katie: So read it again.

Doug: *I am angry at my mom because she uses her mental illness to manipulate me and my family.*

Katie: So, "She uses her mental illness to manipulate you and your family"—is that true?

Doug: It appears that way, yes.

Katie: So that would be a yes.

Doug: Yes.

Katie: Okay. A yes is good; a no is good. This is personal work; it's yours. You may tend to answer the way you've been taught to answer. And maybe there are answers under that, which are available to you if you just wait and allow them to surface. This Work is meditation. This Work is about asking with the intention of allowing what's beneath the surface to come out. It's like, "Come out, come out, wherever you are." Just allow it to take the risk.

So, "Your mother uses her mental illness to manipulate you and your family"—can you absolutely know that it's true that she uses that to manipulate you and your family?

Doug: No.

Katie: And how do you react when you believe this thought and you're alone in your room, you're sitting in your favorite chair, maybe. How do you react when you think that thought and you believe it?

Doug: I want to throw the TV through the window.

Katie: Basically.

Doug: I get really angry, because it's been going on a long time, and I don't know what to do anymore.

Katie: Yes, yes. So now if I were doing The Work, if I were sitting with these four questions, just in that moment as a sidebar, I would write: "I need to know what to do." And I would catch that thought later through inquiry. And "I don't know what to do"—I would question that one later, and turn it around, also.

Some wonderful concepts come up that actually hold up the thought we're working with. It can't exist without those others to back it up. The mind has a job: It's a seeker; it's looking for the truth. So it thinks, "My mother manipulates me," for example. Then pictures and concepts come to enforce that. How else could you believe it?

8. My Mother Manipulates Me

So who would you be without this thought? Close your eyes and look at your mom. Look at her with all those illnesses; watch her try to manipulate without a story. She does her job well, doesn't she? Just look into her eyes, her face, without your story. Drop your story. What do you see?

Doug: I see the whole world there. There's just every emotion, every high, low . . . from the beautiful to the raging. It's just . . . all within her, right there.

Katie: Yes, she's got it all covered.

Doug: Yes, it runs the gamut; it's just all right there. And without the story, I can be present with it; I can just be with it.

Katie: Yes, yes, that's wonderful. Isn't that what you've always wanted, just to be with her without all that *inside* you?

Doug: Yes, but I keep wanting to help her and save her and make it better.

Katie: I would write that one down and do The Work on it later—"I need to save my mother." I would also write down "It's *possible* to save my mother." I would also work with "My mother needs to be saved."

Doug: Everybody else thinks she does!

Katie: That would be them. We're looking at you and what *you* believe. So, "My mother uses her mental illness to manipulate me and my family"—turn it around.

Doug: I use my mother's illness to manipulate my family?

Katie: "You and your family."

Doug: Me and my family—I use my mother's illness to manipulate me and my family. Sure . . . that happens almost immediately. I mean, I just fly into all sorts of stuff.

Katie: So you're doing what your mother does with you and your family. One's enough in the family. Now there are two—using her mental illness to manipulate you and your family.

Doug: So I'm trying to control—

Katie: . . . you and your family through her mental illnesses.

Doug: Yes, I'm just wired to protect.

Katie: Can you find another turnaround for "My mother uses her mental illness to manipulate me and my family"?

Doug: My mother doesn't use her mental illness to manipulate me and my family.

Katie: Now give me an example of how that's true.

Doug: She loves being with us; she absolutely loves being with us. So I know she's there because she has a great time.

Katie: Find another example where she doesn't use her mental illness to manipulate you and control your family.

Katie: She helps out a lot. She can take care of the kids, which is amazing. She can, at times, do that really well. I tell a story about how she can't, but usually she does okay.

Katie: Nice that you should break through your own mental illness for a moment and see that. [The audience and Doug laugh.]

Doug: I really have a mental illness when I think my mom's mentally ill.

Katie: I noticed that. Okay, sweetheart, so you be your mom, just totally wired out, mentally ill, and manipulate me. I'm her son— I'm someone who loves her with all my heart. I'm her son; I'm you.

8. My Mother Manipulates Me

Doug: [as his mother] "I'm not coming over for Thanksgiving because you and Susan are abusive to me and you're abusive to your children, and I can't take it anymore."

Katie: [as Doug] "I really hear that, Mom. I love you're taking care of yourself. Can I bring you some dinner later?"

Doug: "No, because I'm probably going to be in the hospital because of my fibromyalgia, and they'll probably bring me something."

Katie: "Oh, good. I love that you're taking care of yourself, that you would go to the hospital if you need to."

Doug: "I don't have a ride there. So I don't know how I'll get there."

Katie: "Would you like me to take you?"

Doug: "No, I really don't feel like seeing you right now."

Katie: "Would you like me to call a cab?"

Doug: "I don't have money for a cab."

Katie: "Would you like me to call a cab and pay the fare?"

Doug: "You do whatever you want."

Katie: "Mom, you are *so* easy to get along with." [The audience laughs and applauds.]
[As herself] Good old Mom!
[As Doug] "So if you decide that you want to go to the hospital, call me and I'll get a paid-for cab there right away."

Doug: "That would be nice."

Katie: "Okay, Mom, if you need me, call. I'm here. And we're really going to miss you at Thanksgiving dinner."

Doug: "Okay . . . well, I wish I felt better."

Katie: "Well, you know, Mom, that's what I wish, too. I love you. Good-bye."

Katie: [as herself] I didn't notice any manipulation going on from your mother at all. [The audience laughs.] Zero. I heard a very loving son respecting his mother's wishes. Your mom doesn't want to come. She sees you and your wife as unkind to your children. Can you find the place where you're unkind to your children?

Doug: Yes, sure.

Katie: Okay, so you can also say, "Mom, you know, you're right. We *are* unkind to our children sometimes."

Doug: Okay, but if you have a person who takes reality as it is and does whatever she wants with it—even the most benign thing that happens—and if you *say* that to her, it feels like she could really run with that and tell all the aunts and uncles, "Doug finally admitted that he's abusive to his children!" [The audience laughs.]

Katie: Okay, so let's play that one out. So you be all your relatives rolled into one after your mother has brainwashed them. And I'll be you.

Doug: Okay.

Katie: [as Doug] "Ring, ring. Hi, relatives!"

Doug: [as all the relatives rolled into one] "So how are you, Doug?"

Katie: "I'm well. Thank you for asking."

Doug: "Well, you know, your mom is moving here; I sent her a plane ticket to move here. She's leaving you because I hear you're having some family problems, and she says she just can't stand seeing how you're being . . . abusive to the kids, which I find hard to believe; but I haven't seen you in a while, and I just hope everything is okay."

Katie: "You know, it is. It's really kind of you to send her a ticket and help her move to where you are. You're wonderful."

Doug: "Well, I don't want to get into your personal life, but is everything okay? I mean, she also told all the cousins and the aunts, and everyone's concerned that the kids are going to get taken away from you."

Katie: "Well, that's not my experience. Interesting, isn't it?"

Doug: "So the children are fine? There's no abuse going on in the home? This is just Susan going off and everything's fine?"

Katie: "Well, everything is fine, and I've noticed sometimes I become really angry at my children. I can see how Mom would see it that way."

Doug: "Hmm . . . so it sounds like you *are* having problems."

Katie: "Well, no more than anyone else, probably . . ."
[As herself] I can't answer really well here, honey, because I don't know if you strike out at them physically. I don't know any of that, so I can't answer truthfully.

Doug: Yes, I understand that.

Katie: Yes. But if they said, "Did you hit your child?" and I did, I'd say, "I did, and I'm really looking for help."

Doug: Yes, I would. I love The Work. The problem I'm having is doing it around my mom. That's why I'm really glad I got to come up here and do The Work with you. And I know all our realities are kind of made-up projections—

Katie: No, not "kind of." They *are* projected.

Doug: You're right. It feels like . . . it's really scary to be open with her. It's really scary to do what The Work says you should do.

Katie: Well, The Work doesn't say you should do anything. It's just four questions and a turnaround, and you use them or not. That's it. And sometimes I talk about my experience.

Doug: Is there a situation where I should ever feel like it's not safe or good to be around this person right now? I get confused with that, because I feel like it's my thing.

Katie: Well, people *do* feel unsafe around people, and all war belongs on paper. And it's good that you did that, and you questioned it and turned it around, until you could see the difference between what your mother says and what you think she means. Because that's what's going on here. That's your hell, so far.

When we were dialoguing, she wasn't manipulative at all. If I had a mind like yours—an unquestioned mind that would superimpose what you think she really means onto it—then I would begin to manipulate me into believing that it's her and not me. And that's confusion. And if I don't want my mother to know that I was abusive to my children in any way, and she says, "You're abusive to your children!" I might say, "Thank you for your point of view." And then I would really look at it. And I would bear in mind how wise my mother is.

Doug: But she thinks we're abusive to our children because we don't let them see her, because we feel like she's suicidal.

Katie: So, "Your mother is suicidal."

Doug: That's what she tells me.

Katie: "Your mother is suicidal"—is that true? Can you absolutely know that it's true that she's suicidal? I'm not saying that she's not; I'm asking you, can you absolutely know that it's true?

Doug: No.

Katie: And how do you react when you believe the thought "My mother is suicidal"?

Doug: I don't believe the thought; I think she's using it as manipulation. I don't think she'll kill herself because she's said it so many times.

Katie: So how do you react when you believe the thought "My mother is suicidal" and she says, "I'm not coming for Thanksgiving"?

Doug: I get really sad. I get sad, sad; it's sad. It's heartbreaking.

Katie: So who would you be without the thought "My mother is suicidal" when she says, "I don't want to come to your home on Thanksgiving"?

Doug: Who would I be without that thought?

Katie: Yes. "My mother is suicidal."

Doug: And she doesn't want to come for Thanksgiving?

Katie: Yes.

Doug: If I didn't hold it, I'd have a nice Thanksgiving!

Katie: Well, if you didn't believe it, how could you hold it? You can't hold what you can't believe.

Doug: Right, that's exactly the difference.

Katie: So "My mother is suicidal"—turn it around.

Doug: I'm suicidal.

Katie: So tell me about that.

Doug: Yes, sure. Sometimes I just want things to end, to stop.

Katie: Well, you're in the right Work. No one told me that there was a way out, short of death. I thought you had to die of this body to get out of this. And I came to see through questioning my mind that there's a whole other way out. So I really stayed with it, and I found my way out.

So "My mother's suicidal"—can you find another turn-around?

Doug: My mother's not suicidal.

Katie: Could be just as true—who knows? And if you couldn't find another way out? Think about the torture your mind has been sometimes, and there's no way out. These people who kill themselves, they have no other way of dealing with it. And for me, when I had no other way of dealing with it, it looked like an act of mercy. And then I found another way.

Doug: Yes, I know that's what it's about for her.

Katie: Sweetheart, I was looking more at you.

Doug: In the sense that I want to kill myself? I'll have to look at that. . . . Yes, okay, yes.

Katie: Do you know the three kinds of business—mine, hers, and God's?

Doug: No.

Katie: I can find only three kinds of business in the universe: mine, yours, and God's. For me, the word *God* means "reality." Reality is God because it rules. Anything that's out of my control, your control, and everyone else's control—earthquakes, floods, war, or when I will die—I call that God's business. If I am mentally in your business or in God's business, the effect is separation. When I mentally used to go into my mother's business, for example, with a thought like "My mother should understand me," I immediately experienced a feeling of loneliness. And I realized that every time in my life that I had ever felt hurt or lonely, I had been in someone else's business.

So whose business is it if you commit suicide?

Doug: Mine.

Katie: And whose business is it if your mother commits suicide?

Doug: Hers.

Katie: Thank you for knowing the difference. My business is to love. If I'm believing all this, it's hard to love my mother. Let's look at the next statement.

Doug: *I want my mom to see how much we have helped her.*

Katie: Why?

Doug: Why? Because then she would stop attacking us and making us the enemy.

Katie: So "If she saw how much you were helping her, she would stop attacking you"—is that true? Can you absolutely know that that's true?

Doug: No, she probably wouldn't.

Katie: So "Your mother doesn't see how much you help her"—is that true?

Doug: No, no, she might. And she probably does.

Katie: So much for that one. Continue to read.

Doug: That was a big one.

I want her to see how much we loved her, supported her, and tried to understand her. I want her to see that we've bent over backward in an effort to make her happy.

Katie: Turn it around.

Doug: I want me to see that I've bent over backward in an effort to make myself happy? How I'm working so hard to try to make myself happy.

Katie: "Let's change her, then I'll be happy."

Doug: Exactly.

Katie: "I'll devote my life to her happiness, *then* I'll be happy."

Doug: Right.

Katie: I have an expression: Skip the middleman; be happy from here. Have you noticed that your entire life is devoted to your mother's happiness, and she's still not happy, in your opinion?

Doug: It's getting old. *I'm* getting old! I just can't do it anymore—you know, it's been forty years.

Katie: So "You need your mother to be happy"—is that true?
[To the audience] Think of the person in your life that you believe this about. Think of the person in your life that you need to be happy.
[To Doug] "You need your mother to be happy"—is that true?

Doug: I guess not. I wouldn't even know what it felt like. I've never known it.

Katie: So find a moment. Close your eyes, and see if you can find a moment when your mother was happy.

Doug: All right.

Katie: Okay. So did that make you happy? Are you happy?

Doug: Sure! It makes me smile.

Katie: Yes, and are you happy forever?

Doug: No.

Katie: I mean, did that really do the trick?

Doug: No.

Katie: Well, that's it for me and my life. Hopeless.

Doug: Right.

Katie: "You need your mother to be happy"—can you absolutely know that that's true? I love that question. Can you absolutely know it's true that that's what you need?

Doug: No, I can't absolutely know.

Katie: If my mother hadn't been miserable, I wouldn't be able to sit here with you today.

Doug: [laughing] That is true.

Katie: It's the path.

Doug: It seems to be getting worse, though.

Katie: So I would write that down: "It's getting worse." I would work with that later. Really juicy little concepts, right? All universal, no new stressful thoughts, all recycled, nothing new. "You need your mother to be happy"—how do you react when you believe that thought and she's not happy?

Look at your life; close your eyes. Look how you live your life when you believe the thought "I need my mother to be happy," and she isn't.

Doug: I can't even breathe. I just get tight.

Katie: And how do you treat your mother when you're tight, and you believe the thought "I need my mother to be happy"?

Doug: I check out. I'm just not present with her at all. Just like, I'm not going there with you.

Katie: Well, that will certainly bring her happiness. [The audience breaks into laughter.] Spread a little joy, spread a little joy! That will teach her happiness!

Doug: I was hoping she'd see how neutral I am or something. Ah, that's a bunch of bullshit.

Katie: So, "I need my mother to be happy"—imagine your life without that thought. Who would you be without that thought when she doesn't want to come to your house for Thanksgiving? When she says, "I want to go to the hospital"?

Doug: I'd really be happy. I would really be light and happy.

Katie: That's what it's all about anyway!

Doug: Yes, I know. I thought I knew.

Katie: It's like waiting and devoting your life to her happiness so that you can be happy. And who would you be without the thought? Happy.

Doug: Right.

Katie: So, "I need my mother to be happy"—turn it around.

Doug: I don't need my mother to be happy.

Katie: Give me three reasons why that's true. Three examples of why you don't need your mother to be happy.

Doug: Maybe she *is* happy. I really don't know what makes her happy. Maybe all that is happiness to her, I don't know. I really do realize there is no way at this point to make her happy.

Katie: I would say that's two reasons.

Doug: Okay, good. Because I've got a great life, I really do.

Katie: Until you mentally go into her business.

Doug: Yes, yes.

Katie: How do you treat your family when you believe the thought "I need my mom to be happy"? You're having Thanksgiving, it's a really beautiful thing—how do you treat your family when you believe the thought "I need my mom to be happy," and she doesn't want to come?

Doug: I'm tense, and I'm concerned, and I'm worried. I'm running the monologue in my mind of what I'm going to say to her and what she's going to say back to me, and what I'm going to say to her after that, and how I'm going to fix it this time or not fix it or cut her off.

Katie: So you all sit down to Thanksgiving, and you're mentally living wherever your mother is, and your body is there with your family.

Doug: But isn't that exactly what she wants? Isn't that why she *does it?*

Katie: Whose business is that? Boy, that's a good one! I would definitely question that and turn it around.

Doug: Turn it around to "Isn't that what I want?"

Katie: Isn't that why *you* do it?

Doug: Isn't that why I do it to myself?

Katie: Yes, in her name.

Doug: Right, yes.

Katie: Let's look at the next statement.

Doug: *Mom shouldn't attack us when she's not happy. She shouldn't make us the enemy. She shouldn't be so paranoid and should see that people are really being kind to her.*

Katie: So "Your mother shouldn't attack you"—is that true? *Does she attack you?*

Doug: Yes.

Katie: "Your mother shouldn't attack you"—is that true? How many of you have never attacked anyone—would you raise your hands, please? [Looking around at the audience.] That would be zero. . . . Oh, there's one person who misunderstood the question. [The audience laughs.] So . . .

Doug: No, I can't know it's true.

Katie: . . . you're expecting your mother to be different from everyone in this room!

Doug: Right.

Katie: And I've asked this question all over the world. Only the people who misunderstand the question raise their hand. That's the way of it. What is, is.

Doug: Right. She should attack me because she does.

Katie: Beautiful. You've got it. That's what she's done up to now!

Doug: Yes . . . in between some love.

Katie: So, "Your mother shouldn't attack you"—how do you react when you believe that thought and she attacks you?

Doug: I never want to see her again!

Katie: And how does that feel?

Doug: Really cold, really heartless.

8. My Mother Manipulates Me

Katie: And who would you be without the thought, without this lie, "My mother shouldn't attack me"?

Doug: I think I'd feel stronger, because I could handle it.

Katie: If you really want a way out, if you're a truth seeker, if you really want to be free, then welcome attack.

Doug: Yes.

Katie: Because we see people who attack us as enemies, and actually they are friends. They enlighten us to all those deep secrets we're keeping from ourselves. Until those secrets are brought to light, there's no way for us to realize them, so there's no way that our patterns of behavior change. They can't, because the causes are hidden under the surface. The word is denial.

Doug: I see.

Katie: So people who attack us let us tap into that. And mothers are good at that. Your partners are good at that. Your children are good at that. So when you feel attacked, you defend and justify so that you don't have to look. And then you say that they're the ones who are causing your misery, and it's the opposite. It's *you* causing your misery, because you're not allowing your truth to surface.

So an example of that is "Your mother shouldn't attack you." What does she say when she attacks you?

Doug: A lot of times I hear it through my wife or my brother. Is that okay?

Katie: Oh, yes. Attack is attack. And it's coming from your mother, you think.

Doug: Yes. "Doug and Susan don't appreciate me; they don't do anything for me."

Katie: And is she right? Are there times when you don't appreciate her?

Doug: Yes.

Katie: So she's right. "She attacked you"—is it true? She simply told the truth, and that's something you aren't handling well. She said that you don't appreciate her, and I hear from you that she's right. So where's the attack?

Doug: I can see that.

Katie: Give me another example of how your mother attacked you. What else did she say that was an attack?

Doug: "Doug rages at me. Doug raged at me."

Katie: So have you raged at her? Is she right again?

Doug: I guess she could see it as rage.

Katie: So sweetheart—

Doug: But it's like you're down on your back getting beaten. It's like a cry out for—

Katie: You sound just like your mother! Do you rage at her? Have you raged at her? So sweetheart, she's right again. Now, what she's done is told the truth, and what you've just done is found it. Just take a moment for what you're experiencing.

Doug: [crying] It's just heartbreaking—to be able to be open, to take that pain—instead of pushing it out in that rage. And I feel that. I feel that's what I do.

Katie: That *is* what you do, because you don't know another way. And you have to do it, you have to, until you find another way.

Doug: Right.

Katie: I've come to see that defense is the first act of war.

8. My Mother Manipulates Me

Doug: That's it exactly.

Katie: If my mother said to me, "Katie, you don't appreciate me," I could go in and see where she's right. I could go back to a time when I very much didn't appreciate her. It would bring me to tears. That's what it's like to die. That's what it's like when identification begins to die.

"I am the woman who is abused by her mother"—that was my identity once. When that starts to fall away, it's like you're into losing. She wins and you lose. But then it turns into the most humbling, soft experience. It really is a death. And then you go back for more, because she's bringing up all that stuff in you that you couldn't. I couldn't contact it otherwise; I was too dense.

And you say, "Mom, give me more." Just to go back in your heart, or just say, "Tell me everything, I'm open now. I want to hear." And then as she tells you, you're undergoing the same process again. It's like dying, and there's no meanness to it. It's sitting at the feet of the true guru. Your mother, your father, your sister, your brother, your child, your enemy—these are your true teachers.

So if my mother said, "Katie, you don't appreciate me," I would go inside and look. Now we have a lot in common, because I see where she is right, and I say, "Mom, you're right." Now we agree. She sees that I don't appreciate her; I see that I haven't always appreciated her. And there is an intimacy, because we're together in it. And I can ask her to let me know every time she experiences that. Because I need a teacher. That way there are two of us working on me.

Doug: Wow!

Katie: Now here's the other way, the old way. It's what human beings have been doing for a very long time, and we still have war in the world. My mother says, "Katie, you don't appreciate me." And immediately I dig in. "What do you mean I don't appreciate you? I do appreciate you!" And I run my list, and I get my attitude, and I defend and justify.

Who started the war? I did. She just told the truth. And I start to punish her for being more enlightened than I am. If there is a war in my life, I started it. There's no exception. If the war ends in my life, I end it. I end it, or it doesn't end. No exception.

Doug: Just realizing that you could do that feels incredible. That is the ultimate. Just to understand that—and yes, if you could only do that, a little bit.

Katie: People can't *do* it. It's something that you're open to. You question your mind, and you open again. You question your mind again, and you open again. And this gives you what to go back to the enemy with and for. If war doesn't end in you, it doesn't end in the world.

Doug: It just goes on and on.

Katie: That's why I love sitting with you, sweetheart. If you can't do it, it can't be done. That's how it is. There's no hope for your children, there's no hope for anyone, there's no hope for humanity if you can't do it. You're the one. And what I love about it is that you don't *have* to do it. It's in our internal seeking that the enemy holds the answers for us. They have the answers if we're in a hurry.

Doug: You say we don't have to do it. Do you mean it's just going to come to us?

Katie: Oh, yes, again and again. The name for that grace is "Mother." Here she comes through the phone line, through the door. You don't have to know what to do. Life will show you, and with perfect timing, too. You don't have to seek it; it will come. That's why I love that you judge your neighbor; write it down; ask four questions; turn it around.

And sweetheart, there's one more thing I can say. You don't have to end the war. You're not working with your mother; you're working with your mind. Bodies can't get this. Bodies have no use for it. You're working with your mind, and then the love of your mother follows. We can't work with our mothers; you've noticed that.

Doug: Yes. I've tried to make it work.

Katie: And she won't have it. She wants only the real deal, only the genuine.

8. My Mother Manipulates Me

Doug: The more you try, the more it just gets worse.

Katie: Read the whole statement again.

Doug: *Mom shouldn't attack us when she's not happy. She shouldn't make us the enemy. She shouldn't be so paranoid and should see that people are really being kind to her.*

Katie: That's hopeless, hopeless; she does what she does. So turn it around.

Doug: I shouldn't attack us when I'm not happy.

Katie: I shouldn't attack my mother . . .

Doug: I shouldn't attack my mother when I'm not happy, I shouldn't make her the enemy, I shouldn't be so paranoid and should see that other . . . [Crying] God, it's so true . . . and see that other people are really being kind to me. It's true; I shouldn't be so paranoid. That's a good one.

Katie: What are you experiencing now? You seem so vulnerable.

Doug: I'm so aware of the anger and rage, and trying to make everything okay. But I just really understand the beauty of surrender. And when you start to talk about it, it's just too big. It's so much.

Katie: I have an expression for that—it's "Let love kill you."

Doug: It feels like it's trying to. When you say what's true, it's so beautiful. It's so instantly recognizable. It couldn't be any other way. But in a heartbeat, I will spew out my stuff to be safe. I try not to, but I still do, to protect the family, to feel safe.

Katie: To feel safe for what?

Doug: My family.

Katie: Oh, let's drop the family, sweetheart. It's for *you* to be safe. You want your family safe so that you're safe. Your identity—"I am the man with a family"—is safe. It's all about you. I'll keep my family safe, then I'm safe.

Doug: So I'm viewing it as—

Katie: You do with them what you do with your mother.

Doug: Oh.

Katie: When she's happy, you're happy. When they're happy and safe, you're happy and safe. Your life is secure; it's all about you. There's no exception to that. So just notice.

How do I react when I believe the thought "My family needs to be safe"? Oh my God! I am not a pretty sight.

Doug: I see. It's the same.

Katie: I have to manipulate them the way I manipulate my mother. It's hopeless. And then when they're not happy, I'm so shocked—after all that I've done for them!

Doug: Yes.

Katie: So, let's try another turnaround with that same thing.

Doug: I shouldn't attack us—

Katie: I shouldn't attack myself . . .

Doug: I shouldn't attack myself when I'm not happy. I shouldn't make me the enemy. I shouldn't be so paranoid and should see that people are really being kind to me. I would go along with that.

Katie: That's so much wisdom there.

Doug: Yes.

8. My Mother Manipulates Me

Katie: Let's look at the next statement.

Doug: *I need my mom to enjoy what we have to offer, appreciate the time we set aside, to love us as openly as we love her. I need her . . .*

Katie: You sound like a dictator!

Doug: [laughing] It's crazy!

Katie: Read it again; see if you can hear it. "Mom, I need you to . . ." I mean, look what you hand out to this poor woman!

Doug: "Mom, I need you to enjoy what we have to offer . . ."

Katie: "Enjoy what we have to offer or I'll just get—"

Doug: ". . . appreciate the time we set aside—"

Katie: "Or I'll go cold on you!"

Doug: ". . . love us as openly as we love you."

Katie: Boy, what an order!

Doug: "I need you to be sane, not crazy. I need you not to invent a warped reality."

Katie: Not asking for much, are you? [The audience laughs.]

Doug: She's my mom!

Katie: She has a lot to live up to. Living with you is hard!

Doug: Yes. I can see that.

Katie: So you need these things from her—is that true?

Doug: It doesn't seem as true now.

Katie: Can you absolutely know that you need these things from her?

Doug: No. No, I can see that.

Katie: You could sit with that question for a long time when you go home. "Can I absolutely know that it's true that this is what I need in my life?"

Doug: True.

Katie: So sweetheart, who would you be living your life without this thought that you need all these things you're dictating?

Doug: I think that maybe I could just in a real way—not in some manufactured way—be open and big enough to really love her.

Katie: Yes, whether she's happy or not!

Doug: Right!

Katie: Honey, when you're unhappy, do you want someone to be mean to you and cold, or would you want them to be a little more caring?

Doug: More caring, absolutely, yes.

Katie: She's the same way.

Doug: I see that.

Katie: Read that list again, only put in "I need my children . . ." Because if you believe these concepts with one person, you believe them with everyone. Because it's concepts you're dealing with here, not people.

Doug: "I need my children to enjoy what we have to offer . . ."

Katie: They'd better.

Doug: Oh, it's so true. I see that. Boy . . . "I need my children to appreciate the time we set aside—"

Katie: They'd better!

Doug: "To love us as openly as we love them—"

Katie: Oh yes!

Doug: "I need my children to not be crazy and not invent a warped reality."

Katie: Well, they'll live what they live. So let's turn it around and see what's possible. Not possible with your mother—she has her path; not possible with your children, they have their path. Let's turn it around and see whose path you *can* work with. What you can work with is perception—that's *all* you can work with.

Doug: I need to enjoy what I have to offer; I need to enjoy and appreciate the time that I set aside; I need to love me as openly as I love others; I need me to be sane, not crazy; I need me not to invent a warped reality. Yes, that's about it.

Katie: If you work on her, you don't have to work on you. What a set-up! And she's hopeless, so you'll never get to you.

Doug: Funny how we do that. It's so hard to see it when you're in it.

Katie: Well, we begin now. That's what I love about now; this is where we always begin. It's the only place we *can* begin. I can't begin tomorrow, because what is that but a dream? What is that but a theory? And I couldn't begin back in the past, because I didn't. Right now, here is where the power is.
  So let's find another way to turn it around. "I need me . . ."

Doug: I need me . . . I need me to enjoy what we have to—

Katie: "What my *mother* . . ."

Doug: I need me to . . . oh.

Katie: That's the last place we look.

Doug: Wow! I need me to enjoy what my *mother* has to offer and appreciate the time she sets aside. I need me to love my mother as openly as she loves us. I need—

Katie: This is a life's work.

Doug: I need me to be sane, not crazy, and I need me not to invent a warped reality.

Katie: . . . around your mother. So far, I'm just meeting her as a woman who shares with you what she sees, and so far what I've heard is that she's right. She's a very awake woman.

Doug: [laughing] Maybe.

Katie: Let's look at the next statement.

Doug: *My mom is a self-centered, narcissistic, self-absorbed egomaniac.* [The audience laughs.]

Katie: Can you absolutely know that that's true?

Doug: Not absolutely.

Katie: Give me an example of that. Take on her role. Give me an example of how she's self-centered.

Doug: [as his mother] "You know, I'm being a nanny right now with these people. They don't realize that I'm really raising their children, and they don't appreciate me. I'm really the one who taught them to walk and ride the bikes. And they come home and they're angry at me because I made a fort, and the kids don't want to come out of the fort because they know their parents aren't as nice as I am. The parents don't see that *I'm* the reason that their children are as beautiful as they are—they can't see that. But I understand that, but you know that's what it's like to be a nanny!"

Katie: You know what I'm hearing? She could be right! Maybe she's just giving you observations! She could be right—who knows?

Doug: She could, of course.

Katie: Pretty simple, isn't it?

Doug: Very simple, but very huge.

Katie: And you only have to start with one stressful thought.

Doug: When you say you've come to love your thoughts, do you mean even those crazy and sick and insane thoughts?

Katie: What sick, crazy thoughts? I haven't met a sick, crazy thought in years. Thoughts are like children—they're the beloved. They're children. They're screaming to be heard, and they scream and scream and scream. And we shut them up; we send them away; we push them under; we deny them, we try to pretend that they're not there. So when we bring them into the light, as you've done here, and we question them and turn them around, then the children begin to get quiet. And we begin to meet them.
   Let's look at the next statement.

Doug: *I don't ever want to feel her attack me again, get angry and saddened that she doesn't see all the love our family has for her. I don't ever want to feel like I'm the bad guy in her life again.*

Katie: "She doesn't see all the love your family has for her"—is that true?

Doug: No.

Katie: That's very good to sit in. Turn it around. "I don't see all the love . . ."

Doug: I don't see all the love—

Katie: ". . . that she . . ."

Doug: . . . that she has for us, for me . . . yes.

Katie: There's another turnaround. "I don't see all the love . . ."

Doug: I don't see all the love—

Katie: "I don't see all the love that I have for . . ."

Doug: I don't see all the love I have for *her*. Yes.

Katie: Here's what unconditional love looks like. Read your *needs* again.

Doug: *I need my mom to enjoy what we have to offer, appreciate—*

Katie: "I *don't* need . . ." I want you to take it in.

Doug: I *don't* need my mom to appreciate what we have to offer; I *don't* need her to see the time we set aside for her; I *don't* need her to love us as openly as we love her; I *don't* need her to be sane or not crazy; I *don't* need her . . . she can invent warped realities.

Katie: That's unconditional love. And that's how much you love her, and that's the direction you're going in.

Doug: I'm really glad I got to do this.

Katie: I'm really glad, too, honey. You're amazing. Now, do number six, "I'm willing to . . ."

Doug: I'm willing to feel her attack me again, get angry. I'm willing to feel saddened that she doesn't see all the love our family has for her, and I'm willing for her to feel like I am the bad guy in her life.

Katie: Yes, yes. Because as long as you see her that way, you know your Work isn't done. That's what that's about. Now "I look forward to . . ." And read it again.

8. My Mother Manipulates Me

Doug: I look forward to her attacking me again . . .

Katie: Exciting, isn't it? Do you know that no one can attack me?

Doug: That's right. That's right. I look forward to her attacking me again; I look forward to her getting angry.

Katie: What's the worst that she could say to you, like a knife in your heart, if she attacked you?

Doug: "You mean nothing to me. . . ." I look forward to her saying that? [The audience laughs.] Because maybe she will—

Katie: Who knows? You know, if my children said, "Mom, you mean nothing to me," I'd think, "My God, they're finally free!" [Laughter] So, "I look forward to . . ."

Doug: I look forward to her attacking me again. I look forward to getting angry and being sad that she doesn't see all the love that we have for her and the family; I look forward to her thinking that I'm the bad guy in her life.

Katie: That's very exciting. So "she thinks you're the bad guy in her life"—is that true?

Doug: No.

Katie: No. You know what I've gotten from beginning to end here is the way that you love her—it's the thing that shines through everything. That's what this whole thing is about.

Doug: It gets confused.

Katie: Yes, it gets confused. And now we can see how. It's a privilege to sit with you.

Doug: It's been an honor. Thank you so much, Katie.

Katie: You're welcome, sweetheart.

Doug: Thank you.

Katie: If he can do it, we can do it. And he's doing it.

9. Cancer Ruined My Life

You see scars in the mirror, but a mirror can only reflect your thoughts. Only one thing can ruin your life, or even your body, and it's not cancer.

Katie: Okay, sweetheart, what did you write?

Emma: *I am angry at cancer because it ruined my life. I want cancer to never, ever return to me or anyone else. I don't want to live in fear for the rest of my life. Cancer shouldn't leave me so changed, so traumatized, disfigured, self-conscious, and a hermit.*

Katie: So you don't want to live with the fear of cancer. Okay, so tell me, which is more painful, living with the fear of cancer, or cancer?

Emma: Well, I'm only a week out, so I don't know.

Katie: So stop and think about it.

Emma: Okay.

Katie: Your fear of cancer returning, or cancer. Which is more painful?

Emma: Compared to the reality? Compared to how the experience was?

153

Katie: Compared to the reality of cancer.

Emma: They seem equal. I can't even—

Katie: Well, equal. That's amazing.

Emma: Yes!

Katie: So you can take care of half of this.

Emma: I can take care of half of it?

Katie: Yes, if it's equal—cancer and your fear of cancer. You know you can take care of the fear of cancer, and then because there *is* no cancer left, that's done for you.

Emma: Okay, how do I do that?

Katie: Keep reading.

Emma: Okay. *Cancer shouldn't leave me so changed, so traumatized, disfigured, self-conscious, and a hermit. I need to be sure that it's gone and it's not coming back, or to be okay with the thought that it might return. Cancer is hell! It's debilitating, disfiguring, traumatizing, and leaves continued fear. I don't want to have chemo again. I don't want to be bald again. I don't want to feel so weak again. I don't want to hate how I look again. I don't want to lose a year again. I don't want to have so many surgeries again. I don't want my son and my family witnessing all this again.*

Katie: Thank you, sweetheart. So let's start at the top again, okay? And I'd like you to read the whole thing, and then we'll do something else with it.

Emma: Okay. *I want cancer to never, ever return to me.* I mean, *I am angry at cancer because it ruined my life.*

Katie: Okay. Now turn it around. Where you have the word *cancer*, put *my thinking*.

9. Cancer Ruined My Life

Emma: I am angry at my thinking because it ruined my life.

Katie: Is that *as* true?

Emma: Yes.

Katie: That's a lot of it. For me, that's *all* of it. But from where you are, that's a major part of it. So "cancer ruined your life"—is that true?

Emma: Well, I guess I have a life, so—

Katie: "It ruined your life"—is that true?

Emma: Feels like it.

Katie: So is it true that it ruined your life? You came here. You still have your family.

Emma: It *changed* my life. I guess it changed it; maybe it didn't ruin it.

Katie: Is that truer?

Emma: That's truer.

Katie: Yes. How do you react when you believe the thought "Cancer ruined my life"? What happens to you when you believe that thought? What happens to your body? Feel it.

Emma: I hide; I just hide.

Katie: And where do you feel it? "Cancer ruined my life"—where do you feel that in your body? Where do you experience that thought physically?

Emma: Everywhere. It's everywhere. It's just a deadening.

Katie: So "Cancer ruined your life"—does that thought bring peace or stress into your life?

Emma: No, it's ridiculous; it brings nothing but stress.

Katie: So give me a peaceful reason to believe that cancer ruined your life. As you sit here, looking gorgeous. Give me a peaceful reason to believe the thought "Cancer ruined my life."

Emma: There isn't one.

Katie: Who would you be without this thought, "Cancer ruined my life"? Who would you be if you didn't believe that when people said, "Oh, you had cancer."

Emma: I guess I'd be who I am anyway.

Katie: If someone said, "Oh, you had cancer," you might be someone who could say, "Yes. But it didn't ruin my life." "Cancer ruined my life"—turn it around.

Emma: Cancer didn't ruin my life.

Katie: Now name three ways that your life is better because you had the cancer. Three beautiful things that came out of that.

Emma: Well, I healed my relationship with my mom, because she pulled through for me in a way that I never thought she would have.

Katie: Wow!

Emma: Yes, she just completely supported me and my son for a year and slept in the hospital, just showed up in an amazing way. My son, from the ages of fourteen to fifteen, has gotten to step up and help out; and he's really learned what that's about, helping. And I know it will add to my work. I work with Parkinson's patients, so it will only add to my work. And I'll be able to help other women, if I can get through it—when I get through it.

Katie: Well, you're already through it. Except for your thoughts.

9. Cancer Ruined My Life

Emma: Except for my mind.

Katie: Yes. They say you're cancer free, but in your mind, you're not.

Emma: I'm not.

Katie: So even when you don't have cancer, you have cancer. In your mind. It's no good to be cancer free, because you're not.

Emma: Well, I have this gene, and they're just so afraid, and now I'm always going to be tested all the time. Yes, I just need to move on. That's why I'm here, to start the new year, start work again, and just . . . it's like being dropped in hell, and then some giant tongs picks you up and says, "Okay! Go!"

Katie: "This is who your mother is, this is who your son is, and this is what it's for: helping people. So you go, girl!"

Emma: And I'm just . . . I had an image while I was sitting over there of—I don't know why—but a little black, wet cat after a storm, just shivering, just shaking, just going, "Ow!"

Katie: Yes. So what other good things came out of this cancer? Why is it a good thing that you had cancer? What good things came out of it?

Emma: I got closer to my twin sister. She had to have a prophylactic double mastectomy after mine. So she lived with me and used my doctors and surgeons.

Katie: Wow!

Emma: And we reconnected. We haven't lived together in the same state for years and years, so we've both been going through it.

Katie: So "Cancer ruined your life"—is that true?

Emma: No. It just ruined my body!

Katie: "Cancer ruined your body"—is that true?

Emma: Yes! That's definitely true! I look like I met the slasher in the park. It's hard.

Katie: I know, I know, honey. So "Cancer ruined your body"—is that true?

Emma: Changed it.

Katie: "Cancer ruined your body"—is that true?

Emma: Yes! Actually it *is* true! I mean, I guess it depends who—

Katie: So did the surgeon say, "I'm going to operate whether you want it or not"? Or did you consent?

Emma: I didn't have a choice. It didn't work the way it was supposed to.

Katie: And did you consent to go into that surgery, those surgeries? Did you get in the car? You went there, and you *paid* them to do it.

Emma: Yes.

Katie: Okay. So "Cancer ruined your body"—is that true? You said you didn't have a choice. What was the other choice?

Emma: *I* ruined my body, then!

Katie: You said you didn't have a choice. What was the other choice? Do it or . . .

Emma: Death, death.

Katie: So you made the decision. No one made you decide; it was your decision. "Cancer ruined your body"—is that true?

Emma: Well, if I hadn't gotten the cancer, I wouldn't have had to consent to that.

Katie: "Cancer ruined your body"—is that true?

Emma: Still seems so.

Katie: You could have died.

Emma: Yes.

Katie: But what choice did you make? To go into surgery.

Emma: Right.

Katie: What do they do in surgery? They've got knives in there.

Emma: Yes.

Katie: "Cancer ruined your body"—is that true?

Emma: I can't say *no!*

Katie: That's okay. So how do you react when you believe the thought "Cancer ruined my body?" "I didn't do it! I had nothing to do with that surgery, cancer did it!" How do you react when you believe the thought "Cancer *ruined* my body?" You can have cancer and *not* do it.

Emma: I don't recall a choice.

Katie: Dying was the other choice.

Emma: Yes, I didn't choose that one.

Katie: No, you made a very kind choice.

Emma: So, okay.

Katie: Got it?

Emma: Yes.

Katie: Good. Oh honey, there is nowhere we are victims. We are goodness in action. We can never say, "Cancer ruined my body." *I* did that. It was a wise, loving, caring decision. Cancer has no control over me.

Emma: Yes.

Katie: So who would you be without your story, "Cancer ruined my body?"

Emma: I would just be me, probably a little more insecure, but not ruined.

Katie: I just had a picture of you standing naked in front of us, saying, "You see this? I did that. I saved my life. This is what it took. You see this? This is an act of love."

Emma: It's hard to look at in the mirror.

Katie: Well yes, because you thought your body, the other way, would get you something. It's a commodity, for getting love and approval, but you lost your . . . currency.

Emma: Yes, dating's going to be a whole lot different.

Katie: Yes. Can you imagine someone with a mind as open as yours is? You know, if someone doesn't see my body as absolutely beautiful, I think they've got a problem.

Emma: Well, they'd have to be pretty special, too.

Katie: Yes! And isn't that what you want?

Emma: Well, that's all that can be, because that's my reality.

Katie: Oh, really? We'll see. We'll see in a moment. We'll go there. So "Cancer . . ."

Emma: No. I mean the disfigurement is the way it is for me, so it will have to be their reality, too.

Katie: Yes. Well, someone could be with you and not like it. And you could hide it and bribe them some other way.

Emma: [laughing] Okay.

Katie: We never run out of tricks. Until we decide to just settle for the real deal. You know, "Here it is. What do you think?"

Emma: Yes. They don't have to know right away. . . . I don't know. . . .

Katie: No. We don't.

Emma: I haven't really gone there yet.

Katie: Yes, okay. So "Cancer ruined your body"—turn it around.

Emma: I ruined my body.

Katie: Yes.

Emma: I gave it up—

Katie: . . . for a very good cause.

Emma: Yes.

Katie: Now, let's look at this. "Your body is ruined"—is that true? Is it ruined as *currency,* or is it ruined as . . . How is it ruined? What's it going to cost you, other than as currency?

Emma: I wasn't planning on modeling in *Playboy* magazine anyway.

Katie: So "Your body is ruined"—ruined for what? Let's get specific.

Emma: Well, it's ruined because I don't like it. I mean, I don't. I can't even look at it.

Katie: Ruined for what?

Emma: For being naked!

Katie: Yes, because if someone *sees* you that way, you don't get what you want from them. That's what you believe.

Emma: Well, I think it's what happens to me—

Katie: It is. And let's do first things first.

Emma: Okay.

Katie: That's where it's born: in you. I mean, *you* don't like looking at it, so you project that others wouldn't. And when you project that others wouldn't, then you lose what you believe. You lose the security that you imagined you could have purchased with your body the way it was.

Emma: Well, but I *had* it! I had it, you know, it's like—

Katie: You had what?

Emma: A nice body.

Katie: Yes.

Emma: But . . . I know. Oh well, I mean really, you're right. I'm living here to talk about it, so—

Katie: So "Your body is ruined"—is that true?

Emma: I'll settle for "My body is funny-looking."

Katie: Okay. So how do you react when you believe the thought "My body is ruined"? How does that feel *inside* you?

Emma: Oh, it's terrible. I just hide. I just stay home.

Katie: Now close your eyes. What pictures do you see when you believe the thought "My body is ruined"? Where does your mind travel? Look at the stressful thoughts; look at the pictures that attack you.

Emma: It just goes to being alone all the time. Always alone.

Katie: So who would you be without the story "My body is ruined"? Who would you be, living your life without that thought?

Emma: I'd just be—like everyone else. I would just be me again.

Katie: As you're living your life, yes—your very productive, wonderful life, with a body that's strong, that can go to work, that can cook meals, that can take care of itself, that goes where mind tells it to go.

Emma: Yes, I can just move on.

Katie: And with a body that is ready to do it! "My body is ruined"— is that true?

Emma: No.

Katie: No, you have a job to do. And your body is physically able to do it.

Emma: Yes.

Katie: If I think my body is for attracting men, what a limited life! Or attracting friends, what a limited life! We have jobs to do. Our job is to love and to go to work.

Emma: Yes. I don't really think about others as much as noticing what happens to me when I'm in the bathroom, and how I just can't accept—

Katie: What you see.

Emma: What I see.

Katie: And *you* made the decision. You made the decision to do that to save your life! Those scars are how you saved your life, to do your job in this world.

Emma: Yes.

Katie: So now give me three beautiful things about those scars. Three beautiful things about the way your body is after the surgery.

Emma: Well, now you're pushing it. [Laughter]

Katie: So close your eyes, take a look. Three beautiful things.

Emma: There is *nothing* beautiful about them.

Katie: They saved your life.

Emma: Right.

Katie: What else is beautiful about them? All I can see is beauty. Notice how they're healing. Do you see it? Or have you even given them that much attention to see how they're healing, to see the miracle?

Emma: No. One of them is all screwed up: It's rejected everything; it's just completely freaky.

Katie: And is it healing?

Emma: It's not going to heal. If I want to have more surgery, I can, but I don't want to, so I have to just live with . . . the way it is.

Katie: Can you see where it *is* healing?

Emma: I can see the scars healing.

Katie: Good, thank you.

Emma: Sure.

Katie: Don't you find that rather beautiful?

Emma: No!

Katie: That they're healing?

Emma: Yes.

Katie: That's miraculous, that the surgeons cut through us and we heal. I just find that beautiful.

Emma: Yes, I'm getting . . . every day I can move my arm a little bit more.

Katie: Don't you find that beautiful?

Emma: Yes, if I weren't so afraid that I'll never have full mobility.

Katie: As your arm goes a little farther every day.

Emma: A little farther.

Katie: Yes, we won't find that beautiful. We'll think about where it's *not* going.

Emma: Yes. Because you don't know—I don't know—that it will come back.

Katie: Or that it won't.

Emma: Right.

Katie: So your arm—you can raise it a little more, a little more. Don't you find that beautiful?

Emma: Mmm . . . mildly pleasing. [Laughter] As a physical therapist, it's a bummer!

Katie: Is it a bummer that it moves a little farther each time?

Emma: No, that's a good thing.

Katie: A good thing! Okay. I find that amazing. It's amazing! You can't move it at all, and then you can, and then farther and farther. That's amazing.

Emma: Yes.

Katie: But the mind says that it's not ever going to do this or that. . . . When you're stuck in that and your mind is busy proving it, then there's no room for appreciating reality, which is that it doesn't matter what you think, it's still getting better. Despite your belief system, it's still doing its job. Scars are healing. The arm is getting a higher range.

Emma: Yes, I can focus more on being happy for those little steps.

Katie: Yes. It's doing better than *you* are.

Emma: Yes, it is!

Katie: So I love that you're catching up to it.

Emma: Yes, to my mind, yes. To my body.

Katie: To stand in front of a mirror and see the miracle of you saving your life and to see the miracle of it healing: giving back to you everything that it can. And how you don't appreciate it and how you *do* appreciate it. So, "My body is ruined"—turn it around.

9. Cancer Ruined My Life

Emma: It's not ruined.

Katie: Can you give me an example of how that's true?

Emma: Well, it was absolutely the right decision that I made. And I was the one who made it. They didn't do it to me; cancer wasn't out to get me. It wasn't a punishment; it wasn't because of something I did.

Katie: No.

Emma: It's hard to believe that. I know everybody says there's some gift that I'll see from it.

Katie: Well, I heard that from your own lips.

Emma: Relating to my mom and my son?

Katie: Yes.

Emma: My sister . . .

Katie: Yes. And what you have to share in your job.

Emma: Yes. But I could have had that without the cancer.

Katie: Oh, really!

Emma: Yes! I think so!

Katie: "Mom, come down here for a whole year, take care of me, and—"

Emma: She lives here.

Katie: Okay, so "Take care of me for a whole year."

Emma: Yes, financially. Yes.

Katie: And your son, I'm sure he would have just stepped up to the plate without it?

Emma: Taken out all the trash, anyway? I don't know that any of those are worth it, though.

Katie: Well, ask yourself. If that's the only way . . . if that was the only way you could experience how your mother really cares about you, and sees you . . . if that was the *only* way. Play with it. So where is your body not ruined?

Emma: Where is it not ruined?

Katie: Yes.

Emma: My toes . . . everything. Except a bunch of scars, and one of them looks different from the other, and I have two bald spots, and—

Katie: Where is your body *not* ruined? You see, you went into the story.

Emma: Oh, I went into where it's ruined!

Katie: Very good! It's ruined in your opinion.

Emma: Yes. It's not my feet or my legs. I've put on a little weight overall, but my . . . yeah, my legs are fine. My neck is fine. My face.

Katie: Your arms look fine.

Emma: Yes, I just can't use this one as well as I used to be able to.

Katie: You're talking about a large percentage of the world.

Emma: They have something wrong in their bodies.

Katie: Or they can't use one arm that way, at the level they can use the other.

9. Cancer Ruined My Life

Emma: Right, right.

Katie: Okay. So, keep reading. Start at the top again.

Emma: *I am angry at cancer because it ruined my life.* Not true.

Katie: Isn't it nice to know that it didn't ruin your life?

Emma: Yes. I don't have to walk around like that.

Katie: With a ruined life—

Emma: Yes.

Katie: . . . as you live your life.

Emma: Yes, and I don't have to think that I'm starting over. I've had this thought that I'm starting from scratch, and—

Katie: It's absolutely not true.

Emma: No. That's a relief. *I want cancer to never ever return to me or anyone else.* Well, that's pretty unrealistic, but—

Katie: How do you react when you believe the thought "I want cancer not to return"?

Emma: I mean it! I don't want it, I mean, I . . . I have this thought that I can't do that again. That if it comes back, I will end it all.

Katie: Okay, let's look at it. If cancer comes back, you can't do it again.

Emma: I can't. I can't do that again!

Katie: You could be right. I don't disbelieve you. What are you doing, threatening the universe? Threatening cancer, threatening God? What are you doing? Threatening—"I can't do it again!" It just is what it is, honey. "If cancer comes back, you can't do it again"—can you absolutely know that that's true?

Emma: No, I can't know that.

Katie: So just feel that a moment. Notice what it feels like when you believe that thought "I can't do it again. I won't do it again."

Emma: Yes, that's like what you said . . . threatening with myself. It's like giving myself a line in the sand. Just because I can't imagine it doesn't mean I can't do it.

Katie: Very good! So "I can't do it again"—who would you be without that story when you go in for your next checkup?

Emma: Brave?

Katie: Open.

Emma: Willing. Just . . . whatever is up.

Katie: What does it feel like in your body when you have the thought "I can't do it again," and you believe that?

Emma: It just all tightens up.

Katie: Okay. So what does that do to your blood system, and your arteries, and all the places that need oxygen and everything else to be healthy and to keep a healthy immune system—when you believe it or don't believe it? One way, you are courageous and you go in. You don't know if you can do it again or not. The other, it's "I can't do it again," and you're just . . . "Crraaugh."

Emma: Doesn't help, no.

Katie: No. It's very hard to get oxygen through a body like that.

Emma: Constriction. Yes.

Katie: So "I can't do it again"—turn it around.

Emma: I can do it again.

Katie: Could be as true.

Emma: Could be. Oh, God. But I need to stop going there. I mean I need to stop wondering if—

Katie: Is that true—you need to stop wondering "What if?"

Emma: Well, it doesn't make me feel good, but I guess I can't help it.

Katie: How do you react when you believe "I need to stop doing this," and you do it again?

Emma: Yes, and I failed.

Katie: So who would you be when those thoughts come again? "I've got to stop thinking this"—and the thought comes?

Emma: I would be open to the thought if I didn't judge that it was—

Katie: If you weren't trying to fend it off.

Emma: Right.

Katie: Defense is the first act of war. So turn it around—"I've got to stop thinking this."

Emma: I can keep on thinking this. I can keep on wondering if I could do it again.

Katie: Yes. "I don't have to stop thinking this."

Emma: Right. It's probably a normal thought after all, considering what I've been through.

Katie: It's just when you believe it that it gets dishonest.

Emma: Right. It's just the difference between wondering and deciding—

Katie: . . . and dictating your thoughts. Or attempting to. Okay, so keep reading.

Emma: *I don't want to live in fear for the rest of my life.*

Katie: "I'm willing . . ."

Emma: I'm willing to live in fear for the rest of my life.

Katie: "I look forward to . . ."

Emma: Why? Would I look forward to that?

Katie: Well, because—

Emma: . . . because it's true.

Katie: Because people in The Work know what to do with the fear. We look forward to it so we can work through it. It ends fear. So that's why.

Emma: Okay. I look forward to living in fear the rest of my life.

Katie: Yes, that thought. And then whatever is fearful for you, just write it down and question it, turn it around. So read. Start at number three.

Emma: *Cancer shouldn't leave me so changed, so traumatized, disfigured, self-conscious, and a hermit.*

Katie: Turn it around. "My thinking shouldn't . . ."

Emma: My thinking shouldn't leave me so changed, so traumatized, so disfigured, self-conscious, and a hermit. It's not the cancer.

Katie: That's correct.

Emma: But then I'm just blaming myself!

Katie: It's a beginning. Then you can question the thoughts about you. And your thoughts aren't you.

Emma: Yes. That's a good one.

Katie: "You're disfigured"—is that true?

Emma: Yes.

Katie: And how do you react when you believe the thought "I'm disfigured"?

Emma: I cry.

Katie: And who would you be without the thought "I'm disfigured"? What does it feel like when you're not thinking that thought?

Emma: It's just a nonthought. It's just a nonissue. It just doesn't—

Katie: Good. So your body's not the problem. Your *thoughts* about your body—that's the problem. That's what disfigures you. When you're not thinking about it, your body doesn't exist. Good to know, isn't it?

Emma: It's fixable.

Katie: Yes.

Emma: Can't fix the body, might as well fix the thoughts.

Katie: So "Your body needs fixing"—is that true, can you absolutely know that it's true that your body needs fixing?

Emma: Unless I can make it okay the way it is.

Katie: It *is* okay. It's very happy with itself. It's healing. It's going on with its life and its business. *It* doesn't know it's disfigured. It's

173

doing its job. It's moving into the other polarity, the polarity of solution, and strength.

If I focus on body . . . I can't even say "*My* body," because that would assume it belonged to me, and that's crazy. How does it belong to me? "I say so." Other than that, it just goes on and has its life. . . . But if I focus on the physical, I'm focused on an outside cause. This is not me. So I'm out of my business. And when I'm mentally out of my business, that is a lonely experience. So I notice and come back to my thoughts, because that's where the solutions are. So my mind is finding a home in itself, and the body is not its home.

Emma: Right.

Katie: Its home is in itself, in its own wisdom. Mind can never find a home in the body. Bodies die.

Emma: Yes, it was quite fascinating to be bald, and say, "Take my breasts; take my ovaries," and I knew it was still me in there. They can't take that.

Katie: Good to know, isn't it?

Emma: Yes.

Katie: So, to focus on the physical is to focus on an outside cause. It's nice to be kind to it and nurture it and support it. Why not? You know, you like yourself when you do that. It's not personal. Work with that. Work with the mind, then the body follows. What's the worst thing that anyone could say about you?

Emma: The body, you mean?

Katie: Yes, if you took off all your clothes. What's the worst thing that people would say about you?

Emma: Oh, they would just laugh, I think. It's kind of silly.

Katie: So it would be very good if *you* looked at you in the mirror and laughed.

Emma: Yes, it would be a switch.

Katie: Yes, you look in the mirror, and you see how it's healing. And you laugh at the thought that it's not doing what it's supposed to do, that you worried about it. Because it's not you. And if you watch it, it's doing fine.

Emma: Yes, I've even judged myself for being so superficial that I care about my body.

Katie: Whose body?

Emma: This body. I guess if it's not my body, I might not care.

Katie: "It's your body"—can you absolutely know that that's true? [Emma laughs.] That's a very old concept. "This is mine. I say so. That's what makes it true." But just because I say so, think so, believe it, doesn't make it true! If this is my body, what is it doing looking like this? What is it doing at sixty-three? If it's mine, why don't I fix that? *And* my gender, *and* my height. If it's mine, I don't seem to have a lot of control.

Emma: Right. Yes, that would be a relief, actually.

Katie: So how do you react when you believe the thought that it's yours?

Emma: Horrified! I mean just horrified.

Katie: So who would you be without the thought that this belongs to you, that this is you, that this is yours? That you *own* it in some way?

Emma: I'd be separated from it. There'd be a distance, and I wouldn't have such an investment in it. It would be a relief.

Katie: Well, that's the reality of it. It's not yours. Just because you believe it doesn't make it true.

Emma: [to the audience] Anybody want it?

Katie: You know, I could say, "That's mine" [pointing to Emma] just as easily as I could say, "This is mine" [pointing to herself].

Emma: Because we don't know.

Katie: And actually, it's not very interesting. The body is just too much to worry about. And you worry, worry, worry, and it still does what it does. It gets cancer; it gets sick; it gets well; it does . . . it's *doing* all that. It's an amazing miracle.

Emma: It is.

Katie: So, "That's *your* body"—turn it around.

Emma: It's not my body. It's *your* body.

Katie: I'll take it.

Emma: Now it will heal, of course!

Katie: Oh, it's healing anyway.

Emma: Yes.

Katie: When you know that you're not that, you can sit back and watch. It's not personal and you can support it, the way you would help your son and your mother, or your clients when you go to work. You just care for it and nurture it. It's not personal.
  So read the next statement.

Emma: *For me to be happy, I need cancer to be sure to be gone forever.* We handled that.

Katie: Well, this *is* forever, and it's gone.

Emma: Right, that's the future—

9. Cancer Ruined My Life

Katie: This is forever—right here, right now—and the cancer is gone. Are you happy now?

Emma: Yes.

Katie: That's it! And until you project your past experience onto the future, you have a happy cancer-free life, rather than a miserable cancer-free life, because body can't affect state of mind. Mind . . . this is a funny loop, but mind affects body, not through the health or sickness that it generates, but just through the way that it sees it.

Emma: Sure.

Katie: A man could look at your body and say, "Oh, my goodness, I just love looking at where the surgeries were, because that *saved* you for me."

Emma: That saved . . . ?

Katie: That *saved* your life for me.

Emma: Oh, that's nice.

Katie: It is, and that's what happened. You saved you for us. What I really like to say is "You saved 'it' for us." And then as you continue to inquire, you come to see that maybe that's not even true, that it just all is what it is.

Emma: Yes, yes.

Katie: So, let's look at the next statement.

Emma: Oh, what do I think of it? *Cancer is hell.*

Katie: "Cancer is hell"—is that true? Or your thoughts about cancer?

Emma: My thoughts about cancer.

Katie: That's hell.

Emma: Yes, my thoughts put me in hell, my own hell.

Katie: Now go to the worst, the most uncomfortable time with your cancer.

Emma: That's easy; I'm there.

Katie: Where are you?

Emma: I had a hard time with the chemo. It almost killed me.

Katie: Okay, so find a situation where it was the toughest. What's going on? Where are you?

Emma: I was home alone, and I couldn't get off the couch for forty-eight hours, and I couldn't call anyone, and I almost died. I just got stuck in not being able to call, and um . . . then it was an emergency situation, but I thought I was going to die.

Katie: So the worst thing is that you you were on the couch and you couldn't call anyone.

Emma: Yes.

Katie: So "You almost died"—is that true?

Emma: I don't know. That's what they said, but I don't know.

Katie: You either die or you don't.

Emma: Right, it was obviously—

Katie: We love our "almost-dying" stories. But the truth is that we die, or we don't. How do you react when you believe the thought "I almost died"?

Emma: I could go into a mild panic with that one.

Katie: Who would you be without this thought that isn't even true?

Emma: I'd be truthful!

Katie: Yes! "I almost died"—turn it around.

Emma: I didn't almost die.

Katie: No. You . . .

Emma: . . . lived right through it!

Katie: Yes. So you're on the couch and you can't call anyone for forty-eight hours. What is not okay about that?

Emma: According to who? Me?

Katie: What is not okay about lying on the couch for forty-eight hours? Where did you need to go?

Emma: I needed fluids; I needed an IV; I needed—

Katie: Really!

Emma: That's what they say. I mean, it helped, when I did that.

Katie: That's later.

Emma: Right.

Katie: You're on the couch.

Emma: Right. I guess I was doing what I needed to do. I needed to—

Katie: Where's the problem? Don't tell me about what the doctors said or what people said later.

Emma: Yes.

Katie: Close your eyes. You're lying on the couch. . . . Now what's not okay about that?

Emma: Well, not being . . . not being right . . . not being coherent . . . I was out of it.

Katie: That sounds like what people who take drugs want.

Emma: It wasn't a good trip.

Katie: So let's look at your thinking. You're on the couch. What are your thoughts?

Emma: I thought I was going to die.

Katie: Good. So now go back to the couch as though you're there, and answer from that position, okay? "You're going to die"—can you absolutely know that that's true? If you don't get help, and no one's coming, "you're going to die"—can you absolutely know that that's true?

Emma: No . . . I wouldn't know.

Katie: And how do you react as you lie on that couch, when you believe the thought "I'm going to die"?

Emma: Petrified.

Katie: So, without that thought, how does it feel—without the thought "I'm going to die"?

Emma: Just lying on the couch. It's fine.

Katie: So, the worst moment of your cancer—other than your thinking—it's just a woman lying on the couch. So what is terrible about cancer? You're horizontal for forty-eight hours, believing that you're going to die.

Emma: It's more than that, I mean, it's total nausea—

Katie: Then let's look at that.

Emma: . . . and pain, and it was horrible.

Katie: Yes.

Emma: It wasn't just that I couldn't get off the couch, it was just . . . everything was wrong. Everything was just—

Katie: So what's not okay about nausea, other than the physical experience?

Emma: Yes, it was probably just more not okay to be alone then . . . the problems . . . afraid . . . such fear.

Katie: People with hangovers vomit and then they get drunk again the very next day.

Emma: Yes. It's a little different from that. I mean it just literally creates pain through your bones and all that . . .

Katie: Yes, it's very frightening. So I continue to ask you to look at your thoughts about that. Because *that* you can take care of. And in that, the body has the best chance of being a strong, living organism, unless it needs something else. And it does; it always does eventually. It has its own life, and you can't dictate it.

Emma: Yes, I've learned that.

Katie: So other than the nausea and the pain . . . how long did the pain last as you lay there for forty-eight hours?

Emma: It was there the whole time.

Katie: The whole time. Okay. Now, can you track a moment when they came and they found you—what were you experiencing then?

Emma: She used a key.

Katie: And what were your thoughts when you heard her coming? In that moment, did your legs hurt?

Emma: Oh yes, I was in bad shape.

Katie: Okay, you didn't stop to think about it. So just in the moment . . .

Emma: Okay.

Katie: . . . when you heard her turning the key and you knew it was her.

Emma: I remember being surprised that I could even get dressed. I mean I somehow rallied and got some clothes on to go to the hospital.

Katie: Miraculous!

Emma: Seemed like it.

Katie: Yes, you couldn't move for forty-eight hours, and then your mind changed, and you could.

Emma: Yes—because my body probably didn't change.

Katie: No, it didn't. So, you're lying there for forty-eight hours; you could not move. Is that true?

Emma: Don't know.

Katie: Someone walks through the door—you can move. You get up. You can dress.

Emma: Yeah, I'm sure if there had been an earthquake or something, I probably would have gotten up off the couch.

Katie: Just your friend walking through the door, and you got up and dressed and walked out.

Emma: Yes. Got in the car. Poof!

Katie: And you're talking about your worst, the worst time in all the cancer. That was the worst of it. And we're seeing how much of this is what you believe. You believed you couldn't move from the couch. Not true. You believed you were going to die. Not true. And those create all that fear in you, and then it goes like that, and it doesn't help the pain that's already there.

Emma: Right. I don't know what's happening, and my body is—

Katie: So that's where "I'm willing to; I look forward to" comes in, because whenever you're under stress, it's really nice to look at what you're believing. And if you've done The Work enough so that the questions are alive in you—what a trip. What a trip!

Emma: Okay.

Katie: Nice to work with you, sweetheart.

Emma: Thank you so much.

Katie: You're welcome, you're welcome.

Emma: [to the audience] And thank you, everybody.

10. My Sister
the Prostitute

You're worried about her. Her life is hard, dangerous, self-destructive. You have to take care of her. And is any of it true? One of you living her life is enough. You don't both have to live it.

Liz: *I am worried about Ginny because she lives an irrational, crazy, messy, insane, smoke-filled life.*

Katie: Sweetheart, turn it around.

Liz: I am worried about myself because I live an irrational, crazy, messy, insane smoke-filled life.

Katie: Does that ring true about you, also?

Liz: I used to live a smoke-filled life. And sometimes it's insane.

Katie: Are you around her very often?

Liz: No. She lives in New York.

Katie: So, "smoke-filled life"—if it's not cigarette smoke, what other kind of smoke are you filled with?

Liz: I guess Los Angeles smoke.

Katie: And what other kind of smoke? Maybe a smoke screen?

Liz: No . . . maybe . . . no, I don't think so.

Katie: Okay. Is there more?

Liz: Yes. *Her life as a prostitute gave me a deep sadness.*

Katie: Why?

Liz: I think it's because of the pictures I had of her with all these men and the danger she was putting herself in.

Katie: So, "As a prostitute she's in danger"—can you absolutely know that that's true?

Liz: No. I mean, she's no longer a prostitute, and she's fine. But I still see the images of her putting these clothes on and . . . you know, she's my sister, my little sister.

Katie: So "She was in danger"—is that true?

Liz: No.

Katie: No. She made it out okay.

Liz: I know.

Katie: How do you react when you believe the thought "She was in danger"?

Liz: I just get sad—

Katie: Who would you be without this thought, "She's in danger . . . she was in danger"?

Liz: [pause] I'd be lighter.

Katie: So "She was in danger"—turn it around.

10. My Sister the Prostitute

Liz: I'm in danger.

Katie: Now give me three genuine examples of how the turn-around is true in your life.

Liz: How *I'm* in danger? Well, I'm in danger of being miserable because of all the worrying I do about my sister.

Katie: Yes, sweetheart. That's one.

Liz: And I'm in danger of really messing up my sister's life with my worrying. Well, maybe not messing up her life, but adding to her problems.

Katie: That's two. Can you find a third example?

Liz: [long pause] I'm in danger when I imagine her in danger.

Katie: Yes, you're in danger every time you picture her in that room in your mind. She stopped prostituting herself, but you're still prostituting her. You just keep putting her back in a profession you didn't want her to be in. She's doing better than you are. She took herself out of there, and you keep putting her back in. You're in the business.

Liz: There were a lot of men.

Katie: Yes, a lot of dangerous men. But she's out of there, and you're the one keeping her in that room with dangerous men in your mind. And then you—I'll use the term—you blame it on your sister. But it's you: You're the one who's doing that. Let's look at the next statement.

Liz: *I want Ginny to save money, stop smoking and drinking, keep her job, clean up her house, live a normal life, and act appropriately when it's important.*

Katie: My goodness, that's a lot! Let's turn it around and see if you can live it.

Liz: I want myself to save money—

Katie: Yes, *you* save money. How are you doing with that?

Liz: Not very well.

Katie: Do you know about the three kinds of business?

Liz: Yes.

Katie: So whose business is it if your sister does or doesn't save money?

Liz: Hers.

Katie: And whose business is it if you do or don't save money?

Liz: Mine.

Katie: Okay. So just remember the three kinds of business and that will keep you out of her business, because *you* are the one who needs to save money.

Liz: Okay.

Katie: So continue.

Liz: I want to stop smoking and drinking.

Katie: Yes. Stop smoking. Do you smoke and drink?

Liz: No, I'm pregnant.

Katie: That seems very kind, sweetheart.
     And moving to your sister: "Right now, she's smoking and drinking"—can you absolutely know that that's true?

Liz: No, not right now.

10. My Sister the Prostitute

Katie: So where is she smoking and drinking?

Liz: In her apartment.

Katie: No, you said you can't know if she's doing that right now. Where is she smoking and drinking?

Liz: In my mind.

Katie: In your mind. In your mind.

Liz: You know, I wouldn't care as much, but both my parents died of lung cancer . . . or smoking.

Katie: Well, maybe that's not enough for you.

Liz: Hmm.

Katie: Everyone has their own path, and it's all for you. Where is she smoking right now?

Liz: In my mind.

Katie: Yes, so stop smoking.

Liz: Oh God!

Katie: In her name! You're killing yourself with stress over something that you don't even know is happening right now. That stress could take you before it takes her.

Liz: Yes, it's her path. . . . It's a hard one.

Katie: Well, yes! You're living her path in your mind. One of you living it is enough. Both of you don't have to live it. If you want her to stop smoking, turn it around.

Liz: I want to stop smoking. I want to stop thinking about her smoking.

Katie: Yes. That's how you're smoking.

Liz: That's a funny thing!

Katie: Yes. You're not doing what you want her to do—so work on you.

Liz: I get that now, but on my own I would have never have gotten that.

Katie: Well, that's why having a facilitator for this Work is sometimes helpful. It's about you finding your own power.

Liz: I can look at these and say, "Oh, yeah." But the smoking one just didn't come up.

Katie: Well, if you sat with it in meditation, you might find it yourself.

Liz: Okay. I want to clean up my house—

Katie: Yes. Is your house clean?

Liz: No.

Katie: So who could teach her to have a clean house and save money?

Liz: Her house looks like one of those freaky people lives in it—the ones who never throw anything away.

Katie: So let me go into your house and throw out the things that I don't find necessary. [Liz and the audience laugh.] And if you're upset when I do that, I'll just remind you: "You don't need them."

Liz: I agree. I think you're right. But yeah, and I try to go to her house and get rid of her stuff, and—

Katie: Yes, well let her just haul *your* stuff out.

Liz: Okay. You know, I'm an older sister, and I feel like I'm all that's left for her, and—

Katie: Yes. Well, clean up your house so she can see how to live.

Liz: Okay.

Katie: And stop killing her in your mind. When she sees you, she could see a much happier teacher. And start saving money. You're just showing her that it's unnecessary.

We teach the people we love through example. So you don't *have* that to teach her yet. And worry won't do it—it's a killer.

Liz: No. It feels so clean right now. It's like these cobwebs are just everywhere; they're everywhere. I didn't even know they were there.

Katie: Yes.

Liz: [reading from her Worksheet] *I want her to live a normal life.*

Katie: Then find one for yourself.

Liz: And be an example?

Katie: And be the example for that. That's what you want to do: You want to help her. So, who would you be—close your eyes—who would you be without the thought? Picture your sister—you're in her house. Who would you be without the thought "I want her to quit smoking and clean up her house?"

Look at her. Drop your story; just look at her.

Liz: I would just love *her.*

Katie: Yes, yes. Except for your thinking, that's what there is: love. But those thoughts block you from the awareness of it. And you just turn into this disapproving older sister. She picks up a cigarette, and you show her through your words or gestures what you think of that.

Liz: I do. I mean, it's hard when you're in her house, though, and she's smoking, and you don't want to be in that. I mean, that's the other part, but I can just wait outside, I guess.

Katie: Yes. Yes, you might just tell her the truth, if it's true. "Honey, I want to come in, and I'm allergic to smoke." It's all about you.

Liz: It's all about me.

Katie: Yes.

Liz: "I need to act appropriately when it's important."

Katie: Yes. And it's important to you that you save money, that your house is clean and neat.

Liz: Well, this one is about her kicking our cousins at our mother's funeral and crying in the middle of the hospital elevator. I have these images of her just, you know, raging in front of the whole planet with me there. I mean, she can do what she wants when I'm not there, but it's tough when I'm witnessing it.

Katie: It is? So let's go back to the funeral. Close your eyes. Look at her: She's kicking your cousins. Now drop your story and watch her. Watch the cousins; watch the people watching her. Drop your story; look around. Now in reality, is everything okay? Drop your story and look around.

Liz: Everything's okay. She's upset about Mom. I mean, it's okay. It's fine.

Katie: Good to know. It's nice to go back and take another look.

Liz: Yes, that's going to be a little harder to fully let go of.

Katie: Well, you don't have to let go of it. Go back in—is everything okay?

10. My Sister the Prostitute

Liz: Yes, it's fine.

Katie: Well, there's reality for you. How did she kick your cousins? What did that look like?

Liz: It was more me looking at our cousins than at her. Because I'm used to her. It was their shock at the fact that anyone could do such a thing to them.

Katie: Well, tell me what happened. Where did she kick them?

Liz: In front of the restaurant, which was closed, so we had to go find another place to eat.

Katie: And where physically did she kick them?

Liz: In the shins.

Katie: In front of the restaurant, in the shins. How many times?

Liz: Once, really hard. Like, "Go away! I can't be consoled. I hate you people. You've ruined my mother's funeral."

Katie: Well, no wonder that's upsetting for you. Look at those thoughts! The reality is that she kicked one of them in the shins.

Liz: I've loaded all the rest on top of that?

Katie: All of it.

Liz: She kicked one of them in the shins.

Katie: And where did all the excitement come from? It was yours. She kicked one of them in the shins.

Liz: Well, I had to talk to them afterward.

Katie: Really? "You *had* to talk to them"—is that true?

Liz: No, you're right. No.

Katie: So you be the cousins, and I'll be you—clear. Okay? Your sister just kicked one of the cousins. Let's dialogue it.

Liz: [as the cousin] "Your sister just kicked me in the shin."

Katie: [as Liz] "Yes, I saw that."

Liz: "This is an outrage. I'm going to leave the funeral now. I'm not coming to dinner."

Katie: "I understand that."

Liz: [as herself] I think he left at that point.

Katie: Well, that was a smart thing to do! He didn't want to get kicked twice. And it could be that he left because the restaurant was closed. It could be that he had something else to do. It could have been *so many* reasons that didn't have anything to do with being kicked.

Liz: You're right. It could have been other reasons, but I have a feeling it's the kick.

Katie: All he said was, "She kicked me, and this is outrageous, and I'm leaving." And you're not even sure if that's when he left.

Liz: No, there was too much going on—

Katie: Oh, really?

Liz: . . . in my mind.

Katie: . . . in your mind. Very good catch! Okay, honey, it's wonderful that you're learning the difference between reality and imagination. She kicked him. Her mother had just died.

Liz: I understand that.

10. My Sister the Prostitute

Katie: And how forcefully was he coming at her?

Liz: Well, he was just trying to console her and put his arm around her.

Katie: She didn't want to be consoled. She was a poor communicator.

Liz: Yes. That's true.

Katie: And if she wanted him to leave her alone, she was a very clear communicator.

Liz: [laughing] Yes.

Katie: We do the best we can.

Liz: We all do, don't we? She's doing the best she can. That's amazing to me. I mean, I want her to do this [points to the Worksheet], but she can't.

Katie: "I want her to do this"—turn it around.

Liz: I want me to do this.

Katie: Let's look at the next statement.

Liz: *Ginny shouldn't throw tantrums in the middle of the street, cry at the slightest provocation, or smoke. She should take care herself, find family, friends—*

Katie: "She is not taking care of herself or finding friends"—is that true?

Liz: No . . . that's not true.

Katie: Good to know, isn't it?

Liz: I mean, she's alive. She has friends on the phone. She was just alone for Christmas, which made me sad.

Katie: So, sweetheart, what would you be if you were alone on Christmas? Would you be sad if you were alone on Christmas?

Liz: I wouldn't be sad.

Katie: Well, what makes you think she would be? She's not as mature as you are?

Liz: She's in that apartment, and I just—

Katie: So what makes you think that if she's alone on Christmas she'd be sad, if *you* wouldn't be?

Liz: I get that. It makes no sense. I want to be with people on Christmas, but I would be okay if I wasn't. Yeah, she'll be okay.

Katie: Well, it sounds like she has as many tools as you have.

Liz: Yes, I guess she can feed herself. It just looks so messy with her.

Katie: Well, look who's looking: a messy mind, a chaotic mind. She kicks your cousin, and nothing happens. And he expressed what he felt and left. That is not a huge thing.

Liz: No.

Katie: There's a lot of order in it. He's kicked; he expresses himself; he leaves.

Liz: I've had years of thinking of this. There's piles of thinking of this.

Katie: So I would question your thinking until you can see reality. Because you see it very clearly when you close your eyes and you look.

Liz: No, I do see it now. And I'm thinking, "Why have I wasted all my time thinking this?"

10. My Sister the Prostitute

Katie: Because you were believing what you think. So now let's turn it around.

Liz: I shouldn't throw tantrums in the middle of the street.

Katie: Yes, look at the tantrum that *you* threw. Close your eyes and look at you. Look at what you were thinking; look at what you were saying; look at what you were doing. Where did all the chaos come from?

Liz: From my mind.

Katie: Yes, sweetheart. You shouldn't throw tantrums in the middle of the street.

Liz: I shouldn't cry at the slightest provocation.

Katie: No. Someone gets kicked and you lose it.

Liz: I don't know where I got this perfect little girl person.

Katie: A movie.

Liz: Yes.

Katie: Keep turning it around.

Liz: I shouldn't smoke.

Katie: Yes! That advice is for you. You're pregnant; you don't like smoke—so I would say, that's an allergy. If I don't like something, I'm allergic to it.

Liz: I should take care of myself, find family and friends.

Katie: Yes. And one way you can take care of yourself is to stay mentally out of her business. So that when you visit her, you're meeting your sister, not the sister of your imagination. Not the one who throws tantrums in the middle of the street.

Liz: And last time she didn't throw a tantrum. Should I keep going?

Katie: Yes.

Liz: *I need Ginny to stop taking life so seriously, stop smoking, get rid of all her crap, take responsibility at her job*—oh, wow, that's a good one!—*behave when she visits me in Los Angeles to see the baby and to see me get married.*

Katie: Turn it around.

Liz: I need to stop taking life so seriously.

Katie: Yes, and your sister is a part of life. Stop taking that so seriously. She'll live or die. She'll clean her house or not. She'll smoke or not. What's not okay about her dying? The worst thing that happened when your mother died was someone kicking someone. When your mother died, were you okay?

Liz: I grieved for a year and a half.

Katie: Okay, close your eyes. Watch you crying for a year and a half. Now tell me the saddest time. Where are you as you're crying?

Liz: I guess it's right after she died.

Katie: Okay what's going on? Where are you?

Liz: I'm in her apartment. I'm cleaning out her stuff.

Katie: Now find the saddest moment. Where are you? Are you sitting or standing?

Liz: I'm on the floor.

Katie: Okay, what's going on? What are you doing?

10. My Sister the Prostitute

Liz: Well, my sister had just—I don't know if I should bring my sister into it—my sister had just yelled at me while I was talking to someone on the phone. I'm confusing my sister and my mother right now. My grief is . . . my anger with my sister and my anger at my mother.

Katie: So the saddest time is your anger. The saddest thing about your mother's death is your anger as you sit on the floor.

Liz: No, she left me with my sister.

Katie: Who left you with your sister?

Liz: My mother left me with my sister.

Katie: And *who* left you with your sister?

Liz: I left me with my sister.

Katie: Yes, *you* keep leaving you with your sister. Your mother didn't do that; your mother died, and you took it on. It's not right or wrong; it's just what you did. She didn't leave you with your sister. She left you without your sister. *You* left you with your sister. Your mother left you with you.

So the saddest time around your mother's death is you sitting on the floor, imagining that you were left, that she left you with your sister, and anger around that. So what does that have to do with your mother dying? It has to do with you taking on your sister, and you didn't have to. You *never* have to.

Liz: Isn't there a law or something?

Katie: No.

Liz: It feels like there is.

Katie: No. The law is—you love her. But love isn't physical. It doesn't mean you have to take them on. Love is an internal experience. It's an experience.

Look what your brand of love has done. So, you don't want her to die because you could experience another thought that makes you angry. That's what happened with your mother: You experienced a thought that made you very angry. That was the worst time of your grief, according to you.

Liz: No, I think there were worse times, but I'm not sure.

Katie: I asked you for the saddest time: "Where were you?"
"On the floor with the thought 'My mother left me with my sister.'"

Liz: Well, I remember crying so much—just so much.

Katie: So when you go home, break it down the way we just did it. Sit, be still. Find the worst moments in your grief and see what the grief is about. It's not ever about anything but what you're thinking, which isn't even true. "She left me with my sister."

Liz: Or "She left me." How about just "She left"?

Katie: She left.

Liz: "She's not here for me."

Katie: Oh, really?

Liz: It's all about me.

Katie: Yes, it's all about you. But as we talk about it, do you see a picture of your mom? [Liz nods.] So "She left you"—is it true? Where does she live? In your mind. So you just stop and think, "What would Mom say to me?" And boy, will she say it! And she'll come into your mind, and say things you don't even ask for. You can open your mind to it and hear her and her wisdom, and open your heart to it, and allow her to live in you rather than push her away. Those images open your heart when you welcome them, and they'll crack your heart wide open.

I like to say, "Just allow love to kill you." It's an initiation, and there's nothing more powerful. And when there's no separation, she's with you always. Not in a sad way, but in a very wonderful way that leaves a sense of gratitude. And there are a lot of tears with that, too. But they're different tears. They're not all about you. They are, and it's different.

So "My mother left me"—turn it around.

Liz: I left my mother.

Katie: Yes, she comes in, and you become sad because you don't really allow her in. Allow her to merge with you. Allow her to live in you. That way you're never alone. You can say, "Mom, what would you do with her right now? She's smoking, she won't clean her house." And you can think, "Mom, what would you do with me right now? I'm not cleaning *my* house."

Liz: My mother never knew what to do with my sister.

Katie: Yes, she's like you.

Liz: Yes, there's nothing to do with my sister.

Katie: Just love her. That's what to do with her. And then turn it around—and any other thoughts—and do The Work on them. What else?

Liz: Should I go to the next statement, or just keep turning these other ones around?

Katie: Well, read it the way you wrote it.

Liz: *Ginny's a creative World Bank, a—*

Katie: A what?

Liz: A creative World Bank—that means she's got so much creativity in her.

Katie: Ah.

Liz: *She's paranoid, insane, funny, wonderful, a maverick, a delight, a hoarder.*

Katie: Turn it around.

Liz: I am a creative World Bank.

Katie: So tell me about that.

Liz: Well, I'm a filmmaker, and I've published a cookbook. And I have a jewelry company, and—

Katie: You're a creative World Bank! What else?

Liz: I'm a good cook.

Katie: You're a good mommy. You don't drink; you don't smoke; you're a wonderful mommy. And keep reading them, turned around.

Liz: I'm paranoid.

Katie: Yes, especially about your sister. She kicks someone, and you just do this huge thing around it.

Liz: Yes.

Katie: You're a filmmaker! [Liz laughs with the audience.] There are some great stories in there. They're just not real.

Liz: That's true, that's true. I'm insane, for sure. I'm funny, and I'm wonderful, and I'm a maverick. I'm a delight, and I'm definitely a hoarder. . . . That was easy.

Katie: Yes, life gets simple once we begin to understand our mind. And the way we understand our mind is to question it when we're stressed out. Let's look at the next statement.

10. My Sister the Prostitute

Liz: *I don't ever want to be around her tantrums. I don't ever want to lie for her, worry about her health, worry about taking care of her.*

Katie: "I'm willing to . . ."

Liz: I'm willing to be around her tantrums. I'm willing to lie for her. I'm willing to worry about her health. [Crying] I'm willing to worry about taking care of her.

Katie: Yes. Because when it happens again, just know that the tears come, the stress starts, the tiredness takes you over. And let those feelings remind you that you are insane. [Liz laughs.] And then take those thoughts, put them on paper, and bring yourself back to reality.

So, "I look forward to . . ."

Liz: I look forward to being around her tantrums. I look forward to lying for her. I look forward to worrying about her health. I look forward to worrying about taking care of her.

Katie: Yes. "She needs you to take care of her"—is that true?

Liz: No.

Katie: Wow! Isn't that good to know?

Liz: Yes. I feel like there's a part of me that's just going away. It's weird; it's like a shadow part. I don't know, it's . . .

Katie: Say more.

Liz: It's like this part that feels an obligation to my sister—it doesn't have to be there. But it's disorienting. When I'm not worrying about my sister, it's like—

Katie: It's like: Oh my God, I'd have to be happy, and free, and so much less of a burden. You'd be a traitor to misery. "You *have* to take care of your sister"—how do you react when you believe that thought?

Liz: Awful. I feel dreadful because she can't be taken care of. I mean I can't—there's nothing I can do.

Katie: You feel awful and terrible . . . and then how do you treat your sister, when you believe that thought "I have to take care of her" and you feel awful and terrible?

Liz: I treat her like . . . a smaller human being, less than she is. And she knows; she feels that.

Katie: Yes. So, "I have to take care of her"—give me a peaceful reason to believe that thought.

Liz: I don't think there is one.

Katie: Who would you be without this philosophy, "I have to take care of my sister"? Look at your life without that thought. Imagine your life without that thought.

Liz: I would just enjoy my sister.

Katie: Yes. She'd call, and you wouldn't have the slightest thought of having to take care of her. Imagine that freedom. Imagine *her* freedom if she called you and you weren't busy taking care of her at all. Imagine that.

Liz: She could smoke all she wants!

Katie: Well, she does.

Liz: But without my bullshit.

Katie: Exactly. It frees you both up. So, "I have to take care of her"—turn it around.

Liz: I have to take care of myself.

Katie: Yes. You're so focused on her that it doesn't leave you here to mother yourself, to learn how to mother your child. So mother you. Start practicing mothering you so that you'll be practiced at mothering your baby. Just give you everything you would want your mommy to give you if she were here. And give you your mommy, too. Yes, both of you mothering you. What would be the best example to your sister? That woman—or the one she's got as a sister?

Liz: That woman.

Katie: That's the one. That's the one. Okay, so "I have to take of my sister"—turn it around.

Liz: I have to take care of myself.

Katie: And there's another one.

Liz: I don't have to take care of my sister.

Katie: No, you don't. And look at your success so far. She may even kick you if you get too close, and throw tantrums in public.

Liz: Well, she may. And I can just watch them.

Katie: Yes.

Liz: I mean it's interesting if you're not her sister.

Katie: And it's interesting when you know you don't have to take care of her. So, there's another turnaround. "I have to take care of my sister." Would you like to hear it?

Liz: Yes.

Katie: "My sister has to take care of *me*."

Liz: My sister has to take care of me.

Katie: Tell me about that one. Where are you dependent on her?

Liz: Oh! She listens to me.

Katie: What else?

Liz: She sends me all kinds of things that I don't want, but . . . they're wonderful.

Katie: Where are you dependent on her? She listens to you . . .

Liz: Creatively I bounce off of her.

Katie: What else?

Liz: Um . . .

Katie: Start looking at these as motives. It's like, if you don't take care of your sister, then you won't get all these perks! Where else are you dependent on her? And you can look back at the funeral—where were you dependent on her? Where is it that you need your sister to take care of you?

Liz: I guess I could be the good girl at that funeral.

Katie: Yes, she sure makes you look good.

Liz: [laughing] She does; it's true. She always has.

Katie: You might let her know that and thank her for that. When you're talking to her, just say, "You know, I was watching my mind the other day, and I noticed that you help me look good. And that you send me wonderful things. I just love that you do that."
And give her the list of things you love about her, and let her know that you're dependent on her—her marvelous creativity. And just start coming out of denial, and give it back. Pay it back. Play it back. And stay in your own business. "Your sister needs you to take care of her"—is that true?

Liz: No.

Katie: If she ever asks, "Why do you call me?" you can say, "I bounce off your creativity; you send me stuff; you make me look good. I look at your house and my house, and my house is so messy, but yours makes my house look good."

Liz: It's true.

Katie: There could be a lot of humor there. She might appreciate it. But these lists that we find when we're doing The Work, we come to see why we really want these people in our lives: We love them.

And after we look at the perks, we come to appreciate them. And then it becomes visible why you really *are* with her. It's nothing you *have* to do—ever. You don't even have to be there for your baby. It's just that it delights you to do that. Your baby isn't dependent. Your baby doesn't care if it lives or dies; it's all you. You *love* holding the baby; it's about you. What wonderful gifts in the world. But to believe "They need me" takes the joy out of it because it's not clean.

Liz: It does, doesn't it?

Katie: It does. I look at my little grandchildren. They certainly don't need me! If I don't give them what they want, they scream, they tantrum, they forget. They're just having their wonderful little lives.

Let's finish this up. "My sister needs me"—how do you react when you believe that thought and it's Christmas Day and she's alone?

Liz: I just have to let it go. I'm still a little sad about that—

Katie: But how *did* you react on Christmas Day when you believed the thought "She's alone"?

Liz: I was sad.

Katie: How do you live your life when you believe the thought "She needs me"?

Liz: It's dreadful.

Katie: Does that thought bring peace or stress into your life?

Liz: It's so stressful.

Katie: "My baby needs me; my partner needs me. The flowers need me." Does that thought bring peace or stress into your life?

Liz: I didn't mind the baby or the partner or the flowers.

Katie: No, because they haven't interfered with what you want yet.

Liz: Right. I'm sure when the baby is crying and I don't want to get up, it's going to be annoying.

Katie: Could happen. You don't know. It may not happen. To a clear mind, it's a joy if they cry; it's a joy if they don't cry. It's a joy walking to their room, and it's not necessary. When my daughter Roxann's baby would cry—her first one, this was years ago—when the baby would cry and she felt any resentment, she would just do The Work before she went to his bedroom. Because she didn't want the baby drinking her milk until she was clear.

Liz: Wow!

Katie: So she did a lot of Work. She didn't want the baby to wait. She's a wonderful mother, an amazing mother. I really see that in you. So, "My sister needs me"—turn it around.

Liz: I need my sister.

Katie: And then when you're at home, make a list: "I need my sister." And just watch all the things that she gives you that you just love. Because all your other thoughts drown this part out. It hasn't been visible to us because the other thoughts are so loud, and they take over—it's chaos, and it takes over reality, beauty, love.

10. My Sister the Prostitute

Don't let another day go by without making that list, and sit in it. Close your eyes; watch her smoking. Now drop your story. Look at her. She's grabbing the cigarette, and she's smoking, and it's there for her. Who would you be without your story?

Liz: Well, she'd be someone I don't know who's just smoking. I mean, if the smoke doesn't get to me, it doesn't bother me.

Katie: Oh, good, good. The smoke's not getting to you here. And when you first started, it bothered you. You just really wanted her to stop smoking.

Liz: No, it's okay if she smokes.

Katie: Yes. A lot of people who stop smoking begin to drink more or eat more. So when you have the thought "I want my sister to stop smoking," you may want to reconsider. Nothing ahead of its time. *Her* time, not ours.

Liz: Yes, it's her path, like you said.

Katie: "My sister needs me"—can you find another turnaround?

Liz: I need myself.

Katie: Yes. That's the one. You don't want to share your baby with your sister—to share your attention to your baby with your sister when she's not even in the same town. But the way the mind works, you're holding your baby and in your mind you're in New York with your sister, smoking, and you miss the baby!

So, you need *you*. Be present with you, with this gift that's coming, that's always coming, and it's not just a baby. Thank you, sweetheart.

Liz: Thank you so much.

Katie: You're welcome.

11. My Mother Made Me a Victim

Once you realize that you've been living with a fantasy, you may discover someone you can love with all your heart. That someone is you. This is the key to all relationships.

Patrick: *I'm angry at my mom because she's emotionally sick, she started my identity crisis, she made me a victim, she was never a mom to me, and she stayed stuck in her past.*

Katie: "She was never a mom to you"—is that true?

Patrick: [after a long pause] No. That's not true. She was sometimes a good mom. She tried her best.

Katie: Good to know, isn't it?

Patrick: Yes.

Katie: How do you react when you believe the thought "She was never a mom to me"? Close your eyes. "She was never a mom to me." Now watch how you react when you believe that thought.

Patrick: I feel angry at her and incredibly resentful. I start to pity myself. I feel totally powerless. I feel unlovable. If my mom didn't love me, how can anyone else?

Katie: Now watch how your mind travels when you believe that thought, "She was never a mom to me." Watch how your mind proves that to you—the pictures, what she said, what she did—watch your mind annihilate her to be right.

Patrick: I see her yelling at me. I see all the times she was cold or preoccupied or giving her attention to my younger brothers and sisters. I see when she forgot to pick me up from school. I see the time when I was seven and she didn't even give me a birthday party because she said we couldn't afford it.

Katie: So that's how you react when you believe the thought "My mom was never there for me"—because it's a lie.

Patrick: I'll justify it—naturally.

Katie: Well, the mind has a job; its job is to find a home—a place to rest. It can only rest in the truth. So you believe the thought "My mom was never there for me," and your mind does everything it can to prove it, and it can't prove it because it's not true.

Patrick: Yes.

Katie: So get a picture of your mom, and just for a moment drop your story, "She was never there for me." Look at her. Look at her face; look at her eyes. Look at her, just for a moment, without your story. What do you see?

Patrick: What do I see? I see a person who's fought through living hell to be there for her family, to be there for her kids and for me, who has overcome her miserable past to be with me.

Katie: Yes. She's really dedicated. It hasn't been easy.

Patrick: No, it's been horrible for her.

Katie: So turn it around. Turn that sentence around.

Patrick: My mom *was* a mom to me. . . . Wow!

212

Katie: Allow that turnaround to be there for a moment. Can you find three genuine examples of how the turnaround is as true as or truer than your original statement? Close your eyes. Now allow your mind to live in that polarity. Just allow it as it searches for where she was a mom to you.

You have entered a different world, a genuine world—not a world of positive affirmations, but the real deal. Watch and allow your heart to give you what's true. An open heart is not possible to a closed mind. The mind that is stuck in what it believes is a closed mind. It's blind to the world of reality. It eliminates the awareness of it, so you don't get to see love. Love is hidden, because you're believing what you think.

So give me an example of how your mom was a mom to you.

Patrick: She really did love me as much as she could.

Katie: Sweetheart, that's not specific enough. Can you find specific examples?

Patrick: Okay. She did give me birthday parties in other years when she wasn't hurting for money.

Katie: Good.

Patrick: And she fed me and bought me clothes and gave me a good home.

Katie: That's two. Can you find a third example?

Patrick: She almost never spanked me, even when she must have been incredibly annoyed with me. Actually, she spanked me just a couple of times when my behavior was way out of line.

Katie: That's three. Can you find another turnaround?

Patrick: Um . . .

Katie: "I was never . . ."

Patrick: I was never a son to her. And that's probably what I resent.

Katie: I would drop the "probably."

Patrick: That's what I resent.

Katie: Yes. That's what your pain is.

Patrick: That's my pain. . . . Wow!

Katie: So you can begin now.

Patrick: I'm getting it.

Katie: You can just begin to be a son now. Just open your heart to your mom's arms, her cakes, her pies, her wisdom, her love. See what it really is. "My mom was never a mom to me"—can you find another turnaround? "I . . ."

Patrick: I was never appreciative—

Katie: "I was never a mom . . ."

Patrick: To myself.

Katie: Yes. You treated yourself the way you treated your mother in your mind. . . . Okay, let's keep traveling. Read your next statement.

Patrick: [reading from the Worksheet] The next statement? I'm going to turn it around back to me, because that's where it's ultimately going to go, right?

Katie: Okay, let's not take any shortcuts right now. It's powerful to turn the statement around, but when you apply the four questions first, you educate the mind.
[A cell phone rings loudly. It's a ring tone with a lively Latino melody.] I love that song! [The audience laughs.]

11. My Mother Made Me a Victim

When life is so full that you just can't handle any more? Here it comes! That's abundance.

Patrick: [laughing, and shaking his head] That's a hell of a perspective!

Katie: And isn't it true?

Patrick: I'll take your word for it!

Katie: Well, did you enjoy the song?

Patrick: The cell phone?

Katie: Yes.

Patrick: I was ready to shoot the guy!

Katie: You're at war with reality! What were your thoughts about the phone?

Patrick: Annoyed. I was thinking, "What an idiot! You should have shut off your fucking phone!"

Katie: Good. And it's your thoughts that annoyed you. A phone would never be that cruel.

Patrick: I've attached my thoughts to that phone?

Katie: Yes.

Patrick: Oh. So it's not the phone, it's me? Hmm . . .

Katie: The phone is reality. It sings you a song! Do you know what went into that song—the technology, the genius, the creativity? And then to make it available at a price that's affordable, so that you can give it to someone you love or buy it yourself? It brings in the whole world! It will always ring when it's time to ring. That's reality. And for me, it was a beautiful song that came exactly on time. It's your story about it that kept you from receiving the gift of life.

Patrick: My story about the phone or any other disturbance doesn't coincide with reality. Is that what you're saying?

Katie: The phone coincided perfectly with reality. It was your story about it that annoyed you, the story that it shouldn't have rung at that moment. In reality, it *should* have rung, because it did. Why would I let anything untrue interfere with the joy of music?

Patrick: So you truly are that present.

Katie: Well, the song is. Why wouldn't I be? Reality is the teacher.

Patrick: That's amazing. Either you're telling the truth here, or you're the best con artist I've ever met. [The audience laughs.]

Katie: Well, *you* are the best con artist you've ever met, and ultimately you can't con yourself. That's probably what you're learning right now—that you can't con yourself. When you're conning someone else, you have to believe it so hard core yourself that you start losing it. And so you have to jump into the role somehow, as though it's true. But you can't con yourself, and it's really good to know when you ask these questions that you're still vulnerable to what's true. Okay, read the next statement.

Patrick: *I want my mom to be more loving.*

Katie: Why?

Patrick: Um . . .

Katie: Because you're happier that way.

Patrick: Yes, I can see that.

Katie: Yes. Other than that, do you even care if your mom's more loving?

11. My Mother Made Me a Victim

Patrick: No.

Katie: That's good to know. So "Your mom should be more loving"—is that true?

Patrick: No.

Katie: This is about you. It has nothing to do with her.

Patrick: Right.

Katie: How do you react when you believe that thought? How do you treat her when you believe that she should be more loving and she's not?

Patrick: I get angry; I close her out of my life; I don't give her a chance.

Katie: And who would you be without the thought? If you couldn't even believe the thought that your mom should be more loving.

Patrick: I'd probably weigh about a hundred pounds less. Honestly. I wouldn't have the stress that I have. I'd probably—I'd be a free person.

Katie: So close your eyes again—get a picture of your mom. Now who would you be without the thought "She should be more loving"? Just watch her. Drop your story.

Patrick: She just lightens up right in front of me, because I see her as she is.

Katie: Reality. Like the cell phone.

Patrick: I see her as she is. She's as loving as she can be, given who she is. She really does love me. I'm not seeing through my distorted—

Katie: Your belief system.

Patrick: . . . belief system. My story. But my story blocks me from seeing her.

Katie: Very good.

Patrick: My story paralyzes me and never allows me to see anything —except what I want to believe.

Katie: That's all anyone is capable of seeing.

Patrick: And it's constant work. And it's insanity.

Katie: "My mom should be more loving"—turn it around.

Patrick: I should be more loving toward my mom.

Katie: Why?

Patrick: And toward myself.

Katie: Yes. Why?

Patrick: Because that's what it's . . . it's about me.

Katie: What happens when you feel love—how does it feel when you love?

Patrick: It feels great.

Katie: Okay, so *that's* why!

Patrick: When I'm feeling love, I'm feeling at home in the world. It's my God-given birthright, which I've been avoiding all my life.

Katie: So when you're loving to your mother, you're in your birthright—it's not about her. You just love her, and there's nothing she can do about it.

Patrick: And that's the key to relationships! This is amazing! If I'm dating or married or whatever, it's never about the other person. It's *never* about the other person loving me—it's about me just loving the other person.

Katie: Yes, because that's where you're the happiest.

Patrick: Is that what's meant by unconditional love? Amazing!

Katie: To be loving toward your mother and loving toward yourself is where you are the happiest. It's where you are the most balanced.

Patrick: And it's what I avoid the most. Everything else is me directing and controlling their world, not my own.

Katie: Well, *trying* to control their world. Because of course you can't control anything, in reality.

Patrick: Right.

Katie: So, "My mom should be more loving . . ." Continue.

Patrick: Here we go, this is a good one. . . . *My mom should be more graceful when I come to her with problems.* My problems! My story, which isn't real in the first place!

Katie: Yes. What you *take* to her isn't even real. And you expect her to be more graceful with what's not even true for you.

Patrick: God, that's crazy. Because the truth is that nobody can do it but me.

Katie: Yes. When you turn it around, you can see that *you* should be more graceful when your mother is not graceful.

Patrick: Because ultimately people have no power over me—it's just me. People have no power to make me happy. That's amazing!

Katie: People are whoever you believe them to be. They don't even exist for you. You haven't even met your mother—or anyone else in your life.

Patrick: Have you been on *Oprah* yet? [Everyone laughs.] This is classic—God! I've never heard anything like this before.

Katie: Well, you're listening to yourself. There's nothing more powerful than that. That's the power. You're tapping into it.

Patrick: Wow!

Katie: And sweetheart, it's everything. You're getting a glimpse of your ego and how it distorts your world. And when that power moves to another polarity, you start living in a state of clarity and joy. And it's nothing more than being aware of your internal life and knowing what's true and what's not. Not even knowing what's true—just knowing what's *not* true is enough, because what that leaves is the great surprise. And all you can know about it is its nature. And so you begin to live a fearless existence. . . . Okay, let's keep moving.

Patrick: *She has to stop being so harsh with me.*

Katie: Turn it around.

Patrick: I have to stop being so harsh with myself, with her, with the world and everyone in it.

Katie: For your own sake.

Patrick: I'm a terrorist.

Katie: To yourself.

Patrick: Correct . . . and to the world.

Katie: You're a terrorist to the world that you see.

11. My Mother Made Me a Victim

Patrick: I want her to be more graceful and not as judgmental toward me.

Katie: So "She shouldn't be so judgmental toward you"—is that true?

Patrick: No, it has nothing to do with it. She's not the issue; I'm the issue. I'm the problem.

Katie: And people are wonderful; their projections are wonderful. What does she say about you that hurts?

Patrick: Oh, that I'm lazy.

Katie: And are you?

Patrick: [laughing] Yes.

Katie: So she's right. You *are* lazy—sometimes. What else does she say that hurts?

Patrick: [after a pause] Nothing. I can hear her say, "You should get married. You should have a better job," and none of it hurts. I can find where she's right. She has a point. And she's just saying that because she's worried about me.

Katie: I think you've met your mother. You know, before I did this Work, I was motherless. And then I did The Work and I had a mother. Just like that: Boom! Let's move to the next statement.

Patrick: *I want my mom to accept that I make mistakes, know that I'm in God's hands, that I am lovable, not to put pressure on me, and allow me to go out and fall on my face.*

Katie: "Your mother doesn't know that you're lovable"—is that true?

Patrick: No. It's a lie.

Katie: Nice to know—nice for you to know.

Patrick: That's what *I* believe. I believe I'm not lovable.

Katie: And so you have to project it onto her.

Patrick: But how do you get past that?

Katie: "You're not lovable"—is that true?

Patrick: [after a pause] No.

Katie: And how do you react when you believe the thought "You're not lovable"? How do you live your life?

Patrick: I shut down the world and people around me. I withdraw. I feel like a toad. I never trust a woman when she says, "I love you."

Katie: So that's how you create yourself as unlovable. When you believe it, you have to create it. And then you're feeling that way, and someone says "Hi!" or a cell phone rings, and you get annoyed. So who would you be without this thought in your life, "I'm unlovable"?

Patrick: I would be a person who's just free, who doesn't need to be all caught up in the drama of other people, someone who could be content. I could just be by myself and not think I need other people and not go out of my skull with anxiety. Does that make sense?

Katie: Yes, it does. The reason people don't like to be alone is that they're alone with their own thoughts. And if you aren't at peace with what you think, you don't like the company you keep.

Patrick: How do you break those patterns?

Katie: We're doing it.

11. My Mother Made Me a Victim

Patrick: Just by asking questions?

Katie: It's the truth that sets you free. Every time you answer a question honestly, your own truth sets you free. "I'm not lovable"—turn it around.

Patrick: I'm a worthwhile person.

Katie: No. Keep the turnarounds very simple. "I'm not lovable."—what's the opposite? "I'm lovable." Now give me three lovable things about you—three things that you love about yourself. This is where you come out of denial. Denial doesn't serve. What do you love about yourself?

Patrick: I love that I'm Irish. And what I mean by that is the creativity, the humor, the ability to laugh at myself.

Katie: So "If you were not Irish, you would have no humor"—is that true? [The audience laughs.] "If you were not Irish, you would not be as creative"—is that true? Can you absolutely know that that's true?

Patrick: No, that's not true.

Katie: So what I'm hearing is that you love your creativity, and you love—

Patrick: I love my heart. I love how I love people. I love how I try to do good despite myself; I love that I love the power of women in the world, the sensitivity that they have to heal the world.

Katie: "You're not lovable"—is that true?

Patrick: No.

Katie: Good. So you continue to name things and notice things that you do throughout your life that you love about you.

Patrick: Okay.

Katie: And then, when someone says "I don't love you," and you never even for a moment think that has anything to do with you, "I'm lovable" is experienced through your whole being. Until we're really aware of the truth, when we try positive affirmations and say we're lovable, it's a lie. We don't truly believe it. This is about the genuine thing. So read what's left. "My mother is . . ."

Patrick: *Mom is harsh, strong, loving, powerful.*

Katie: Turn it around.

Patrick: I am harsh, strong, loving, powerful.

Katie: So those thoughts were really about you.

Patrick: Right. All thoughts are about me.

Katie: They're directed outward, but it's all coming from you. What you believe is all you *can* project out, as long as you believe it. After you question it, you cannot project out what you don't believe any longer, so your whole world changes—when mind changes, world changes. And the next time a stressful thought appears, you may not experience stress around it. You may even experience laughter. After today, if you ever believe the thought "I'm unlovable," you may just burst out laughing, because you know what's also true: You're very lovable. And if someone says, "You're unlovable," you might think, "Isn't that interesting, I used to think that too," rather than get angry at them, because you've realized the truth for yourself.

So are you going to question your stressful concepts as they surface, or not? Are you going to question them and turn them around? Are you going to sit with them like a student of yourself and read the book of you? And you'll notice that sometimes you do, sometimes you don't—at first. And if you have The Work for breakfast every day, it starts waking up in you. You no longer do it; it does you. The only concepts that come back to you are the ones that need your understanding. I see all thoughts as the beloved.

Patrick: As the what?

11. My Mother Made Me a Victim

Katie: As the beloved, or as my dearest, dearest children. They arise in my care. And I meet them with understanding, because until I do, they scream and they come back, begging for my attention. And I question them and turn them around and come to see that all thoughts are friends—there's not one thought that's an enemy.

But we try to think differently, we try to change them, to replace them with positive thoughts, and it just doesn't work. It just shoves them away for a while, but eventually they come back. But when we meet our thoughts with understanding, there's no stress.

That's why you can put me in a hole somewhere, in prison, in solitary confinement, and I'm in there with good company. I love being with me. And when I'm with anyone, I'm with me. For twenty years I haven't met a thought I didn't love. And because I love my thoughts, I love what they project. So I live in heaven; I live in a perfect world. There are even cell phones here, ringing for me. It rang for you, too. How do I know? You heard it.

Patrick: How can I live that way?

Katie: Work with your mind and see what's already there! You had a perfectly graceful, lovable mother, and you couldn't see her. But once you questioned your mind, she became visible to you. Before, you had the mother from hell; now you have the mother from heaven. Work with your mind and the world will follow. That's it. But I don't have a goal. Why would I cheat myself? Why would I think so small?

Patrick: Because the ultimate happiness is being at peace with yourself.

Katie: When you're at peace with yourself, you're free to see what's already here, and there's nothing you need. Everything you need is right here; it's just that you can't see it because you're believing what you think. Your mother was right there in front of you all your life.

Patrick: And I didn't see her.

Katie: You didn't see her. So you question your mind and all of a sudden you have a whole new mother. Why would you plan that? How *could* you plan that? The little boy prays, "I want another mother; I want a graceful mother; I want a mother who loves me"—well, you got her in twenty minutes. That's the power of going inside to that wisdom inside you.

Patrick: Thank you so much, Katie.

Katie: Thank you. It's a privilege to sit with you.

12. My Husband Shouldn't Have Left Me

People come and go, doing the things they believe they should do. They're not the ones you have to deal with.

Joyce: *I'm angry at Duncan because he left me after sixteen years of marriage and being partners.*

Katie: "He left you"—is that true?

Joyce: Yes.

Katie: Okay. "He left you"—can you absolutely know that that's true?
[To the audience] I love that you all follow this.
[To Joyce] "He left me"—can you absolutely know that that's true? And how long can you sit in that: three days, four days, five days? To wait for answers that may be under the surface, for realizations that could blow your world apart and wake you up.

Joyce: No. I can't absolutely know for sure.

Katie: Where did you find your *no?* Where did that come from?

Joyce: Just my pattern of feeling a victim and lesser, not good enough. Old patterns.

Katie: Where did that *no* come from?

Joyce: Because I've done this many times, and I know that I left him many times.

Katie: So you left him before he left you?

Joyce: In a sense, yes. There were ways that I left him before he left me.

Katie: So you left him. Wonderful. And the reason I see that as wonderful is because you're awake to it. You're aware of it, and then you don't have to live that out with other people.

Joyce: I don't have to?

Katie: Well, you're aware of it. When we see our patterns and we're awake to them after the fact, then we tend not to make the same mistakes again. And when we do, we're aware of them. And it changes everything.

Joyce: I've been blaming myself for it, not him so much.

Katie: So, as we speak of him, do you see him in your mind's eye? [Pause] "He left you"—is it true?

Joyce: No.

Katie: No. He's right here in your mind. Now when you were in the kitchen and he was in the bathroom—where did he live?

Joyce: In my mind.

Katie: You just imagined him in the bathroom. For all you know, he was in the backyard. But you imagine him, and he lives inside you. That's why people cannot die. When they're alive, they live here [pointing to her head], and when they're dead—as we say— they live here, inside you.

He is no more and no less than your imagination. No two people have ever met. You can be married sixteen years and *never*

228

know whom you're married to. And you wonder why we don't get along. Someone can say, "You don't know me at all," and you say, "Yes I do!" But he could be right when he says that to you.

So how do you react when you believe the thought "He left you," and he lives with you all day long, in your mind?

Joyce: I'm terrorized, depressed—

Katie: And alone!

Joyce: Yes.

Katie: While he's in your mind, which is where he was when he was in the kitchen and the bathroom and you thought "He's in the bathroom—I'm not alone."

Who would you be without the thought "He left me," when the images come? This is so important, because it's the power of love. You're thinking "Ohhhhh, he left me," as you see him in your mind.

So the image of him comes, and you immediately go into sadness or bereavement or pictures of you living alone for the rest of your life, and all the good times you had, and what he did—as you stand there doing the dishes at the kitchen sink. It's not him leaving you that's so painful; it's the thoughts running through your mind.

So when that image comes, rather than go through all the stories, if you open your heart to the visit, then—like me—you'll never have anyone who can leave you again. No one can divorce me; they don't have that power! I've got three husbands living right here [pointing to her head], and they're all welcome. [Joyce laughs with the audience.] And each time one appears, I just experience this amazing gratitude and laugh. It's amazing how they tolerate it.

So who would you be without the thought "He left me"?

Joyce: I'd be present in my body, doing whatever I'm doing in that moment. I'd feel more powerful.

Katie: Close your eyes and watch yourself, living your life without that thought.

Joyce: I'd put a lot more energy toward healing myself and taking care of myself than in him.

Katie: And notice when he comes to your mind and you see his image without the thought "He left me"—watch how he's with you throughout the day.

[Joyce begins to cry.] You really love him, huh?

Joyce: Yes . . . I didn't expect divorce. I didn't know he was so unhappy and stressed out and in debt. I didn't know because he didn't really communicate much. He's very British, and he keeps everything in.

Katie: Yes.

Joyce: So it's beautiful to see the men in this workshop come up here and cry, because I've never seen him cry in sixteen years.

Katie: But you can see him in your mind's eye, honey, as you take care of yourself, as you do what you know to do.

Joyce: Yes, but I don't know how to deal with the love that's still there for him. It's like, I love him, but I hate him!

Katie: Well, let's keep moving. That's how I deal with it. Because thoughts are what we have to deal with—not people. I love how people come and go. It shows us what's left if freedom is our purpose and if loving people unconditionally is our focus. And it certainly is, because that's where we're the most comfortable. And then it's wonderful that people come and go. We get to see what our Work is.

So "He left me"—turn it around.

Joyce: I left him.

Katie: Tell me how that started.

Joyce: Well, he tried to communicate some things, and I was trying to get us to counseling. I didn't know about The Work.

12. My Husband Shouldn't Have Left Me

Katie: That's a good thing, or he couldn't have left. I mean, everything has to happen the way it does, so things happen as they should. Conditions have to be perfect so he can leave you, so you can have this.

Joyce: I couldn't have both?

Katie: No. Not on *your* path.

Joyce: I guess not, because that's not what the reality is. This is reality.

Katie: Your path is showing you what's necessary. It had to be him. So he tried to tell you, and . . . what, you didn't listen?

Joyce: I didn't listen. I had certain beliefs. He was saying, "Don't spend so much money." I didn't know he was so deeply in debt. I asked for us to sit down and have weekly financial meetings, just to see where we were. And he didn't want to do that, not even once a month.

Katie: Okay, so let's start the conversation right now. You be him, and I'll be someone who is listening—someone who is not going to leave him.
So [as Joyce]: "Hi, honey."

Joyce: [as her husband] "Hi."

Katie: "Look at everything I bought at the yard sales!"

Joyce: "We don't need any more stuff. You've got so much stuff already. What are you out buying more stuff for? Where are we going to put it?"

Katie: "Those are very good questions. Oh, my goodness! Let me see, there's one thing here I do need."
[As herself] Was there ever one thing you needed?

Joyce: [as herself] Not really. Not when I look back.

Katie: So he was right.

Joyce: He was right.

Katie: And where *are* you going to put all that stuff? He has some wonderful questions, but you left him for your own ideas. And rightly so, because that's where you were at the time. Okay, so keep going—about the money.

Joyce: [as her husband again] "You know, we don't have that much money, and I don't want to talk about it."

Katie: "Okay. You don't have to talk about it much. What I hear is we don't have that much money. Are you saying that we need the money I spent at this yard sale?"

Joyce: "I don't want to talk about it. Just understand we don't have that money for you to spend. You don't need that stuff; we have enough as it is."

Katie: "Okay, you're right. We don't need it; I can see that. We do have enough as it is. I can hear you. Okay. I hear you say that we don't have enough money. So how much can I specifically spend that would work for you?"

Joyce: "Well, you use your own money, whatever money you make from your own business."

Katie: "Oh, that's excellent. Thank you. That works for me."

Joyce: "And if you don't make the changes, maybe we should get a divorce."

Katie: "I don't want that. So I'm going to spend only what I make. I love these conversations. What I love about you is you're so open. You offer information that is so clear."

Joyce: [as herself] I wish I *had* said that.

12. My Husband Shouldn't Have Left Me

Katie: Well, you didn't have that to say. Your concepts were overriding your husband's communication.

[Joyce begins to cry.] Honey, look at me. You do that with everyone if you do that with him. And you also override your own wisdom. If you didn't listen to his, you didn't listen to your own.

So let's keep traveling, because when you go into the past—"I wish I had said that then"—you can't begin now. It's okay to sit and just experience that and cry and cry and cry for hours. And when you come out of it, you begin again. And as you're sobbing, write down through your tears those concepts that come up. Your hand will get a life of its own and just fly—just nonsense, that can give you your life back. And is it nonsense? Well, it's not. Just write it all down. It will pour out of you.

Can you find another turnaround to "He left me"?

Joyce: I left me.

Katie: *You* left you. Yes. Give me three genuine examples of how the turnaround is true in your life.

Joyce: Well, I circled my life around him. His friends were my friends. I dropped all my old friends, and we had spiritual friends that we hung out with.

Katie: So you totally traded your life for his. That's one.

Joyce: Whatever money I made from my business went into building up *his* business.

Katie: Good. That's two.

Joyce: I didn't know he was going to buy a two-acre property on Maui. We couldn't afford it, and we went deeply into debt. It was just about when I was to have surgery. . . . We are in deep trouble financially, and we have to sell.

Katie: Well, sweetheart, that sounds very exciting.

Joyce: And he also says it's my fault.

Katie: I would look at the places where he is right. I would just look at those places. Okay, so [dejectedly] "We have to sell the property in Maui."

See if you can hear this turnaround, okay? [Excitedly] "We have to sell the property in Maui!"

Joyce: [laughing with the audience] Anyone want to buy a property?

Katie: Okay, let's look at the next statement.

Joyce: *I want Duncan to realize that divorce at this time in my life would leave me without retirement or savings and without the ability to do work full-time.*

Katie: Okay, so "You are not going to have the ability to work full-time"—is that true?

Joyce: Yes. I don't have the ability right now.

Katie: Oh, really. What are you doing full-time?

Joyce: The Work! Although it doesn't seem like it at times.

Katie: Well, it seems like it to me.

Joyce: And just taking care of myself and my cat and the property, the one that we have lived on for sixteen years. I have tenants, and I'm trying to take care of it.

Katie: So let me get this straight: You're doing The Work; you're taking care of tenants; you're taking care of the property; you're rehabilitating that body—and you're not working full-time?

Joyce: I *am* working full-time.

Katie: So, "I'm not going to be able to work full-time to support me"—is it true? Your answer is *no*. And all you've done is notice. Not only *can* you work full-time, you *do!*

12. My Husband Shouldn't Have Left Me

Joyce: Well, I can't get alimony, so everything has to come out of the second property, and—

Katie: "You can't get alimony"—is that true? Who told you that?

Joyce: My attorney. Hawaii is a no-fault state, and since he doesn't have a whole lot of money either, he doesn't want to have to pay alimony for the next five years. He's a contractor, and—

Katie: I hear what he wants and doesn't want. And "You can't get alimony"—is that true?

Joyce: [after a pause] I can, if I give up my home.

Katie: So "You can't get alimony"—is that true? Yes or no?

Joyce: No.

Katie: Very good! I hope you pin yourself down and don't give yourself any slack when *you* give you The Work.
    "You can't get alimony"—is that true? Notice when you go into your story and can't get honest with yourself, the way you couldn't get honest with him. Hear yourself, the way you couldn't hear him. That's what being married to him was about; that's what your life is about—growing, living in the unlimited, an unlimited life. So "You can't get alimony"—how do you react when you believe that thought?

Joyce: Fear, can't sleep, I worry about the future.

Katie: So who would you be without the thought "I can't get alimony"?

Joyce: Someone who would be scrambling to find ways to support herself financially.

Katie: Or at least having more restful sleep at night.

Joyce: That would be big.

Katie: Really, it would.

Joyce: Yes, I've been having to take medication to sleep. I've never had to before in my life.

Katie: So who would you be without the thought "I can't get alimony"? My goodness, the truth is that nothing's changed in your home other than your thoughts.

Joyce: Well, he paid most of the bills.

Katie: So your thoughts didn't go there. Okay, let me say that more clearly: You're in your home; you're in your bed; you're in your kitchen; you're with your things—just the way you were when he was there and he was off to the market. So nothing has changed except your thoughts. There's nothing different in that home but your thoughts.

Joyce: I can feel it in my mind but not in my cells.

Katie: Okay, you have the rest of your life to sit with this.

Joyce: I hope it doesn't take that long.

Katie: Well, enjoy the journey, because the end is not what matters; it's the trip. So, "I can't get alimony"—turn it around.

Joyce: I can get alimony.

Katie: Tell me about that.

Joyce: Well, alimony is basic living expenses. I have a little bit of Social-Security disability, I get that. I'm a milliner—I make hats— and I've started a Website, and I've gotten three orders out of sending out eight hundred flyers. But that's three orders, so—

Katie: So how can you get alimony?

Joyce: You mean direct alimony?

Katie: Yes.

Joyce: Give up my home: sell my home, my property, and I'd get alimony.

Katie: Yes.

Joyce: But I'd prefer—

Katie: Very good!

Joyce: . . . to keep the home, rent the home—

Katie: So *he* doesn't want to give you alimony, and *you* don't want to give you alimony. You're perfectly compatible!

Joyce: [laughing] Yes, we do have that in common. Well, I want to try anyway. And if I can't, I'll have to sell. And in the meantime, I'm trying to rent and take care of two houses on the property.

Katie: But this is your preference. That's what's important for you to know, because it leaves the two of you compatible and thinking the same way. And you don't have to be bitter around it. You can say, "We really agree!"

Joyce: Actually, from the sale of the Kula property—it keeps being extended because of the buyer. It's a contingency sale, and he has changed his attitude quite a bit. He was saying I was riding his back, ripping him off, and so forth. And then one day we were arguing about the settlement, and I walked him through The Work with my first belief, "Duncan is abandoning me." And he just listened. Before, he didn't want to even listen to anything about The Work. But I just walked him through. And we came to the turnaround—the one we just did—"I left him." And I told him how I left him. [Crying] And he was very quiet.

And then a few days a later, his offer changed quite dramatically so that I might be able to get a very big mortgage and be able to save the house. And that was really amazing. And he really supported my coming here, and I paid my own way *and* he supported me.

Katie: I love that you both have that in common, too. You both support you. Let's look at the next statement.

Joyce: *Duncan shouldn't have left me without clearly communicating his unhappiness, fears, and debts, and without making an attempt to heal our relationship.*

Katie: "He didn't communicate clearly with you"—is that true?

Joyce: I wasn't listening clearly.

Katie: You go to a yard sale. You come home. He's upset, and he tells you, "We don't need these things." He's communicating very clearly. "We can't afford it." That's clear.
   How do you react—in your marriage—when you believe the thought "He doesn't communicate clearly, he's British"?

Joyce: [laughing] I treat him badly; I try to get him to go to therapy; I try to drag things out of him.

Katie: Oh, that must have been pleasant. [The audience laughs.]

Joyce: [laughing] Not for him. Yes, it wasn't pleasant. We had some pretty bad fights—mainly in the last three years when my health went downhill. We had a really good relationship until then.

Katie: So I would question that thought, too. With this physical change of yours, it could be a good journey walking through that one.
   So "He didn't communicate clearly." Close your eyes and continue to report as you watch the images and pictures. How do you react when you believe the thought "He doesn't communicate clearly"? Watch you wanting to take him to therapists, and—

Joyce: I thought it was his fault, his problem; and I had my own problems and I shut down.

Katie: Look at what you said to him; look how you treated him.

12. My Husband Shouldn't Have Left Me

Look when he communicated clearly what he did not want—how you overrode it. And look at his face, watch. That's how you react when you believe the thought "He doesn't communicate clearly." [Joyce sobs.]

So sweetheart, watch *exactly* the same thing, only who would you be without that thought, "He doesn't communicate clearly; I need him to communicate clearly"? So close your eyes, and watch your life with him.

Joyce: It would be totally different. I would be listening to him; I would be respecting him.

Katie: Yes, watch him when he told you he didn't want to go to therapy—whatever that scenario was—watch him. You, without the story "I need him to communicate clearly."

Joyce: I would see in myself the problems that I saw: buying real estate, taking a gamble. A lot of things, it was just my . . . [She sighs.]

Katie: Now look at him communicating. Drop your story and look at him.

Joyce: I think *I'm* British. [The audience laughs.]

Katie: So "He doesn't communicate clearly"—let's just turn this whole thing around.

Joyce: He *does* communicate clearly.

Katie: Yes. I'm even getting a sense that maybe he wasn't even that secure about buying the property.

Joyce: Yes. I was pushing him to buy a property—investment property—and then I got so deeply into my pain and disability thing. And then he went off on his own and found a property with a client of his, and they were so enamored of it. And I said to him, "No, I don't think this is a good time to buy property, I'm about to have surgery." Then he was talking to someone, and I realized he said, "This is my dream. This reminds me of my homeland." And I thought I should support him because he was supporting me, so I signed the papers.

Katie: So you signed the papers, and your motives were?

Joyce: To support my husband. He wanted this property.

Katie: And what would have happened if you had *not* signed it? Because you did *not* think it was right?

Joyce: I don't think he would have bought the property.

Katie: So who bought the property?

Joyce: We did.

Katie: Drop the "we." He couldn't do it without you.

Joyce: I did. Yes.

Katie: "I wanted to support my husband"—turn it around.

Joyce: I wanted him to support me. Yes. He's a fabulous contractor.

Katie: But you signed it so he would support you. And you knew not to do it.

Joyce: And I also sold our property—on paper. I had the deal already in hand. He walked in before the final inspection and said, "I want a divorce." He also fell in love with his young office girl. She had come to stay on our property, and right before she left, he said, "I want out."

Katie: Okay, so read that one again, turned around.

Joyce: Duncan *should* have left me without clearly communicating his unhappiness and without making an attempt to heal our relationship.

12. My Husband Shouldn't Have Left Me

Katie: Yes, he should have! Give me a genuine example of how that is as true as or truer than your original statement.

Joyce: Well, because that's what happened.

Katie: And why else is that true? . . . Because when he tries to communicate, you override him.

Joyce: . . . yes. I just got it—I do override him.

Katie: Read it again, just like that.

Joyce: Duncan *should* have left without clearly communicating and without making an attempt to heal our relationship. So then I'm into beating myself up again because it was my fault!

Katie: Oh well! You have The Work. And it's not your fault. Here's how to deal with it: When you were signing the papers, for example, or when he was telling you that you can't afford this garage-sale stuff—that you don't need it, that you have everything you need—you would do it anyway. So go to the place inside you—either where you're signing it or going to the garage sale. Okay, find one of those places where you did what you're feeling guilty over now, what you're beating yourself up over . . . okay? Which one would it be? The time where you signed to buy the property?

Joyce: Yes.

Katie: Okay, close your eyes. Now look at what you were believing at the time. You see what you were believing before you signed it? Okay. So how could you have done anything different in that moment? How is it possible when you look at what you were believing?

Joyce: I think if I hadn't been so buried in drugs or pain. I was on drugs for pain—

Katie: That has nothing to do with it.

Joyce: It doesn't?

Katie: The world would tell you it did. And I'm asking you to go back in there and look at what you were believing just before you signed it. Now, with what you were believing, how could you have done anything else?

Joyce: [hesitantly] If I was believing that we needed an investment . . .

Katie: Which you were . . .

Joyce: . . . or that we need a new home? Or that I could support my husband? Or that I needed to support him?

Katie: Okay. So believing all those thoughts, how could you *not* have signed the papers?

Joyce: Yes. I did what I had to do . . . I guess.

Katie: I would drop the "I guess." Go in and see if it's true. Test it: In that moment, with what you were believing, there's nothing you could have done not to sign that paper. The world has a term for that: "doing the best you can." You did exactly the best you could do, given what you were believing in that moment. There were no other options.

[To the audience] How many of you were taking that trip? Okay, so for those of you who were not, I invite you to take it—with all those things that you did that you shouldn't have done. "Why did I do that?" Because you were believing your thoughts in the moment. Is there anyone who doesn't understand that? That leaves you guiltless. That leaves you in forgiveness. That leaves you in the experience of someone who never underperforms—if you really sit in it. That is the proof that in every moment of your life, you have always done the best you could do. In every moment. And as long as you believe your thoughts, your life must be lived out of that. You believe what you think or you question it—there's no other choice. Pretty simple stuff.

[To Joyce] So what we're doing here, what you're doing here, is taking 100 percent responsibility without the guilt. And if someone says, "You shouldn't have signed it," you might just smile and think, "If they were believing what I was believing, they would have signed it, too." And yes, you were taking drugs. And rather than take responsibility for ourselves, we say, "It was the drugs; it was the accident!" and then we go on and there's no resolution. So get really close when you're doing this Work, as you do so well.

Joyce: Should I go on?

Katie: Yes, that's what the mind does—it goes on and on. And until you love everything you think, your Work's not done.

Joyce: What does that mean? I've heard you say to hold your thoughts like your very dearest child.

Katie: My thoughts *are* my dearest children. There's nothing else to love. Mind is everything. So if I don't love my thoughts, it is mind not loving itself, not understanding itself. It's mind not meeting itself. The end of war is where the mind meets the mind, where it's no longer separate. Where it's absolutely free to do what it loves to do, and that is to create.

Joyce: As long as we question.

Katie: As long as it's free, but when you're stuck in a belief that's stressful, then it's stuck there. It's got to spend its life proving that it's the drugs; it's him; it's the accident. And it's stuck proving what can never be proven.

So when you question what you believe, the mind is free, and it's no longer at war with itself. And it's unlimited—genius is an understatement. But we're still stuck like dinosaurs in "He doesn't care about me. She should do this. He should do that." And then proving it and then getting people to agree with us, and if they don't, we get angry with them and we find people who do. And we get religions, and we get all our little ducks in order, and then *that* doesn't work, and then . . .

Let's look at the next statement.

Joyce: *I need Duncan to provide enough from the sale of our second property to take out a second mortgage and save my home.*

Katie: Okay, turn it around.

Joyce: I need me to provide enough from the sale of our second property to take out a second mortgage and save my home.

Katie: Yes. So that is your occupation right now, to stay as on top of your property as you can in the sale. And I hear that he has contingencies, and what do you think about it? It's your property, too. But I'm sure that's okay with you, because that's the way it is, and you haven't done anything successfully to change it.

Joyce: Hmm. I haven't done anything successfully to change it?

Katie: Yes. You haven't done anything to sell it to someone without contingencies.

Joyce: Well, I've been asking the Realtor to get backup offers, and—

Katie: Well, you're the owner. So, you might just call daily and ask, "Are there any backup offers? Are you advertising? What can we do? How can I help?"

Joyce: Good idea.

Katie: Put it out on the Internet.

Joyce: Put it on Craigslist.

Katie: Yes—get backup offers. You know what to do with real estate: You buy it, and you become enlightened! [Everyone laughs.] Let's look at the next statement.

Joyce: *Duncan is cold, cruel, cowardly, and a betrayer.*

Katie: Turn it around.

Joyce: I am cold—

Katie: When it comes to *him* and what he has to say.

Joyce: Yes. I am cruel . . . toward myself, too. Yes.

Katie: So now your Work becomes about identifying specifically where, and apologizing and making it right.

Joyce: To him and to me?

Katie: Yes. And that's where we step into it. And oh, life is so exciting in that place—apologizing and experiencing that, and asking how you can make it right and doing everything you can to make it right. It's an amazing journey.

Joyce: I've been doing that with him.

Katie: Well, you have some more to do with him. "*I* signed those papers. *I* did that. And if you're in trouble with it, then I sincerely apologize. I wanted you to support me, and I was afraid not to sign those papers. It was like an insurance policy that didn't work. You left me anyway."

Okay, the next statement.

Joyce: I am cowardly.

Katie: Yes, you think you can't support yourself, and you're doing well.

Joyce: Yes. It feels like I've been coming out of a lot of fear: fear of supporting myself physically and financially, fear of taking care of the mortgage and the tenants. And they're all things that I'm kind of doing.

Katie: I'd drop the "kind of." You're doing them!

Joyce: [laughing] Yes. This is so wonderful! I've been watching you do this Work every day of this workshop, and now I'm doing it with you!

Katie: And you're really doing it. And the next word?

Joyce: I am a betrayer.

Katie: Do you betray yourself?

Joyce: How did I betray myself? By not listening to myself, by not listening to him.

Katie: By knowing what to do and overriding it with motives—fearful motives.

By knowing what's right and then overriding it like with the Maui property—you overrode it. To your mind it wasn't okay. You couldn't afford it, and you overrode that with your motives of wanting his love, approval, appreciation, and support. So you overrode him simply because you were afraid.

Read the next statement.

Joyce: *I don't ever want to go through the anguish, heartache, and work of a divorce again.* It's a lot of paperwork. It is! It's a lot of work!

Katie: Who wants the divorce?

Joyce: He does, definitely.

Katie: Then why are you doing all the paperwork?

Joyce: Well, I have to do the paperwork for my attorney and if I go to court—which he threatens me with. So from day one I said I'm not going to court. He said, "Don't challenge my business. Don't you touch my business—you had nothing to with it." And I was like hypnotized; I was terrified.

We were involved in a spiritual practice together. And my teacher told me: "Don't go to court; don't ask for alimony. Sell the two properties and split it down the middle; you don't have kids." And I was terrified that I was going against my husband and my spiritual teacher. [She breaks into sobs.] I thought I would get karmically punished if I did anything other than that. However—

Katie: So he gets the business, and what do you get?

Joyce: He gets the business, and three-quarters of his business debts. I had no idea he had those business debts—no idea. Because I didn't look at the figures, I never looked! That's another way that I betrayed me.

12. My Husband Shouldn't Have Left Me

Katie: So he gets three-quarters of the debt and you get the other quarter?

Joyce: He gets three-quarters of his debts paid off from the sale of the second property. Plus he gets the business, and I get monies to put down toward a mortgage on the first house, my home, our home for sixteen years. And out of that money—I also have to use that money as alimony. I'm not going to get extra alimony.

Katie: So, sweetheart—

Joyce: And health insurance. He's also offered health insurance.

Katie: So sweetheart, what I'm hearing is that you're doing the same thing in the divorce with his business that you did with the Maui property when you bought it.

Joyce: Signing it? Signing it away? Well, this is what my attorney said. Because it's a—

Katie: Does your attorney go to his teacher? [The audience laughs and applauds.]

Joyce: She's supposed to be a bulldog. Her point was because Hawaii laws are so no-fault, number one, and number two—

Katie: Is there a community-property law in Hawaii?

Joyce: I don't know what that means.

Katie: It's where you each own half of everything: the home, the business, the—

Joyce: Yes, it's kind of like that, but see, the thing is he's a contractor. He can hide a lot of money. And she said that she's tried contractors before. It's a lot of work. You have to pay five to ten thousand dollars to someone who's not just a CPA but a specialist, have to go look into the books, go see what he's made over the last few years, and project what he *can* make. He could shut his business down, the courts could say "You owe your wife"—

Katie: Honey, I hear all this. It could be bad news. And do you want half of his business? No. Do you want half of *your* business, the business that you own together, the business that you gave him money for from your business to build his business? Do you want half of that business?

Joyce: She says I could only get half of his tools, and his truck. That's how it is with contractors. . . .

Yes, I would like to have some of it, for alimony, so I wouldn't be terrorized on how I was going to do it. But I'm going to do it anyway, I mean whether I get alimony or not, I'm just going to do it. I have to.

Katie: Well, all I know is that half of that business is yours. And if you want it . . . well, whether you want it or not, it's yours until you sign it away. You have experience there, and you can be informed. And the beautiful experience is that when you signed the papers to buy the Maui property, you were believing your thoughts at the time, and so you signed them. And you knew not to do it. And now you're in a divorce where paperwork is involved, and are you repeating the same thing again? That's all.

Joyce: Well, I stopped the drugs, except for one sleep aid.

Katie: Are you taking care of yourself? Or are you taking care of *him,* as a trade-off so that he will think well of you? So you are going to use your half of the business to buy his goodwill, which didn't work last time. But just know that. That way, when you sign one-half of your business away to him, then you know. Just be awake to it. And if your motives are to win his approval or the teacher's approval or the society—his society that you admire—to get back in their good graces, then you may want to take a look at that. And support yourself! And I'm not talking about the money anymore. Support yourself. You are a victim as long as we can buy you with our [in a cheerful, sing-song voice] "Hi! I really like you! You're wonderful!" That's a big ticket in your world.

Joyce: Yes, it is.

Katie: I often say, "Personalities don't love—they want something." So if you want to please me, give me something. Just don't take it away once you give it.

Joyce: Well, if I question my attorney, I'd have to start all over again with another attorney. [The audience applauds loudly.]

Katie: And there's another way if you're serious about it. You just walk in and you say, "I've made up my mind: That's my business, also, and that's what I want. That's half my house, and that's what I want. I want that down the line. And I want to know, just very simply, one reason why not." And then your attorney will give you the short version. And then you can just ask her for the odds. So maybe a different approach.

Joyce: She says we could go to court, and it may take time, and we may get alimony, but we wouldn't get the property possibly.

Katie: I don't know. Either way, it doesn't matter. Just know where you are selling out for love, approval, and appreciation. Just know that it's very expensive, and you've proven that to yourself.

Joyce: Yes, I have.

Katie: "Who are my friends?"
"Oh, the ones I buy."
Okay, so what did you write as the last statement?

Joyce: *I don't ever want to go through the anguish, heartache, and work of a divorce again.*

Katie: "I'm willing to . . ."

Joyce: I'm willing to go through the anguish, heartache, and work of a divorce again.

Katie: "I look forward to . . ."

Joyce: I look forward to going through the anguish, heartache, and work of a divorce again.

Katie: Yes. You may not experience any more stress over it at all. And you don't *have* to do that paperwork. You do it because it's how you support yourself financially. Your job is to take care of you. Nice Work, sweetheart.

Joyce: Thank you, Katie.

13. I'm Not Enough—
and Some People Are
Better Than Others

"I'm not enough" is one of the most painful stories of all. But if you know that peace happens inside you, you can enjoy the world as it lives you. If we all understood what success is, we would all love ourselves.

Jonathan: I wanted to ask if you could help me with a belief that persists in spite of any number of Worksheets and facilitations.

Katie: If I can, I would love to. That's what I was born for.

Jonathan: This belief seems to be in the middle of most of my conflicts with other people and with myself, too. It comes down to "I'm not enough." And combined with that is a feeling that some people are better than others. And then conversely, of course, some people are less than others.

Then that also results in two things for me. One is this feeling of always being up against it. And second—what's maybe worse—I'm always having to find where I am in the hierarchy, no matter where I am. And it's just relentless, and I'm so sick of it.

Katie: So sweetheart, why don't you come up to the chair and we'll see if the answers that live inside you can help you out.

Jonathan: The other problem with that is the turnarounds. First of all, question four—"Who would you be without that thought?"—just seems like science fiction. I can do it, but it doesn't connect very much with my reality. And then the turnarounds seem like a bunch of ooey-gooey happy talk.

Katie: So, step into my parlor. [The audience applauds.] Gooey happy talk. Boy oh boy! [Jonathan walks up to the stage and sits down.] So you're not enough.

Jonathan: Yes.

Katie: For what?

Jonathan: This is going to be hard, because I'm already sort of spinning with it . . . because you know, I've been through this part of it. And it all becomes so circular after a while.

Katie: Now let's move back to the question.

Jonathan: I can already tell where we're going with this, and like—

Katie: So let's move back.

Jonathan: [in a tone of self-parody] I know, I know: I'm enough to be sitting here. Like, *so what!*

Katie: That's *it! That's* what's so what! You're enough to be sitting here. That's the whole point, and when you really get that point, it will blow your mind!

Jonathan: Yes . . . it's pretty small—

Katie: So slow it down a moment.

Jonathan: It's pretty small potatoes, isn't it?

Katie: Let me know when you really get it. For me, it wasn't small potatoes. It was a revelation. It was the most profound realization I could have given myself after decades of despair, convinced that I wasn't enough; never had been; and never, ever would be.

Jonathan: Uh-huh.

Katie: So just feel the support of the chair that's holding you. Just relax into it. Now if you had a billion dollars . . . if you were the most successful person in the world and you were sitting here in this chair—

Jonathan: It's hard to feel that because it's not the money. It's something—

Katie: If you were the most important person in the world and everyone knew it, the whole world knew it, God knew it, would the chair feel much better?

Jonathan: Yes!

Katie: Is that true? The chair would be much better?

Jonathan: Yes.

Katie: Can you absolutely know that that's true, that the chair would feel better? You're the most successful person in the world. God knows it. Every human being knows it. All the cameras are on you. And does the chair really feel much more comfortable in that position? If you are the man sitting there in that position, can you absolutely know that that's true?

Jonathan: Well, no.

Katie: Thank you for not doing the ooey-gooey thing.

Jonathan: I mean the chair remains the chair. It has nothing to do with it.

Katie: And thank you for getting real. It's not just the chair, is it? It's the mind that's sitting in the chair.

Jonathan: Right.

Katie: So how do you react when you believe the thought "I'm not enough," and you're sitting in this chair? For all you know, you *are* the most important human being in the world, and you're just not aware of it. You don't know; you *can't* know. It's only your mind that tells you otherwise. You're just believing what you think. It's okay; I'm just running that by you. How do you react when you believe the thought "I'm not enough"?

Jonathan: Can I just ask you how could that be? How could I not know that? How could there be no evidence of it?

Katie: The proof is that you *don't*.

Jonathan: Oh.

Katie: And how do you react when you believe the thought? See, when you don't know the truth, you have a very troubled mind. It's a confused mind; it's a frightened mind. That's what a lie feels like. But it's not a lie to you, because you're believing what you think. *That's* how it's possible.

So who would you be sitting in this chair right now without the thought "I'm not enough"? Sit there as the successful man. Sit there as the failure. Sit there as every man that you wanted to be, or woman or child or you. Sit there and experience who you would be sitting in this chair without the thought "I'm not enough." [Long pause] Just feel the support.

Jonathan: I mean—

Katie: Feel the support of the chair.

Jonathan: It's difficult.

Katie: Allow it to support you—because that's what it's doing whether you're aware of it or not. And experience the breath that's breathing you and the ground that's supporting the chair. Feel what's supporting your arms and the support under your skin.

Jonathan: [after a long pause] At that point, it's . . . it's the body that's just sitting here.

13. I'm Not Enough . . .

Katie: Whoever you are.

Jonathan: Yes . . . exactly. I mean, it's just—

Katie: Is it enough? Just right now. I'm not talking about later.

Jonathan: Yes . . . it's more than enough. It's actually awe-inspiring . . . and it's just one moment. That's the magnitude of all of it, just sitting in little, little flashes, like a stop-action movie. And it's okay then. It's more than okay; it's beyond okay.

Katie: Yes. So "I'm not enough"—turn it around

Jonathan: I am enough.

Katie: Okay, now give me three reasons why that's true. And you know how you don't like ooey-gooey reasons. You want the real deal, because that's all you're going to believe. . . . Name the reasons—in your own truth—why it is enough to be the man sitting in this chair right now. Even more than enough.

Jonathan: [after a long pause] It kind of comes and goes. All I can really say is there isn't anything more to have.

Katie: There's not. There's not.

Jonathan: It comes and goes, though, because there's an immediate fast-forwarding.

Katie: That fast-forwarding would take the awareness from you. And that's okay, just notice. What does it have to do with reality?

Jonathan: It must have something to do with why so many of us are just in there churning away, climbing, and—

Katie: I would drop the "so many of us." Why are you?

Jonathan: Yes, why am I?

Katie: So ask yourself. Why are you? It doesn't matter how hard you work or how hard you strive, you end up in a chair somewhere.

Jonathan: Yes . . . yes. [Laughing]

Katie: Alone!

Jonathan: Yes, I was thinking of it kind of like pinball. The ball always goes down the hole in the end.

Katie: Yes, it has to rest somewhere. . . . Why is it enough to just sit here?

Jonathan: It actually isn't enough. Because I feel like I need to "get it" right now. You know what I mean? I'm on the spot, so I need to have my epiphany now. [The audience laughs.]

Katie: Okay, so that's a thought. Now, come back to the question. Why is it enough just to sit here now without an epiphany?

Jonathan: The best I can come up with is that I don't have any other choice. What other choice *do* I have? I can be somebody else. I can be somebody that I'd rather be in the future, or somebody that I wish I hadn't been in the past. But I don't have any choice . . . here.

Katie: And isn't it wonderful that you can do all that as you sit—in this support? Isn't it amazing that you don't have to live all that out? You can just sit here and imagine. This is so much kinder. You doing this; you doing that; you striving; you failing at that—isn't it kinder just to have what you have right now: the support as you sit with nothing to do, no one to be?
It was so wonderful when I really understood that I was mediocre. Oh my goodness, what a balance! If I want to be a very important person, can I just follow the first direction first? Can I learn to sit? If I'm *so* important and *so* awe-inspiring and *so* special, at the end of that—can I rest? Well, if I can't do it from here, how could I do it from there? You know, those great jobs in the world that you want to do? The good news is, you don't have to. You've

been spared. It's someone else's job: all those great scientists and actors and doctors and saints. You don't have to do that—you've been spared, so that we can sit here now and know that it's all being taken care of. Why would I take on that job when they're so willing? I'm spared to just be here now.

Jonathan: That just doesn't ring true for me. I mean, look at Miles Davis. There's no way I can say we're equals. In every way he's better than I am. What he did was more. His experience must surely be so much more. And it must be so much better to be him than to be me. How could that not be true when you listen to his music? How could it not be? It's just so transcendent.

Katie: Who is Miles Davis if you're not a listener? What good is it if there's no one to listen? Who makes him great?

Jonathan: I think he'd be great if he were all alone on a desert island.

Katie: I would turn that around.

Jonathan: I'd be great. Yeah, but only because no one else was there. [The audience laughs.]

Katie: If you were Miles Davis and there was no one listening to your music, how great would you be? If you have your story and there's no one to listen to your music, how great are you? And some of you know that's exactly what's going on right now.

Jonathan: It's hard to imagine. I don't know.

Katie: So let's look at it again. With your thought system—with what you're believing—if you were Miles Davis . . .

Jonathan: Yes, it probably wouldn't be good enough.

Katie: I would drop the "probably."

Jonathan: Yes. And that's how that works. What arrogance.

Katie: It's pure arrogance.

Jonathan: Wow! Yes. Miles Davis isn't good enough—

Katie: It doesn't matter how talented he is, how gifted he is—he's just not good enough. That's it. He can't rest; he can't sit; he can't receive the support of what *does* exist in reality.

Jonathan: Yes, if I were Miles Davis, it would ruin me to be thinking that way. Yes.

Katie: [after a long pause] You know, all that's required of me is that I be good enough just to sit in this chair now. It doesn't matter what my mind says. That's all that's required of me. What am I to do, jump up and save the world? Not yet. Be there for my daughter? I don't think so. It's not required of me right now. And when it is required? Can I do that as well as I sit here? Yes.

Jonathan: What if it is being required and you're not doing it?

Katie: Then you're confused. You're tormented. . . . Only a huge ego could say that you're supposed to be doing something that you're not doing. If it's required, just start moving toward it—get the job done. And if you can't get the job done, it's because it's not required. It's your attempt to mess up the universe, and the universe won't have it. It would prefer perfection. It does its job. The universe does what's required. It spits you out—have you noticed?

Jonathan: Yes.

Katie: It will not give you the talent for that. It will not give you the mind for that. It will not give you the body for that. It's not your job. Fight *that*. Your job is to sit here now until you stand—fight *that*. See what happens.

Jonathan: And why would it give you the mind and talent for something but not the means to actually pursue it and do it?

13. I'm Not Enough . . .

Katie: Because it's not your job. You obviously don't have the mind and talent for it. And if you do, it's just not time. The universe won't allow it.

If I'm good at something, I don't give it to the world. I give it to my daughter; I give it to you. I give it to the one in front of me, because I've received it myself. I have the ability to do that. If I have the most sweetheart thing in the world, it's not for everyone. It's for the one in front of me—it's for me first and then you. That's it. That's all that's required. No push, no pull.

It's not for a grand scale. It's just for this, the one in front of you. That's your job. And if you believe it's otherwise, you torment yourself with the mind that's not in reality—the mind that won't just sit, notice, appreciate, be supported. And I'm good enough to do this. I know my job. My job is to sit here comfortably now. I'm doing my job.

There are two ways to sit here—tormented, or accepting my job. And suppose I had the thought "I want a sip of tea" [there is a cup of tea on the table beside her] and I couldn't do that. "Oh my God, I'm not doing my job. I'm a failure. I'm not enough. I'm not good enough even to have a sip of tea. God, it's painful to sit here as a failure. All it would require is for me to reach out, get the cup—but no! This is hell!"

We'll just stay with that metaphor. "I want a sip of tea and I'm not doing it." Who the hell do I think I am? *It* doesn't move until it moves. And then I'd answer the question—who the hell *do* I think I am? And then I get real: I'm the woman sitting here—tealess. Can I love it?

There are two ways to sit here: suffering or not. And then if I reach out for the cup of tea and I pour it and I spill it: "Oh my God! Life is tough—I failed again." But you know, how else can the tea spill? I'm needed for that. When the tea spills, that's when I'm a success. When it doesn't spill, that's when I'm a success. I'm doing my job.

And something else that's delicious: living as a secret. No one else has to know what a success I am. They don't have to know. That's like the icing on the cake.

Jonathan: Why is it conventionally so different? I'm having to exercise a good deal of restraint to stop myself from objecting the whole time you're saying this. And I do understand it. . . . Well, obviously I don't, really.

Katie: Yes, it's the truth in front of your face. You don't have to accept it.

Jonathan: Observing other people, they seem pretty much like me. It's not the way we act.

Katie: You keep bringing other people into it. Does that make you feel better?

Jonathan: Well, yeah, because then I don't feel uniquely awful.

Katie: What if you were the only one in the world who believed that? All the rest of us are living happy lives, and you're the only miserable person in the world. And you just keep holding on to your beliefs, and people laugh and say, "How can you believe that?"

Jonathan: It does seem that way a great deal of the time, yes. That's part of the whole thing: that sense of something that I'm just not getting.

Katie: Oh, you're getting everything you need. You're just not noticing. And when you believe what you think, you *can't* notice. You're blinded. Your mind's busy proving that what it believes is true.

Jonathan: How do I get that to stop?

Katie: Put the thoughts on paper, and you sit with them. And you question them and turn them around—or not.

Jonathan: It works on some things, but it doesn't work on this.

Katie: I would work on what it worked on. That's the way of it. It'll never work on what I *want* it to work on, because my answers will come out of the motive.

13. I'm Not Enough . . .

Jonathan: Yes, I can see that.

Katie: So work on what it will work on. And watch the mind disassemble itself where it's able to. That would be living like a kind human being, to just work on what the mind *can* work on. And each time you do that, the mind begins to open up, until pretty soon the things that were like cement are like the ones you started with. Mind begins to trust that what it is without its story is not an unsafe thing to be—is not an unsafe experience.

Jonathan: Okay. Because my intuition is that there's something really core and fundamental that would be the one to try to explode, and the others would fall into place.

Katie: Oh, the mind loves that story. "I think I won't do The Work; I'll just look for the shortcut. When I find that core belief, I'll just blow it all at once."

Jonathan: That's right.

Katie: "I'm still waiting for that one core belief, and now I'm eighty years old. Now I'm ninety." [The audience laughs.] "Now I'm dead."

Jonathan: Okay. All right. I mean, I can do the easy ones.

Katie: Yes. That's where I started; I could do those, too. But the truth is, I could do the tough ones. I was in a hurry. The stressful thought that came up—that was the one. And I knew I could always do it. Why else would it come up?

But I didn't pick and choose. When it came up, stress would let me know, and I'd just do it. And then as life came to me, it was amazing. Where my freedom was had nothing to do with the thing I'd just worked on.

Jonathan: Yes . . . okay.

Katie: It's very dear to sit with you, sweetheart.

Jonathan: So if you run into a belief that is not giving up, that you're just sort of not getting anywhere with . . .

Katie: Well, I would question that one. There's nothing I wouldn't question. "I'm not getting anywhere"—how would I know? I question what I believe and turn it around. I never know *what's* going to happen afterward.

Jonathan: Okay . . . it's the same thing again. It's me setting the terms for what constitutes getting somewhere.

Katie: And what's important.

Jonathan: . . . and mapping out another future that will never come.

Katie: It will or it won't. Who knows?

Jonathan: So if you run into one that you keep stubbing your toe on—

Katie: I don't see how you could ever undo that thought, because the motive that you're coming out of won't allow what is underneath the motive to surface. And when you have a motive and you ask, you're just that much under the surface—because when anything else comes up, any other answer comes up to meet it, it won't meet your motive. So why would you ask in the first place? It's using The Work to get money or to lose weight or to heal cancer or whatever it is. How can that work? All the answers are going to come out of your motive.

Jonathan: Yes, that's right. A lot of my inquiry starts from a place of bad faith, actually, where it's not honest. It's not looking for the truth; it's looking for what I want. So rather than being honest, what I want is to be better, whatever that is.

Katie: People are so used to self-help workshops and positive thinking—and ultimately that's hopeless. Because when you get what you want, here you are, sitting in the same mind. Miles Davis—totally inadequate! Van Gogh chopping off his ear.

13. I'm Not Enough . . .

Jonathan: Right.

Katie: Start like a child, honey. Just be a child. Go in for the love of truth. I've found that it's the truth that sets us free. The very simple little truths. And when you really question a concept that's no big deal, you would be shocked at the power of it. Because you're not—your ego isn't—threatened by the answers.

Jonathan: Yes, and when I said I wasn't getting anywhere with this, it's not true. It's that I'm not getting where I want to go with it. You know, it's not turning me into the person I thought I ought to be, and so that's why I think it's not working.

Katie: Yes. That's why I love The Work. It will turn you into the person you want to be—it's just that you didn't know who you wanted to be! So you get it. But you can't plan it, because you don't know what it is. How can you plan for what you don't know? I love who I am. I never thought it would be this.

Jonathan: Right. Could you go through one more time why that is all so frightening—that sense of some little mistake? Why is it frightening to not know?

Katie: Well, let me move back to what I interpreted. So what is it that you want?

Jonathan: Are you asking me that specifically—not just rhetorically, but specifically?

Katie: Yes. What do you want? Do you want to be a success? I know what a success is, but you don't realize what a success is yet or you would love yourself. You would really love yourself! But you think you want something else and that something will *bring* you self-love. There's nothing between you and that—except imagination. And that imagination is what blocks you from realizing that everything you want, you already have.

So what is it that you want? What is it that you think will bring you whatever it is you think you want? You think that will bring you peace. It always gets back to that, but you put so many stumbling blocks in the way to peace that it's a hard trip. It's an impossible trip. So would you agree that you want that success because you think that then you'll be peaceful?

Jonathan: Yes, right. That's the thing.

Katie: So as you sit in this chair and experience the support all around you, get what you came for—without that huge trip the body has to make before it can have what you *already* have. And if it's peace that you're looking for—and I hear from you that's what you're looking for—you find it *inside* you.

And these questions—they're the invitation for the answers to surface. And it's quiet; it's clear; it never says you have to accept it. Just allow it to live. Allow those answers, those truths, to live in you. You can throw them away later. But just allow them. And skip all the hard work, and find it from where you're sitting, through The Work. The Work is meditation. It's the fast way. And then you may notice how simple your life becomes. But you can't even credit it to The Work. You just know your life is changing.

The simple version of what I just said: Look for peace from here now, not in the world. And then enjoy the world as it lives you. When you meet a stumbling block, just question your thoughts about what's going on. Don't expect anything.

Jonathan: I think that for the very first time I got a little glimpse that these tormenting thoughts actually are . . . just okay. You know, that's what I've got. Because even this whole time that I've been sitting here talking to you, there's that sense that I have to fight thoughts off somehow. But that's not it; that's not it.

Katie: [making the sound of a big kiss] Mmmmmmmmwah!

Jonathan: So it's *not* a mistake. It's not a mistake to be thinking this stuff that I think.

Katie: Oh, honey! [Jonathan laughs.] Thoughts are friends; they're not enemies. I would meet them at the door with open arms—and I do. Because until I do, they just keep knocking—and rightfully so. They're the key to my heart. Why would I close the door on them?

13. I'm Not Enough . . .

Jonathan: Yes . . . yes, I see that. I see. Thank you, Katie.

Katie: You're so welcome.

14. My Father Abused Me

The memory is eating at you. You wish you could let go of it. But it's not your business to let go of it, only to question your thoughts about it. If you question them deeply enough, <u>they</u> let go of <u>you.</u>

Katie: So sweetheart, let's hear what you've written.

Stan: I have to acknowledge that I'm very nervous.

Katie: Yes, well we have so many stories about what it means to sit here: "What will people think?" And some of us think, "Will I do it right?" These thoughts keep spinning in our minds. A feeling for me is like a sweet gift that says, "Maybe inquiry will help." So let's see what you have here.

Stan: This is from the past, so should I make it like it is the present?

Katie: No, just read it the way you wrote it. We don't care about time or space; we just write it down. Does the mind care? When we think of something that happened thirty years ago, forty years ago, it's like it's happening *now*. Sometimes we can even smell the smells. So that's what this Work does—we go back.

Stan: Okay. *I'm angry and saddened at my father because I never got to really know him. He never kept his word with me. The only times I got* *to be with him were when he took me to the bars and we played shuffle-board. He never listened to me, was patronizing, and sexually abused me when I was about eight years old.*

Katie: I love that you are here for the real thing. You are one courageous man.

Stan: This is the first time I've ever acknowledged it in front of anyone.

Katie: Yes, you're amazing. You show us what we are—courage. Let's keep going. You've come to the right place, my friend.

Stan: *He was drunk and abusive, took no interest in my life or the lives of my siblings. When he wasn't drunk, he wimped out with my mother and everyone. His drinking was the dominant cause of daily fights and disharmony in the home. And I miss him.*

Katie: Yes, we are love, and there's just nothing we can do about it.

Stan: You want me to continue?

Katie: I do. Isn't that what the mind does? Here it comes, so we may as well.

Stan: *I want my father to stop drinking, pay real attention to his other children and me, stand up to my mother, keep his word with me, take more interest in me and what my life is about, take better care of his health, demonstrate his love for me, and be less selfish.*

Katie: Continue.

Stan: *My father should stop drinking, stop lying, should have more backbone, be more confident, stop smoking, talk and listen to me— really—be assertive when not drunk, encourage me to realize my dreams.* Should I read the next statement?

Katie: Yes.

14. My Father Abused Me

Stan: *I need my father to spend some real time with me, acknowledge me, demonstrate he really loves me, cares for me, supports me, help me dispel the confusion, be there for me for real instead of in the bars, to play shuffleboard, go hiking, play ball, and so on. My father is a drunkard, a selfish bastard, a loner, a wimp, totally inattentive to the rest of his family and to me. I don't ever want to accept his lies; I don't ever want to be sexually abused by him; I don't want to go to the bars in order to be with him; I don't want to have those daily fights that created such tension in the house.*

Katie: Quite an exorcism, sweetheart.

Stan: Yes.

Katie: [to the audience] I invite you all to go to the place where you relate to this in your life. And as we go through the inquiry, I invite you to go inside and give you your own freedom—don't wait for his. Find your own.

[To Stan] So sweetheart, let's begin. Let's move to the *shoulds,* because they seem to get right to it. Read the first statement.

Stan: *My father should stop drinking.*

Katie: Is that true? And go back to . . . what age are you? Pick an age here where it's the most painful.

Stan: Eight, nine years old.

Katie: Okay. So, little boy, "Your father should stop drinking"—can you absolutely know that that's in his best interest or yours? Can you absolutely know that that's true?

Stan: No, I can't know that for sure. No.

Katie: Yes, we just can't know more than God. We can't *know* what is best for our path; all I can know about my path is I've had the perfect one for me.

Little boy, what happens inside you when you believe the thought that he should stop drinking, and he doesn't?

Stan: I feel sick; it's painful.

Katie: And how do you treat him when you believe that lie? How do we know it's a lie that he's supposed to stop drinking? He drinks—that's it. That's what he does. A dog barks; a cat meows; he drinks.

How do you treat him when you believe the thought "It's supposed to be different, he's supposed to stop drinking"—and he doesn't stop; he comes in drunk?

Stan: Angry.

Katie: So close your eyes, little boy.

Stan: Distancing.

Katie: Yes, keep going. How does it look? Get more specific.

Stan: I'm abusive to him.

Katie: Yes.

Stan: I don't want anything to do with him. I curse at him.

Katie: Yes. Now how does it feel, little boy, inside you when you treat him that way?

Stan: Sick. Really sick.

Katie: Sick. Can you see a reason to drop the story "My father should stop drinking"? And I'm not asking you to drop it, little boy. I'm just asking if you can see a reason to.

Stan: Yes.

Katie: Little boy, can you see one good reason to keep the story that does *not* make you sick—one good reason to keep the story "My father should stop drinking"?

Stan: I can't see any reason to keep the story. But I'm not sure it's going to go away just because I've decided I don't want to keep the story.

Katie: And that's what I love about this Work: It *never* asks you to drop it. It doesn't even imply that you should drop it. That's the power of investigation.

Stan: I mean, I'd like to drop it, but I doubt if it's—

Katie: . . . your business? It's not my business to drop a story. Mankind's been trying to do that for centuries! It doesn't work. So don't even go there. Letting go is an outdated concept.

Stan: It would be great if you *could* let go, but it's not . . .

Katie: It's not what we do. But investigation—self-realization, realizing for yourself what is true—dispels the illusion. So I've got this little secret, and everyone's welcome to it: I inquire.

It's as simple as this: Can you see one reason, little boy, to keep the story "He's supposed to stop drinking," one good reason that's not painful inside you?

Stan: The only reason that I can come up with is that by keeping it fresh in my mind, I can . . . no, no, I just keep getting angry. No, I can't see any reason.

Katie: Yes—not one good reason. I couldn't either. So little boy, eight years old, who would you be without your story?

Stan: Who would I be?

Katie: Yes. How would you live in that house without your story? Who would you be without the story?

Stan: I really don't know.

Katie: Isn't that fascinating? That's been our entertainment, but *only* our whole life. We don't even know! I was a child at forty-three; I came to see that I didn't know anything. I had this Work. I didn't know how to live, and then I noticed I was being lived. I was like a child, a toddler. When we stay in The Work, we come to see we don't *have* to know anything. The whole world will give us everything we need.

"My father shouldn't drink"—turn it around.

Stan: I must acknowledge that I've been in AA for eight years.

Katie: Oh good, angel.

Stan: I drank and did all the drugs I could get my hands on for a long time.

Katie: Oh.

Stan: I destroyed my family.

Katie: Isn't that *fine?*

Stan: [laughing] I'm not sure that it was, but—

Katie: Well, honey, anything that brings us together—I'm for it.

Stan: [laughing] Yes, that's true. It got me here.

Katie: Yes. So "My father shouldn't drink"—turn it around.

Stan: I shouldn't drink.

Katie: Yes. *You* live it; that's for *you* to live, not him. There's another turnaround. "My father shouldn't drink"—what's the opposite polarity?

Stan: I shouldn't drink.

Katie: Okay, and sometimes there are six of these turnarounds that are truer than what we wrote. "My father should . . ."

14. My Father Abused Me

Stan: My father should drink.

Katie: Yes. Now give me three genuine examples of how that turnaround is true.

Stan: Because that's his way?

Katie: Yes—because it's what is. I mean, what's the truth of it? Did he drink?

Stan: Yes.

Katie: "He should drink"—that's it. And a second example?

Stan: [pause] Because in the long run I can't know what's best for him. I can't know if or when he should stop drinking.

Katie: Yes. What are you going to do, dictate to God? "Excuse me, God, he really should stop drinking right now. You're doing it wrong." Am I going to tell God how to run the show? Not likely. I don't even know how to run my own.
Can you find a third example?

Stan: Well, if he keeps drinking and I stop putting my "shoulds" onto him, maybe it could really change our relationship.

Katie: Very good. Let's look at the next statement.

Stan: *He should stop lying.*

Katie: "Fathers shouldn't lie"—what's the reality of it? Let's start playing with a full deck. "Fathers shouldn't lie"—what's the reality of it? Do they?

Stan: Well, my father did.

Katie: That's it. That's your experience. Do fathers lie? Yes. Welcome to reality. So what happens when you argue with reality? How did you treat him when you believed that lie, the lie that fathers shouldn't lie?

Stan: I wasn't very kind.

Katie: And how did it feel when you were unkind?

Stan: Painful.

Katie: Can you see a reason to drop this mythology, "Fathers shouldn't lie"?

Stan: Yes.

Katie: Can you see one stress-free reason to keep the story that anyone on this planet is not supposed to lie—news commentators, presidents, popes, children—one good reason to believe the story that *we're* not supposed to lie?

Stan: It would be better if we didn't, but—

Katie: Can you really know that that's true?

Stan: Hmm.

Katie: I don't believe that anymore. How do I know it's in my best interest that people lie? They do. I need to get a clue here! Have you ever lied?

Stan: Yes.

Katie: Well, there it is. Can you see one good reason to keep the story "People shouldn't lie" that is not stressful inside you?

Stan: I can't think of any.

Katie: Boy, it's so fine to lose our self-righteousness. It's the first act of humility.

Stan: Yes. I'm pretty self-righteous. I mean, I have been.

Katie: I don't really get that from you—and that's just silly me. I just get a humble man. Who would you be without the story, little boy, that fathers shouldn't lie?

Stan: A lot lighter, I think.

Katie: Turn it around.

Stan: I shouldn't lie.

Katie: That's it. It doesn't get any better than that. I work on me. That's a full-time job; it's a life's work.

Stan: I shouldn't lie, and I *do* lie.

Katie: Yes! I lie when I think my father shouldn't lie, for starters. You punished him when he lied, and it didn't work. It never taught him a thing.

Stan: Right.

Katie: So that's hopeless. So when I turn it around—"I shouldn't lie"—I have an agreement with myself that not till I learn how not to lie myself will I try to teach the world not to lie. And I'm not there yet. This is a life's work. Let's look at the next statement.

Stan: *He should have more backbone.*

Katie: So "Your father should have more backbone"—can you absolutely know that that would be in his best interest on his path?

Stan: I can't know that, no.

Katie: And how did you treat him when you believed the thought "He should have more backbone"?

Stan: With contempt.

Katie: And how did that feel inside you?

Stan: Painful, sad.

Katie: Can you see a reason to drop this story?

Stan: Sure, yes.

Katie: Can you see one reason to keep the story that is *not* painful?

Stan: No.

Katie: Who would you be without this story?

Stan: I don't know.

Katie: Isn't that fine? That's what's meant by ageless—there's no age in that. There's no age in "I don't know."

Stan: Does it mean that? It sounds really good *now*, but it's going to crop up again.

Katie: Can you really know that?

Stan: No.

Katie: And how do you react when you believe the story?

Stan: Restricted.

Katie: Who would you be without it in this moment?

Stan: I don't know!

Katie: My favorite position.

Stan: But there's something in the answer to that that leaves me like I'm nowhere.

Katie: That's where you've been all your life! [The audience laughs.]

Stan: [laughing] That's true.

Katie: It's just that now you know it.

Stan: Yes.

Katie: Life is so simple: We walk; we sit; we lie horizontal. That's about it. Everything else is a story about what's going on while we're doing it.

Stan: It's almost like the stories make my being real. [The audience applauds.] And without the story, I wouldn't be real.

Katie: And you've never been real. You know that.

Stan: Yes. I've been at the forefront of the story. [He gives a low whistle.] Holy shit! [The audience laughs loudly.] Wow! My hairs are standing up. Is that significant? [More laughter.] Oh my God, that's really true. Without my stories, there's really nothing here.

Katie: Yes.

Stan: And the stories are actually what make me—

Katie: Exist?

Stan: . . . exist. I mean *every* story, not just this story. There's something that I attach to what happens that makes me feel real. Is that so?

Katie: I hear from you that it is, and that's my experience, too.

Stan: Yeah. So what would I be without it? I mean it's like, who am I?

Katie: None of my business. I am.

Stan: Just am?

Katie: And who would you be without *that* story? The story that you even are.

Stan: Just—

Katie: Silence.

Stan: Yes.

Katie: Silence apparently talking, apparently sitting. That's all.

Stan: [laughing] That's great!

Katie: What's your first name?

Stan: Stan.

Katie: Stan, it's a privilege to sit in the presence of truth.

Stan: Yes, it is. Yes, it is.

Katie: Let's look at the next statement.

Stan: Okay. *He should be more confident.*

Katie: "He should be more confident"—is that true? Can you really know that that's true?

Stan: I can't know that, no.

Katie: Turn it around.

Stan: I should be more confident. And he shouldn't be more confident. It's okay for him not to be confident.

Katie: It must be. He wasn't.

Stan: He wasn't. Jesus!

Katie: I mean, who's going to argue with a tree?

14. My Father Abused Me

Stan: Damn! This really is amazing! Just answering the questions.

Katie: You know, when we were children, the world said the sky is blue. So we said, "The sky is blue." We didn't stop to go inside and ask ourselves. We didn't know how. So we're still children, and we begin now. But when the mother says, "The sky is blue; it's a sky," a wise child goes inside. "It's blue—can I really know that that's true? No. And I can see it's my mother's religion; it just doesn't happen to be mine." And what she's got is as valuable as what I've got. So we love. She says it's blue; I say "I understand." And I don't bother to tell her that it's not blue, in my experience. And if she asks me, I'm going to say, "You know, Mother, it's not my experience, and I love that you see the sky as blue." We're compatible.

Stan: It seems that agreeing that the sky is blue is a way to get by.

Katie: Yes—like incest.

Stan: Yeah.

Katie: It's love. We don't know how to do it. So we begin now. But incest is very interesting, like every other symbol. All being equal, we all receive the one we need for this moment now. But you wanted something from him. And that's what it was about. What did you want from him?

Stan: I wanted acceptance.

Katie: Yes. And did you get it?

Stan: I don't think so.

Katie: So you wanted acceptance. And love?

Stan: Yes.

Katie: And appreciation?

Stan: Yes, and acknowledgment, support.

Katie: So that's what we'll do for love: anything. And we're confused—we say they did it to us. But we didn't run away. And if we did, we didn't run away again, and if we did, we didn't run away after that. We didn't say no, some of us. We were too frightened, because we wanted something. First we wanted security, second comfort; and then, when we get that all controlled, we wanted pleasure. And all pleasure is pain. Self-love is as good as it's ever going to get. But that's what the little boy was up to. "I will do *anything* for love."

I often say, "If I had a prayer, it would be this: 'God spare me from the desire for love, approval, or appreciation. Amen.'"

Stan: Whew! It took a lot of years to get that.

Katie: Ah, we don't care. The best thing about the past is—it's over.

Stan: [laughing with the audience] And not re-creating the past over and over.

Katie: None of my business. I just inquire. Because, like you, I know the power of that. Let's look at the next statement.

Stan: *He should stop smoking.*

Katie: Is it true?

Stan: He still smokes. So do I.

Katie: "He shouldn't smoke"—turn it around.

Stan: I shouldn't smoke.

Katie: Yes. And when you get it all wired, then go teach the world about smoking. This is it, you know—you smoke for this experience of humility. This is a life's work, and it's not *ever* about not smoking. It's about self-realization.

Can you see a reason to drop the story "He shouldn't smoke"? This is terrifying for people! This is where we get to the *real* courage of inquiry, when you're dealing with the thing you're attached to. You think you're attached to it, but it's just a story of things that you're attached to. No one's attached to a thing. A thing is nothing more than your story. You found that.

Can you see a reason to drop the story "He shouldn't smoke"? And I'm not asking you to drop it. Can you see one good reason to keep the story that is not stressful?

Stan: No.

Katie: And isn't that when you want to smoke?

Stan: Yes, it is.

Katie: And when we're stressed, we smoke. It's the same with all addictions—drinking or obsessive sex, the same with any reach for an outside cause. Who would you be without the story "He's not supposed to smoke"?

Stan: I don't know! It's that big "I don't know," that empty space "I don't know."

Katie: It sounds a bit sweeter than shame and guilt. What do you think?

Stan: [laughing] Yeah.

Katie: So, "He shouldn't smoke" is just a lie, and "I shouldn't smoke" is, too, when you're smoking.

Stan: Right.

Katie: "He's a smoker"—is it true? How can you know in this moment? Maybe he quit a month ago, and you haven't spoken to him for six months. "I'm a smoker"—is it true? Like, right now?

Stan: No. Not right now.

Katie: No. So you're a nonsmoker. How do you react when you believe the thought that you smoke, which can only happen in a future?

Stan: If I say I'm a smoker right now? And I'm not smoking?

Katie: Yes.

Stan: It makes me a liar.

Katie: That's right. And how does that feel?

Stan: Not good.

Katie: And what happens is that you attach to a whole future of when you're smoking. And you're sitting here not smoking! It's a *wild* trip out and away, so that we don't have to experience this sweet moment now, just two friends sitting together, just hanging out. No smokers here. We're in the presence of peace.

I smoked very heavily, I chain-smoked. Our house smelled like it—everything, all my clothes. But when I found this Work, I would pick up a cigarette and I'd say to myself, "She wants to what, with what? She's going to . . . what?" And I'd never light the cigarette. I couldn't see the sense in it. In the presence of peace, it has its own life. And that is none of my business; it's just none of my business. My thinking is my business.

When I believed my thoughts, I used to rape my physical health by saying my body should be more beautiful; it should be healthier; it should be taller, shorter, fatter, thinner, younger. I took a perfect body and trashed it in my mind. And then, in an instant, I became a friend. And all I did is what you've done today: I just met my thinking with a little understanding. I no longer saw it as an enemy that needed to die, go away, be—what was the term we used?—let go of. Why would I let go of one of my children? Does that make sense? Our thoughts are our children. Why would we want to banish them? Why can't we just join with them? And that's what this Work does: it meets every concept with under-standing.

14. My Father Abused Me

There are no accidents. This thought appears now, perfectly, to be met finally after all these centuries. It's been like an orphan out there. Have you ever felt like that?

Stan: Yes.

Katie: Well, that's what beliefs are, and when we meet them with understanding, the mind gets *really* quiet.

Stan: Yes. Sometimes the quiet can be frightening, too.

Katie: What does the quiet mean?

Stan: It's unfamiliar space.

Katie: So "Quiet is unfamiliar space"—is that true?

Stan: For my busy mind it is, yeah.

Katie: Do you sleep every night?

Stan: Yes.

Katie: So, is quiet an unfriendly, unknown space?

Stan: No.

Katie: You're a friend. You do it well every night. That's as bad as it gets. You wake up where you left yourself. The worst that can happen is that you're going to find yourself where you were. It's such fun! Who we are without a story is where we are every night. In the silence. We can be used there; we're servants there, true servants.

Stan: That's what I want to be, but I've chased gurus all my life and religions and this whole thing, and I still haven't found it.

Katie: Well, you're the guru you've been waiting for. He was right under your nose! Let's look at the next statement.

Stan: *He should talk and listen to me—really.*

Katie: Is that true—did he?

Stan: No.

Katie: Welcome to reality. Little boy, how do you react when you believe the thought "He should listen to me—really," and he doesn't, ever?

Stan: It doesn't feel good.

Katie: How do you treat him when you believe that story?

Stan: With anger.

Katie: How does that feel?

Stan: Doesn't feel good.

Katie: Can you see a reason to drop the story that anyone should listen to you, ever, under any circumstances?

Stan: This is one of my big issues, when people don't listen to me.

Katie: Look how you treat them when they don't and you think they should!

Stan: I see.

Katie: It's a flat-out lie.

Stan: Well, it's not just listening, but it's having a communication when there's no communication.

Katie: You're right—there isn't any.

Stan: And that's okay? That's what it is.

14. My Father Abused Me

Katie: It really works when you know that everything you say to him is for you to hear. Who's not listening? That's why I love that this is being recorded! Everything you ever said to him was for you to hear—*are* you? Stay in inquiry, and the inquiry is what's important for you to come to know what's true. And I hear you. So let it fall over you like a bath. Don't even try to hear it.

Stan: Yeah, it just feels good. It's refreshing.

Katie: I would go with that. Let's look at the next statement.

Stan: *He should be more assertive when not drunk.*

Katie: So he should be more assertive, is that it?

Stan: He should be more assertive when he isn't drunk. He doesn't have to be drunk to be assertive. When he was drunk, he was very assertive.

Katie: So you want him to be assertive when he's not drinking—for what? Why?

Stan: Well, so I could feel respect for him. Yes, that's basically what it was.

Katie: And then when you feel respect for him, what would you feel?

Stan: What would I feel if I respected him? I would feel good, I guess.

Katie: And look how you treated him to teach him this. Look what it cost you when he wasn't assertive. And if you just dropped *him,* the stories of him, then you would have that happiness that you wanted *through* him. . . .

The short version is, we can just drop the middleman and be happy from here. The other way is such a long route. "After he's assertive, after he's sober and stops lying, then I'll be happy." Instead, you start looking at the list, and you say, "Gosh, maybe I'll just give the guy a break," and notice your own happiness as a result of that.

Stan: So when someone is lying and not being assertive, it's okay?

Katie: It's perfect. It's my favorite part—it's what is. I'm a lover of reality.

Stan: But what if it affects where you're at?

Katie: It can't.

Stan: It can't?

Katie: Cannot. Your story about it is what's affecting you. *No* one can affect you. Your story about their actions affects you. That's it. No one has ever done anything to me. No one *can* do anything to me. I tell the story of you, and I heaven me or hell me. And I call it your fault, or to your credit.
Let's look at the next statement.

Stan: *He should encourage me to realize my dreams.*

Katie: So "Your father needs to encourage you"—is that true?

Stan: Yes. Well, it would have been nice if he did.

Katie: Can you absolutely know that that's true?

Stan: Can I know that it would be true if he did encourage me?

Katie: Can you know that if he encouraged you, your life would be much better?

Stan: Yes!

Katie: Can you absolutely know that that's true?

Stan: No, I can't know that for sure.

Katie: What is in my life is the right path. So *"He* would be much better off if he encouraged you"—can you absolutely know that that's true?

Stan: No, I can't.

Katie: So how did you treat him when you believed the thought "Fathers should encourage their sons"?

Stan: Hmm. I felt diminished. I felt unwanted.

Katie: How did you treat *him?*

Stan: How did I treat *him?*

Katie: When you believed that story?

Stan: With anger.

Katie: And how does that feel?

Stan: Not good.

Katie: Can you see a reason to drop it?

Stan: Sure.

Katie: How did you treat *you* when you believed that story and he didn't comply?

Stan: I withdrew.

Katie: So can you see one good reason to keep the story "Fathers should encourage their children," one reason that isn't painful?

Stan: No, I can't see one reason to hold on to it.

Katie: Who would you be without that story, that anyone should encourage you?

Stan: I don't know. I mean, I really don't know.

Katie: I really hear that. Turn it around.

Stan: I should encourage myself to realize my dreams. Yes, I should encourage myself.

Katie: It's not a father's job. That's a myth. If you want encouragement, give it to yourself. That way you always have it; you don't have to wait.

Stan: But what about when you're a child?

Katie: Children don't know these things. So we begin now. That's what I love about this Work—we can write from a three-year-old perspective if we need to. It's timeless.

Stan: It actually seemed kind of silly to go back and do all this. But I felt I needed to, because this is something that was incomplete for me, an opportunity for me to say something about my father that I've never said before.

Katie: Yes. There's another turnaround for that one.

Stan: I should encourage my father. I should encourage my father to realize his dreams.

Katie: Yes.

Stan: I should encourage my father? How does that work out?

Katie: Well, you expected *him* to know! I think you're just like him. Maybe he didn't know either.

Stan: No, he probably didn't.

Katie: The next time that that thought comes to you: "They should encourage me"—it could be a child, your children, a relative, someone you're close to—it doesn't matter. And you have the thought in their presence "They should encourage me"—turn it around. And encourage *them*—for your sake.

Stan: It's like creating good karma for yourself.

Katie: But there is just the karma of this thought—there is no other karma. There's no past life; there's only a belief appearing now, and we attach to it so deeply that it gives us the illusion of a story that's real. There's only this. That's all that has ever been.

Stan: Yes. I'm following my thoughts. I'm in the shadow of my thoughts. It's really true.

Katie: Yes, all these spiritual concepts you've heard? You could write the book now. You're the book to read. No other.

Stan: It's true. My thoughts are leading me through life. All my beliefs, my feelings. They're in the forefront, and I'm traveling right behind them. And the inquiry kind of stops that. It brings it right here. I mean, it's amazing. And it doesn't matter that it's even future or past. It's happening now.

Katie: It wasn't just a concept. It's true.

Stan: Yes. Wow! Does this stay with you?

Katie: None of my business.

Stan: I have a feeling. I mean, it feels good right now. I'm really getting it, but I'm afraid that when I walk away and go out back into life that it's going to say, "Pshooosh!"

Katie: Let's look at statement number five. [The audience laughs loudly and applauds.]

Stan: *My father is a drunkard, a selfish bastard, a loner, a wimp, totally inattentive to his family.* C'est moi. I mean, blazingly! My wife had the good sense to divorce me. [The audience laughs.] I blamed her for a lot of years, but she was right.

Katie: Yes. And you might write her a letter just to let her know she was right. Get this stuff done. You write the letter for your sake. "You were right; I was the last to know. I hear you now." If you want it all, live it.

Stan: Goose pimples again.

Katie: Yes.

Stan: It's true. I couldn't understand why she would put me out of the house just because I took a trip to India and got drunk and was stoned out of my mind. I couldn't understand it.

Katie: Yes.

Stan: This drunkard, selfish bastard, loner, wimp, totally inattentive to his family—that was me.

Katie: And if you attach to the story "My father shouldn't drink"? He's drunk with his drinking; you're drunk with your thinking.

Stan: Oh my God.

Katie: Of *course* he should drink—it's what he did. I mean, are you going to take someone's breath away from them? We don't drink by accident. Nothing before its time.

Stan: You could actually get addicted to the thinking.

Katie: That's the *only* addiction. It's always been the only addiction. We're addicted to these concepts, and we become confused because we don't know how to meet them with understanding. We can't let go of them, because they're reality for us, and letting go just doesn't work. Only the truth can set us free. Let's look at the next statement.

Stan: *I don't ever want to accept his lies again.*

Katie: Okay. So "I'm willing . . ."

14. My Father Abused Me

Stan: I'm willing . . .

Katie: . . . to accept . . .

Stan: To accept his lies.

Katie: Yes. "I look forward to . . ."

Stan: I look forward to accepting his lies.

Katie: Yes, because they could appear again in your mind. The little five-year-old, the eight-year-old, the nine-year-old. That story could appear again about how he lied to you. You feel the stress, and the feeling is the reminder to investigate the story you're in.

Stan: So I'd actually be grateful if he lied to me again, because it would give me an opportunity to confront this.

Katie: To do The Work. That's what number six is all about. And the next statement?

Stan: *I don't ever want to be sexually abused again.*

Katie: And you could attach to that story again. "I'm willing to . . ."

Stan: I'm not sure I'm willing to.

Katie: You may as well be. It could appear again in your mind.

Stan: Um. I'm *willing* to be sexually abused by him?

Katie: Yes. "I look forward to . . ."

Stan: I don't know if I could say that.

Katie: I hear that. And here it comes—two o'clock in the morning, four o'clock, I don't think it cares—here it comes. It's a possibility. Undo it—or not. You see, if it's two o'clock in the morning and the incest thing came to you in your mind, I would sit down and judge him again. I would inquire, and I would look forward to it happening again—all night long.

How do I know when it's time to do The Work? I don't even have to know what to do The Work on—it appears. The story comes, and if it's not totally comfortable, undo it—or not.

Stan: Well, I'd really like to get through this.

Katie: So go back to the worst incest you experienced. What room is it in? What house? Can you find the house in your mind and the room?

Stan: Sure.

Katie: Okay. Where are you?

Stan: It never left my mind.

Katie: Yes. So how old are you?

Stan: Maybe eight years old.

Katie: And where is he? Where are you, before it begins?

Stan: I was lying next to him in the bed.

Katie: Okay. And did he come to the bed, or did you go to his bed?

Stan: I lay down with him on a Saturday. He was drunk and sobering up from the night before.

Katie: Okay. So, little boy, little eight-year-old, did you know before you went into that room that it might happen?

Stan: No.

Katie: No indication whatsoever? Okay, so now you're lying in bed with him. Now what happens? How does it begin?

14. My Father Abused Me

Stan: I was on his right side and I fell asleep, and when I woke up, he was . . .

Katie: [after a long pause] It's okay.

Stan: He was touching me.

Katie: Yes. Now, he was touching you. [Stan sighs heavily.] And what did you do? What are you doing now, little boy, and what's going on in your mind?

Stan: I made believe I didn't know it, and I got out of bed. I made believe I wasn't aware of it, and I just got out of bed.

Katie: Okay, and did you go through any more, or just the touching and then you got up?

Stan: I was totally confused.

Katie: Okay, so see if this is accurate. You woke up with him touching you. And you let it continue, and then you got up as if it hadn't happened.

Stan: Yes.

Katie: So when you woke up and experienced it, you didn't leave the bed, because you wanted something from him: What was it? You were afraid you would lose something.

Stan: Oh, I was afraid. Like now I would say, "What the hell are you doing?"

Katie: No. I'm talking to the little eight-year-old.

Stan: No, I couldn't do that. I would be afraid of being alienated from him.

Katie: Good. So "He molested me"—turn it around.

Stan: I molested me?

Katie: Yes. You didn't get up. And I'm not saying you did it wrong; I'm not saying you made a mistake. You did the best you could at the time—that's not the point. But *you* molested you: you didn't get up. This is not about right or wrong. You didn't get up because you wanted his . . . what?

Stan: Acceptance.

Katie: Acceptance. So you molested you to buy his acceptance.

Stan: Yes.

Katie: And we go through our whole lives thinking, "He molested me." And there's another turnaround.

Stan: He molested me. I molested me. . . . I molested him?

Katie: Yes. You used your body to get his approval, to get his acceptance.

Stan: This never occurred to me.

Katie: Well, sweetheart, it's the last place we look—to ourselves. This is a surgery. We go in and get it all.

Stan: I was willing to be sexually abused in order to have his love and attention?

Katie: That's what I hear from you. I know *I* was. I'd do anything for love—at three years old. When I was three years old, I let this man who was repairing a house next door touch me. I would walk over there, and the man hurt me. I was three!

Stan: Oh my God.

Katie: I'd do anything for love, but I didn't know it until I was *forty*-three. He did it to me—yes, that was a good one. I walked over there. I was confused at three—or four, maybe four. And I could say that until I was forty-three, every year of my life—most days—I would do something to manipulate a person for approval or acceptance or love.

Stan: It's true.

Katie: But only everyone. I was just a walking scam. And when I didn't get their love or acceptance, I would say how they did it to me. And I lived my life that way.

Stan: Yes, it's true.

Katie: And that's why it's so hard to talk about, because when you really look at that, *you* are revealed to your wonderful self. And that feels really painful at first. It's like a surgery when the surgeon goes in and opens you up and then they sew you back together. You're going in and you are getting it all, not just part of it. And so you're sore for a few days. And with this maybe the knees get weak, and you're exhausted for a few hours. But oh, when you come back, it's pure light.

Stan: Yes. Yes, I see that more clearly. It's amazing.

Katie: So now let's see if we can do that "I look forward to."

Stan: I look forward to being sexually abused by my father.

Katie: Yes, so you can come to play with a full deck. I often say that forgiveness is simply seeing that what you thought happened, didn't. And we think we have to name it something, so we call it forgiveness.

Stan: I see that.

Katie: It's a beginning.

Stan: Whew! Powerful medicine.

Katie: Yes—you.

Stan: The inquiry.

Katie: Yes.

Stan: Telling on yourself and acknowledging what's so.

Katie: Let there be light.

Stan: Amen.

Katie: Yes. Wonderful Work, sweetheart.

Stan: Thank you, Katie.

Katie: Welcome, angel. My experience is that God is everything. That's the direct route. People who have that don't need this Work. God is everything. Add an "o" for those of you who don't do the G-word. What is, is.

So God is disguised as your father, giving you everything you need—*everything*—giving you exactly what you need to come home. What does it take? This now! I'm willing; I look forward to it, all of it. Nothing ever happened but a concept. There's nothing to manipulate, to change around, nothing to do, just to do The Work on the concept.

And we're unlimited. And sweetheart, as far as ambition goes and jobs and things like that, with this Work you can shoot for the moon, because you can no longer fail. The worst that can happen is a concept! And what is so sweet is that it moves without harm as a servant. And it moves perfectly as you do.

Stan: This is really amazing. I just moved out from Jersey. I lived in New York and I went through the program in New York—detox, the whole thing.

Katie: Ahh, are you good!

Stan: I went through rehab. And I've been looking all my life for that sense of peace that would allow me to be of service.

Katie: Yes, angel.

Stan: And I just had to close everything, close my life, totally shut down. And I thought, "Well, I'm going to come out to California and live in the desert." And that's when I found The Work: in Barstow. You know, I just heard about it.

Katie: Oh, my. That's where I found it, too, sweetheart! [The audience and Stan laugh.]

Stan: It's only by grace . . . I mean it's nothing that I could deliberately do to get me to be here. This would be the last thing that I would conceive of. I even tried to talk myself out of it. I even got lost and got here an hour late in order to avoid confronting myself, as I see it now. And I'm so grateful that you're here. You can't imagine how grateful I am!

Katie: I think I can.

Stan: Yeah. You can.

Katie: Yes, we've all been hanging out in the same places. There's no new concept, no new thought. They're all recycled; they're not even ours. We're not doing them on purpose. So today we meet them with understanding.

Stan: Thank you, Katie.

Katie: You are so welcome.

15. Scared and Angry at God

*"I need to know what's next. I need to control my life and death"
—is that true? Even the most frightening thoughts, when questioned, dissolve into a delighted not-knowing.*

Marcia: *I am scared and angry at God because I am dying and because I don't know what's next.*

Katie: "You're dying"—is that true?

Marcia: I feel it.

Katie: Can you absolutely know that it's true that you're dying?

Marcia: No, I can't absolutely know that.

Katie: You know what I heard this morning on CNN? For years they've been treating people for heart attacks who actually have not been having heart attacks. Someone's business is having a rough time or he's getting divorced or his daughter's getting married, and he becomes so stressed out that it shoves the blood to the heart, and the heart can't pump and stops. And then they treat him for a heart attack, because it looks the same. But there's no long-term damage. And they go on treating him as though he had a heart attack. And the heart begins to pump again, because he passes out. And the doctor on CNN was saying, "Just relax your mind." Well, wouldn't we if we could?

I work with people who have done meditation for thirty or forty years, and when they get out of the meditation mode, they still see problems in life. And everyone would see differently if they could. But we have to live our lives out of what we believe. If you want to know what you believe, look at your life. It's a mirror image of what you believe.

So "You're going to die"—is that true? A lot of you are thinking, "Well, of course it is! Everyone dies!" Maybe you're right, and look again! Do you believe everything you think? Did you ever stop to ask *you?* To really sit in that? "You're dying"—can you absolutely know that that's true?

Marcia: No.

Katie: Where did the no come from?

Marcia: Deep inside. From some place in that presence.

Katie: Yes. And how do you react when you believe the thought "I'm dying"? How do you live your life?

Marcia: I get really scared. I get really contracted. It's almost like I'm already dead. It's not a physical dying.

Katie: Who would you be without the thought?

Marcia: Very calm. I'd be happy, just living my life.

Katie: "I'm dying"—turn it around.

Marcia: I'm not dying.

Katie: Could that be as true or truer?

Marcia: Yes. I can't really know. But what comes next is the fear about what *is* next, and that I don't know.

Katie: So "You need to know what's next"—is that true?

Marcia: I'd like to.

Katie: "You *need* to know what's next"—is that true?

Marcia: No, it's not true. It's not what I really need.

Katie: How do you react when you believe the thought "I need to know what's next," and you don't know?

Marcia: Really tied up, really feeling tied up. Not fluid at all.

Katie: And this is where a lot of us panic. This is where we go to the refrigerator. This is where we light a cigarette or drink alcohol or where we raise our voice to our children or our partner. When we don't know and we think we need to know, we feel out of control. We become frightened. So who would you be without the thought "I need to know what's next"? Who would you be without that thought in your everyday life?

Marcia: Clear. Really clear. There would be just what's next.

Katie: That's exciting.

Marcia: Yes.

Katie: So I see that as you question what you believe, you don't *need* to know what's next, because it's always here! Next, next, next.

Marcia: Yes, I can do that. But there are times it goes away. It just goes away, and then I get angry at God because it goes away.

Katie: Yes. So "what's next" goes away—is that true?

Marcia: No.

Katie: That's not possible. The next thing is always here. [Marcia and the audience laugh.] "I need to know what's next"—turn it around.

Marcia: I don't need to know what's next.

Katie: No! Because what's next is next. The next thing comes, and the next, and the next. And it's so exciting not to need to know. Because there's nothing that comes next that you're not prepared for.

Marcia: [convulsed with laugher and snorting] Oh my God, that's hilarious! It's so true. I didn't plan to come up here on the stage and snort, but oh well! [The audience laughs.]

Katie: "I'm going to die"—turn it around.

Marcia: That one is a little harder.

Katie: What's the opposite of "I'm going to die"?

Marcia: I'm not going to die.

Katie: Yes, now give me three ways that that could be true. . . . Just finding a turnaround is not enough. Find three ways, three reasons that the turnaround could be true. This is meditation. Find *one* way.

Marcia: Well, nothing dies really. Its physical form changes. But it's that hanging on to some kind of structure.

Katie: An identity. It's only an identity.

Marcia: Yes. A bio-body suit.

Katie: Who would you be without your story? Who would you be without the story of you? The story of us?

Marcia: You'd just meet every moment. It's just different moments like that, and then it comes back. It's just this. It's really an energy form just meeting other energy forms.

Katie: Who would you be without *that* story?

Marcia: I don't know. I don't know.

Katie: That's exciting!

Marcia: Yes, I see that.

Katie: What's next? You don't need to know, because *that's* what's next. And when you're dead, it's not a problem, because there's no one to know you're dead.

Marcia: Hmm.

Katie: How would you know you're dead if you're dead? Let's see, if you die and you go to heaven and take this thought system with you, you wouldn't even know you were in heaven! [The audience laughs.] Heaven, when you put your belief system onto it, is hell. I call it earth.

Marcia: [laughing] Wow!

Katie: Let's look at the next statement.

Marcia: Oh, I can't read it. Oh yeah, this is a good one. *I want God to reveal to me what's next so I won't be afraid.*

Katie: No, no, no. Turn it around. God's too busy to reveal anything to you—he's too busy rolling around heaven all day.

Marcia: I want me to reveal . . . but I also feel there's another turnaround.

Katie: So just do one at a time.

Marcia: I want *me* to reveal to me what's next. But I don't know that that's possible; it's just next. I can't reveal that; I can just *be* it.

Katie: You're the one that sees it.

Marcia: Hmm.

Katie: What's next is only what you perceive. Can you hear that?

Marcia: Say it again?

Katie: What's next is only as you see it. The next thing happens, and if there are four hundred people in this room, four hundred different things happen.

Marcia: Hmm.

Katie: The way we see it and what we think about it and the meaning of it is different for each of us. So four hundred different things happen.

Marcia: Ah.

Katie: So *you* reveal to you what's next. Read it again, and see if you can hear it. You're the one who says what's next. Your belief system determines it.

Marcia: And what if you have no belief system?

Katie: Then where's the problem? [The audience laughs.]

Marcia: There isn't any! Oh! Can we just do a hard-drive crash and start over again and still be in a body? That's really what it is.

Katie: But you know, it's not like a hard-drive *crash*—it's just undoing one belief at a time. When you find yourself believing a thought and it's stressful, question what you're thinking.

Marcia: Uh-huh.

Katie: And if your thoughts are beautiful and the world's a wonderful place for you, don't bother questioning them. Just have a happy life. So it's not like a hard-drive crash. It's just questioning one, one, one.

Marcia: Got it.

Katie: Okay.

Marcia: Should I read the next statement?

Katie: Yes. That's what's next.

Marcia: Oh.

Katie: So read it.

Marcia: *I need God to communicate with me more clearly so that I won't be afraid of dying.*

Katie: Why are you afraid of dying? What do you think will happen?

Marcia: Just nothingness.

Katie: Okay, so you're afraid of nothing? How can you be afraid of nothing?

Marcia: I don't know! I don't know how to answer that!

Katie: If there's nothingness, there's nothing to be *afraid* of!

Marcia: I hear what you're saying. I do hear it.

Katie: But I'm only coming from your words: "I'm afraid of nothing." Can you hear yourself? Those were your words. They're on tape. "I'm afraid of nothing." So there's nothing to be afraid of in nothing. There's nothing! That's just a game the mind plays. What is it without its identity? The only way mind can live is as an identity. You know, if it didn't believe it was a you, it could just jump into this flower and say, "Oh! Life is really good from here. I love my color. . . . I like hanging out with these guys." It would just adjust—mind adjusts to anything.

Marcia: I like that.

Katie: Well look, it has adjusted to a *you*. That's major.

Marcia: I get it. Thank you.

Katie: You're welcome.

Marcia: I get it. Yes. Okay, so what I just need to do is to be in the moment.

Katie: "I need God to communicate with me clearly"—turn it around. "I need myself . . ."

Marcia: I need myself to communicate with me clearly.

Katie: Yes. That's what you're looking for. It's within you.

Marcia: Uh-huh.

Katie: And turn it around again. "I need to communicate . . ."

Marcia: I need to communicate with God clearly.

Katie: It's all within you. A connection with the source of everything. Its nature is love. It wouldn't be what the mind would lead us to believe. That's why I love these four questions and turnarounds. It's like we're disassembling hell.

Marcia: I feel that. I don't feel so scared.

Katie: Read your last statement.

Marcia: I don't ever want to be afraid of dying.

Katie: "I'm willing . . ."

Marcia: I'm willing to be afraid of dying.

Katie: "I look forward . . ."

15. Scared and Angry at God

Marcia: I look forward to being afraid of dying.

Katie: Now that's exciting.

Marcia: It is!

Katie: That way you won't miss your own death. [The audience laughs and applauds.]

Marcia: Thank you so much.

Katie: You're welcome, sweetheart. You know, The Work is like this. You're walking through the desert and it's a beautiful day; and you look down and see a big fat rattlesnake, and you're terrified of rattlesnakes. You jump back, your heart is racing, your pulse is beating, you're paralyzed with fear, sweat on your brow. Then the sun goes behind a cloud and you look again, and it isn't a snake after all—it's a rope.

Now I invite you to stand over the rope for a thousand years and make yourself afraid of it again. You can't. This is self-realization. You have realized for yourself what is true. And you can never be afraid of that rope again. That's the power of questioning your mind.

So what we've been dealing with this evening are apparent snakes. And I can tell you that in twenty years, I have never met a thought that is in reality a snake. They've all been ropes. Every single stressful thought I have ever encountered has been a rope. There's no exception to that. And I love that you've begun to find it out for yourself.

AFTERWORD

by Carol Williams

I hope that reading this book will inspire readers who have never done The Work to begin, as well as help people who have been doing The Work for some time to see possible new routes for their inquiry.

If you have never done The Work and would like to try, download a Worksheet from **www.thework.com**, or copy the one in this book. Then find the thought that is making you unhappy *now* and write as freely as you can.

Sometimes it is easiest to start with matters that are trivial but annoying: Teenagers and next-door neighbors are wonderful subjects for The Work. "She should tidy up her room." "They should be more considerate." Or it could be best to dive right in and inquire about the most painful thought you have—the one you'd rather not even think.

As many of the dialogues in this book show, the thought that is causing you the most pain is sometimes not the one you first think it is. If you ask the questions diligently, your answers will reveal other thoughts that seem questionable. Notice those. Then jot them down, too, and inquire about them next: *Is it true? Can I absolutely know that it's true? How do I react when I believe that thought? Who would I be without the thought?* Then turn the thoughts around and find three genuine examples of how the turnarounds are true in your life.

It can be good to do The Work with a trusted friend asking you the questions. Then you switch around and ask them. Some

309

people do better on their own. The important thing is to do The Work slowly. As Katie often repeats in these dialogues, The Work is meditation. Don't second-guess or think you know. Instead, wait quietly for your answers.

The wonderful thing about The Work is that if you do it for a while, eventually *it* starts doing *you*. It simply becomes harder and harder to believe the thoughts that are not true for you. The freedom and happiness that this brings pervade every part of your life.

APPENDIX

The following Judge-Your-Neighbor Worksheet is what participants are asked to fill out before their conversation with Katie. It is also what you fill out when "asking you"—when you do The Work at home on your own or with a friend. The instructions are simple:

Fill in the blanks below, writing about someone (dead or alive) you haven't yet forgiven one hundred percent. Use short, simple sentences. Don't censor yourself—try to fully experience the anger or pain as if the situation were occurring right now. Take this opportunity to express your judgments on paper.

Katie explains the process at greater length in her book *Loving What Is:*

> The first step in The Work is to write down your judgments about any stressful situation in your life, past, present, or future— about a person you dislike or worry about, a situation with someone who angers or frightens or saddens you, or someone you're ambivalent or confused about. Write your judgments down, just the way you think them. (Use a blank sheet of paper; or, if you have access to the Internet, you can go to **http://www.thework. com**, to the Resources section, where you'll find a Judge-Your-Neighbor Worksheet to download and print.)
>
> Don't be surprised if you find it difficult at first to fill out the Worksheet. For thousands of years, we have been taught not to judge — but let's face it, we still do it all the time. The truth is

that we all have judgments running in our heads. Through The Work we finally have permission to let those judgments speak out, or even scream out, on paper. We may find that even the most unpleasant thoughts can be met with unconditional love.

I encourage you to write about someone whom you haven't yet totally forgiven. This is the most powerful place to begin. Even if you've forgiven that person 99 percent, you aren't free until your forgiveness is complete. The 1 percent you haven't forgiven them is the very place where you're stuck in all your other relationships (including your relationship with yourself).

If you are new to inquiry, I strongly suggest that you not write about yourself at first. If you start by judging yourself, your answers come with a motive and with solutions that haven't worked. Judging someone else, then inquiring and turning it around, is the direct path to understanding. You can judge yourself later, when you have been doing inquiry long enough to trust the power of truth.

If you begin by pointing the finger of blame outward, then the focus isn't on you. You can just let loose and be uncensored. We're often quite sure about what other people need to do, how they should live, whom they should be with. We have 20/20 vision about other people, but not about ourselves.

When you do The Work, you see who you are by seeing who you think other people are. Eventually you come to see that everything outside you is a reflection of your own thinking. You are the storyteller, the projector of all stories, and the world is the projected image of your thoughts.

Since the beginning of time, people have been trying to change the world so that they can be happy. This hasn't ever worked, because it approaches the problem backward. What The Work gives us is a way to change the projector—mind—rather than the projected. It's like when there's a piece of lint on a projector's lens. We think there's a flaw on the screen, and we try to change this person and that person, whomever the flaw appears to be on next. But it's futile to try to change the projected images. Once we realize where the lint is, we can clear the lens itself. This is the end of suffering, and the beginning of a little joy in paradise.

People often say to me, "Why should I judge my neighbor? I already know that it's all about me." I say, "I understand. And please trust the process. Judge your neighbor, and follow the simple directions." Here are some examples of people you may want to write about: mother, father, wife, husband, children, siblings, partner, neighbor, friend, enemy, roommate, boss, teacher, employee, co-worker, teammate, salesmen, customers, men, women, authorities, God. Often, the more personal your choice is, the more potent The Work can be.

Later, as you become skilled in The Work, you may want to investigate your judgments about issues such as death, money, health, your body, your addictions, and even your own self-criticisms. In fact, once you're ready, you can write about and inquire into any uncomfortable thought that appears in your mind. When you realize that every stressful moment you experience is a gift that points you to your own freedom, life becomes very kind.

THE WORK OF
Byron Katie

Judge-Your-Neighbor Worksheet

Judge your neighbor • Write it down • Ask four questions • Turn it around

Fill in the blanks below, writing about someone (dead or alive) you haven't yet forgiven one hundred percent. Use short, simple sentences. Don't censor yourself—try to fully experience the anger or pain as if the situation were occurring right now. Take this opportunity to express your judgments on paper.

1. Who angers, frustrates, or confuses you, and why?

I am _____ at _____ because _____
(name)

_____

(Example: I am *angry* at *Paul* because *he doesn't listen to me, he doesn't appreciate me, he argues with everything I say.*)

2. How do you want them to change? What do you want them to do?

I want _____ to _____
(name)

_____

(Example: I want *Paul* to *see that he is wrong.* I want *him* to *apologize.*)

3. What is it that they should or shouldn't do, be, think or feel? What advice could you offer?

_____should/shouldn't _____
(name)

_____

(Example: *Paul* should *take better care of himself. He* shouldn't *argue with me.*)

4. What do they need to do in order for you to be happy?

I need _____to _____
(name)

_____

(Example: I need *Paul* to *hear me and respect me.*)

5. What do you think of them? Make a list.

_____ is_____
(name)

_____

(Example: *Paul* is *unfair, arrogant, loud, dishonest, way out of line, and unconscious.*)

6. What is it that you don't want to experience with that person again?

I don't ever want to_____

_____

(Example: I don't ever want to *feel unappreciated by Paul again.* I don't ever want to *see him smoking and ruining his health again.*)

The four questions:

1. Is it true?

2. Can you absolutely know that it's true?

3. How do you react when you believe that thought?

4. Who would you be without the thought?

Turn it around.

(Find three genuine examples of how each turnaround is true in your life.)

INDEX OF TOPICS

(The following are dialogue—not page—numbers.)

Abuse: 8, 14

Addictions: 6, 14

Adultery: 4, 12

Alimony: 12

Anger: 1, 5, 6, 7, 8, 9, 10, 11, 12, 14, 15

Approval: 3, 9, 12, 14

Body image: 1, 2, 9, 12, 14

Boundaries: 4, 8, 10

Cancer: 9

Cell phones: 11

Chronic fatigue syndrome: 2

Communication: 10, 12, 14, 15

Comparisons: 13

Contempt: 4, 14

Control: 2, 6, 8, 9, 15

Co-workers: 1, 7

Criticism: 8

Death: 15

Debt: 12

Dependence: 6, 10

Depression: 2, 12

Disability: 12

Disease: 2, 6, 9

Divorce: 12, 14

Fairness: 5

Fathers and daughters: 5

Fathers and sons: 14

Fear: 2, 4, 6, 9, 12, 15

Friends: 1, 5, 7, 8, 12

Future: 9, 13, 14, 15

Goals: 11

Government: 5

Guilt: 1, 6, 10, 12

Homelessness: 6

"I'm not good enough": 4, 13

Incest: 14

Jealousy: 4

Law: 5

Listening: 1, 6, 8, 12, 14

Loneliness: 9, 10

Lying: 2, 13, 14

Manipulation: 8

Marijuana: 4

Masochism: 14

Medications: 2

Mediocrity: 13

Money: 5, 10, 12

Mothers and daughters: 3, 10

Mothers and sons: 6, 8, 11

Music: 3, 11, 13

Obligations: 8, 10

Obsessions: 6

Pain: 6, 9

Parents and children: 3, 6, 8, 10, 11, 14

Raising children: 10
Relationships: 4, 11, 12, 14
Respect: 4, 5, 6, 7, 14
Responsibility: 1, 7, 8, 10, 12
Sadness: 6, 8, 10, 14
Sex: 4, 14
Sexual abuse: 14
Sisters: 9, 10
Sleep: 2
Smoking: 4, 10, 14
Success: 13
Suicide: 6, 8
Unconditional love: 1, 4, 8, 11
Victims: 5, 9, 11, 12

ABOUT THE AUTHOR

Since 1986, **Byron Katie** has introduced The Work directly to millions of people throughout the world at free public events; in prisons, hospitals, churches, corporations, universities, and schools; at weekend intensives; and at her nine-day School for The Work. She is the author of the best-selling books *Loving What Is; I Need Your Love—Is That True?; A Thousand Names for Joy;* and, with Hay House, *Question Your Thinking, Change the World.*
Website: **www.TheWork.com**

Visit **www.TheWork.com** and change your life:

- Learn more about **The Work.**

- Download **audio and video clips of Katie** doing The Work with others.

- Print out **Worksheets** for daily use.

- Establish a practice on the **NetWork,** find a **facilitator,** or call the free **hotline.**

- See Katie's **schedule of events.**

- Find out about the nine-day **School for The Work with Byron Katie.**

- Visit the store for Katie's **books, CDs,** and **DVDs.**

We hope you enjoyed this Hay House book. If you'd like to receive
our online catalog featuring additional Hay House books and products, or
if you'd like information about the Hay Foundation, please contact:

Hay House, Inc.
P.O. Box 5100
Carlsbad, CA 92018-5100

(760) 431-7695 or (800) 654-5126
(760) 431-6948 (fax) or (800) 650-5115 (fax)
www.hayhouse.com® • www.hayfoundation.org

Published and distributed in Australia by: Hay House Australia Pty. Ltd.,
18/36 Ralph St., Alexandria NSW 2015 • *Phone:* 612-9669-4299
Fax: 612-9669-4144 • www.hayhouse.com.au

Published and distributed in the United Kingdom by: Hay House UK, Ltd.,
292B Kensal Rd., London W10 5BE • *Phone:* 44-20-8962-1230
Fax: 44-20-8962-1239 • www.hayhouse.co.uk

Published and distributed in the Republic of South Africa by: Hay House SA
(Pty), Ltd., P.O. Box 990, Witkoppen 2068 • *Phone/Fax:* 27-11-467-8904
info@hayhouse.co.za • www.hayhouse.co.za

Published in India by: Hay House Publishers India, Muskaan Complex,
Plot No. 3, B-2, Vasant Kunj, New Delhi 110 070 • *Phone:* 91-11-4176-1620
Fax: 91-11-4176-1630 • www.hayhouse.co.in

Distributed in Canada by: Raincoast, 9050 Shaughnessy St., Vancouver, B.C.
V6P 6E5 • *Phone:* (604) 323-7100 • *Fax:* (604) 323-2600 • www.raincoast.com

Take Your Soul on a Vacation

Visit **www.HealYourLife.com®** to regroup, recharge,
and reconnect with your own magnificence.
Featuring blogs, mind-body-spirit news, and life-changing
wisdom from Louise Hay and friends.

Visit **www.HealYourLife.com** today!

Mind Your Body,
Mend Your Spirit

Hay House is the ultimate resource for inspirational and health-conscious books, audio programs, movies, events, e-newsletters, member communities, and much more.

Visit **www.hayhouse.com**® today and nourish your soul.

UPLIFTING EVENTS

Join your favorite authors at live events in a city near you or log on to **www.hayhouse.com** to visit with Hay House authors online during live, interactive Web events.

INSPIRATIONAL RADIO

Daily inspiration while you're at work or at home. Enjoy radio programs featuring your favorite authors, streaming live on the Internet 24/7 at **HayHouseRadio.com**®. Tune in and tune up your spirit!

VIP STATUS

Join the Hay House VIP membership program today and enjoy exclusive discounts on books, CDs, calendars, card decks, and more. You'll also receive 10% off all event reservations (excluding cruises). Visit **www.hayhouse.com/wisdom** to join the Hay House Wisdom Community™.

Visit **www.hayhouse.com** and enter priority code 2723
during checkout for special savings!
(One coupon per customer.)

CPSIA information can be obtained
at www.ICGtesting.com
Printed in the USA
FSOW01n0117240316
18374FS